OUT OF SLAVERY

LEGACIES OF WEST INDIAN SLAVERY
Lectures and conference papers given during the
William Wilberforce 150th anniversary celebrations
at the University of Hull, July 1983

OUT OF SLAVERY
Abolition and After
Edited by Jack Hayward

ABOLITION AND ITS AFTERMATH
The Historical Context 1790–1916
Edited by David Richardson

DUAL LEGACIES IN THE CONTEMPORARY CARIBBEAN
Continuing Aspects of British and French Dominion
Edited by Paul Sutton

THE CARIBBEAN IN EUROPE
Aspects of the West Indian Experience in Britain,
France and The Netherlands
Edited by Colin Brock

OUT OF SLAVERY
Abolition and After

Edited by
JACK HAYWARD

Professor of Politics
University of Hull

LONDON AND NEW YORK

First published 1985
by Routledge

2 Park Square, Milton Park, Abingdon, Oxon OX14 4RN

711 Third Avenue, New York, NY 10017

Routledge is an imprint of the Taylor & Francis Group, an informa business

First issued in paperback 2016

Copyright © 1985 Frank Cass & Co. Ltd.

British Library Cataloguing in Publication Data

Out of slavery: abolition and after.
1. Slavery—Great Britain—Anti-slavery movements
I. Hayward, J. E. S.
322.4′4′0941   HT1163

ISBN 0-7146-3260-0

All rights reserved. No part of this publication may be reproduced in any form or by any means, electronic, mechanical, photocopying, recording or otherwise, without the prior permission of Frank Cass and Company Limited.

ISBN: 978-0-714-63260-5 (hbk)
ISBN: 978-1-138-97782-2 (pbk)

Typeset by Williams Graphics, Abergele, Clwyd

To
Sir Roy Marshall,
Vice-Chancellor,
University of Hull,
1979–1985
Formerly Vice-Chancellor,
University of the West Indies,
1969–1974

CONTENTS

Notes on Contributors	ix
Preface *Lord Wilberforce*	xi
1. The Utility of Commemoration: Reflections on the Enduring Scourge of Servitude *Jack Hayward*	1
2. Slavery: the Underside of Freedom *Orlando Patterson*	7
3. Freeing the Slaves: How Important Was Wilberforce? *James Walvin*	30
4. William Wilberforce: 150 Years On *Fiona Spiers*	47
5. Wilberforce the Saint *Ian Bradley*	69
6. Abolition and the National Interest *Howard Temperley*	86
7. Emancipation from below? The Role of the British West Indian Slaves in the Emancipation Movement, 1816–34 *Michael Craton*	110
8. West Indian Society 150 Years after Abolition: a Re-examination of Some Classic Theories *Lloyd Best*	132
9. 'Some in Light and Some in Darkness': the Long Shadow of Slavery *Shridath S. Ramphal*	159
10. The English Judge and the Ethnic Minorities *Lord Scarman*	193

CONTRIBUTORS

Lloyd Best, United Nations Project Co-ordinator in the Central African Republic, economist and formerly Leader of the Opposition in the Senate of the Republic of Trinidad and Tobago

Ian Bradley, teacher and journalist, formerly on *The Times*

Michael Craton, Professor of History, University of Waterloo, Ontario

Jack Hayward, Professor of Politics, University of Hull

Orlando Patterson, Professor of Sociology, University of Harvard

Shridath S. Ramphal, Secretary-General of the Commonwealth

Leslie Scarman, Lord of Appeal in Ordinary

Fiona Spiers, Co-editor of William Wilberforce Editorial Project

Howard Temperley, Professor of American History, University of East Anglia

James Walvin, Reader in History, University of York

PREFACE

Dr Fiona Spiers at the start of her lecture well reminds us that anniversary celebrations provide a useful focus and fulfil a need among scholars to concentrate on a series of related problems and to take stock of current trends in research. The death of William Wilberforce on 29 July 1833 and the passing in that year of the Act of Parliament abolishing slavery in the British colonies were commemorated with enthusiasm in 1933, the centenary year. The University of Hull took the view that 1983 – the sesquicentenary – should not be regarded as merely the same event fifty years on. The background from which we now look at the history of the end of the eighteenth and the beginning of the nineteenth century has radically changed. We have passed through the period of decolonisation; we are well advanced in the period of widened recognition of Human Rights; the economic and social consequences of what was done, and left undone, by the Abolitionists and Emancipators and of the situations which they faced are being newly revealed.

All these changes seemed to call for a reappraisal on broad lines of the problems of slavery and freedom from slavery as they can now be seen and of the contribution and personality of the Abolitionists, particularly of their leader and spokesman William Wilberforce. We have urgent new questions to ask to which we seek answers relevant to our time. The University of Hull, which through its present Vice-Chancellor, Sir Roy Marshall, has strong links with the West Indies, felt qualified to attempt this reappraisal and, through an initiative taken by its Department of Politics led by Professor Jack Hayward, it commissioned these lectures as a coherent piece of research.

The lectures cover a wide field. They attempt to consider the institution of slavery as it existed in the early nineteenth century; the forces making for its survival, as well as the forces, social and economic, making for its disappearance; the part played by

West Indian slaves in the emancipation campaign; the aftermath of slavery and the substitution by law of freedom in the West Indian colonies; the stresses in West Indian society created by this substitution and their consequences in the modern age. They probe and test the validity of arguments that by the end of the eighteenth century the slave trade and the institution of slavery were already under overwhelming pressures, social and economic, which would have brought them to an end independently of the Abolitionist movement; that the latter at most accelerated and may even have retarded reform; that abolition was brought about by capitalist attack, or alternatively by the movement towards worker equality following the Industrial Revolution; that the policy of the British government in forcing emancipation on the colonies was shortsighted and niggardly.

These lectures also examine the record of the Abolitionists and evaluate the techniques and arguments used in their campaign. They discuss in depth the personality of Wilberforce, that remarkable, complex, exposed character. Was he a saint or a hypocrite? Was he truly a believer in freedom? Was he a competent parliamentary leader? How does he stand in relation to other contemporary issues? Are there inconsistencies in his attitudes, and if so how are these to be explained? On all these and on many other important issues, the reader must make up his/her own mind.

This particular reader believes that in the end, across all the tangled web of human imperfection, there is justification for regarding the movement which culminated in 1833 as one of the great movements forward of humanity and for maintaining Wilberforce – mythical and humanly imperfect a figure as in some respects he may be – upon the pedestal on which history has set him. Whatever view each reader may ultimately take, it is safe to say that these lectures provide a fascinating study of the kinds of forces and arguments, moral and material by which human beings are moved.

One final remark. If, as we all believe, celebrations are to have more than a festival character or charismatic significance, the two final lectures, by Lord Scarman and Sir Shridath Ramphal, point to the vast contemporary problems which need to be met by a renewal of the spirit and faith which so strongly moved those who realised the reforms of 1807 to 1833. Injustice

Preface xiii

and inhumanity tend to leave, long after their apparent removal, a legacy equal in scale, if different in character, for which later generations have to pay. The Secretary-General of the Commonwealth, in his wide ranging and sympathetic survey of the trauma of his own country, concludes with an appeal for a fresh, convinced and principled crusade against those forms of inhumanity and deprivation which, as our consciences tell us, are so unworthy of the post-abolition age.

Lord Wilberforce

1

The Utility of Commemoration: Reflections on the Enduring Scourge of Servitude

JACK HAYWARD

In 1933, the centenary of the abolition of slavery in the British colonies and of the death of William Wilberforce, the University College of Hull had only been in existence for five years and was not able to mount a suitable commemoration of these two events, which historical accident had appropriately conjoined. Slavery itself was far from dead. Dr Temple, Archbishop of York, speaking at the centenary commemoration in Hull in July 1933, regretted that slaves were still captured and sold in some parts of the world and similar sentiments were vigorously voiced half a century later in 1983. Whilst lending its nascent support to the commemorative campaign to remind people of the continuing scourge of human servitude, the newly created University College hoped to benefit from the centenary. A National Wilberforce Memorial Committee launched an appeal for £25,000 to endow a Wilberforce Chair of History, scholarships and an annual lecture. Despite the patronage of the Duke of York (later George VI) and the leaders of the Conservative, Labour and Liberal Parties — signatories to an appeal published in *The Times* — only a fraction of this sum was raised.[1] Still facing harsh times that recall in some ways the 1930s, the University of Hull — without setting aside any funds specially for the commemoration — was able to mount an extensive programme of sesquicentenary activities. This was possible, thanks to external financial support — notably from the Noel Buxton

Trust for the lecture series published in this volume and from the Commonwealth Foundation for the conference on 'Legacies of West Indian Slavery', whose papers are published in the three volumes associated with this book — and to the voluntary activities of devoted colleagues. Particular mention must be made of Dr Paul Sutton, Lecturer in Politics at the University of Hull, who initiated the original suggestion that a conference should be held and who played an energetic part in many aspects of the commemorative activities; Dr James Walvin, Reader in History at the University of York and a leading authority on the history of slavery and abolition, who provided invaluable advice as well as one of the lectures printed in this book and Mrs Beverley Culley, who was the tireless secretary of the university working party that planned and organised the activities which I shall briefly describe.[2]

On 3 March 1983, the lecture series was launched by Sir Roy Marshall, Vice-Chancellor of the University of Hull and former Vice-Chancellor of the University of the West Indies, while on 5 March the Hull Bach Choir and the University Choir and Chamber Orchestra with soloists gave a performance of Handel's *Israel in Egypt*. (The theme of achieving freedom from slavery is sufficiently strong for this oratorio to be performed annually in Freetown, Sierra Leone, with which the city of Hull is twinned.) After the first half of the lecture series, devoted to the historical dimension of the *Out of Slavery* theme, focusing particularly upon the role of William Wilberforce, an operetta by Derek Scott, *Wilberforce*, was performed at the university's Middleton Hall. The theatrical aspect of the commemoration took the form of two productions. The first consisted of a play entitled *Toussaint*, inspired by C. L. R. James's account of the life and role of Toussaint L'Ouverture in the San Domingo revolution, *The Black Jacobins*.[3] The leading part was played by J. D. Douglas, who wrote the script. The play was performed by the Faceless Theatre company from Cardiff. The University of Hull's own Drama Department put on a memorable production of the Nigerian dramatist Wole Soyinka's *Death and the King's Horseman*, which focuses upon the tragic consequences of the conflict between traditional African and Western colonial values. The intertwining of cultural and political themes, inseparable from the history of West Indian slavery and its

The Utility of Commemoration

contemporary legacies, which was the *leitmotif* of the international conference held at the University of Hull, was thus exemplified in the activities that preceded it.

Culture and politics are also closely interrelated in the West Indian devotion to cricket and no one has expressed this better than C. L. R. James in his classic *Beyond a Boundary*.[4] He showed that if one wishes to understand that cornucopia of city states, it is to the Athenian commitment to self-government and to publicly organised sport — his own life-long passions — that one must look. However, umpires have all too often been superseded by dictators (as Lloyd Best's discussion of 'doctor politics' in this volume shows) and the Westminster style has even more difficulty in surviving abroad than does cricket. In any case, the connection between cricket and politics has been a persistent source of controversy in the 1980s, with the issue of South African racism sometimes sharply opposing the sons of the slaves and the sons of the slave-owning countries. The University of Hull organised a Wilberforce Commemoration cricket match between the West Indies World Cup touring team and the Yorkshire County Cricket Club but the issue of two Yorkshire players who had taken part in representative matches against South Africa prevented the game from taking place. A late substitution of Lancashire County Cricket Club (which did not raise this problem) was not able to save the match, the English weather having the last word. All that sadly remains of what had been intended as an opportunity to celebrate a sporting rivalry that unites millions of people in a common love of the game is a splendid commemorative brochure[5] and a reiteration of the inseparability of issues of humanity from the way in which sporting ties are sustained. Inadvertently, the inability to hold the match as originally planned demonstrated why it had been desirable to organise it. Issues of principle stubbornly resurface often in unlikely places, and a waterlogged pitch does not wash them away.

The commemorative activities culminated at the end of July, to coincide with the sesquicentenary of the death of Wilberforce. The city of Hull also mounted its own programme of events at that time during its civic week. An important feature of this civic programme was the opening of a refurbished permanent exhibition in Wilberforce House devoted to the history of the slave trade and the Abolitionist movement. In addition to a temporary exhibition in the Brynmor Jones Library at the University of Hull, organised by its archivist Norman Higson, illustrating the life of William Wilberforce and his fight against the slave trade and slavery itself, a three-day international conference was mounted at the University on 'Legacies of West Indian Slavery'. Three companion volumes set out the results of this conference, so its themes and associated events will only be briefly touched upon here.

Before the academic proceedings commenced, an illustrated lecture of his opera *Toussaint*, inspired by a reading of James's *Black Jacobins*, was given by the composer David Blake, the opera itself being successfully revived at Covent Garden in September 1983. The international conference, with over a hundred participants, was opened on 27 July by Sir Roy Marshall and was devoted to the historical dimension of West Indian slavery, seen in the comparative perspective of the British, Dutch and French colonial experience. A party of visiting dignitaries from Freetown, whose establishment as a settlement for freed slaves was assisted by William Wilberforce, attended part of the first day's proceedings. On the second day, the focus switched to the contemporary economic, political and social legacy in the Caribbean, including in the afternoon the conferment by the university's Chancellor Lord Wilberforce of an honorary degree of Doctor of Letters on C. L. R. James, who responded by offering some trenchant reflections on matters that doubtless will be discussed at greater length in his autobiography. The conference concluded its proceedings on 29 July – the sesquicentenary of Wilberforce's death, three days after the second reading of the Bill abolishing slavery in the British colonies – by considering the impact of the West Indian social, economic, cultural and educational impact upon contemporary Europe.

The lectures that follow present nine different views on what the theme *Out of Slavery* means retrospectively and prospectively. What it definitely does not mean is that the fight for human rights is over because the battle is won. The actual emancipation of the slaves in the British West Indies had to wait until the end of apprenticeship in 1838, and significantly the Anti-Slavery Society for the Protection of Human Rights was founded a year

The Utility of Commemoration 5

later in 1839 to continue the fight. It still has to battle against serfdom, debt-bondage and child labour. Many will go further and agree with the Secretary-General of the Commonwealth that the fight against South African apartheid is one of the foremost battles against state-organised servitude in our time. It was therefore exemplary that the Lord Mayor and City Council of Hull should choose 18 July 1983, the sixty-fifth birthday of the imprisoned leader of the African National Congress, Nelson Mandela, to give his name to the ornamental gardens adjacent to Wilberforce House and to place the following inscription there, extracted from the lecture delivered by Shridath Ramphal at the university on 24 May 1983 and printed in this volume.

> I invite each and every one of you, citizens of Hull and other friends, to question whether any can take pride in the work and achievements of Wilberforce and the Anti-slavery Movement if as individuals, as a nation, as a world community, we fail to take a righteous and uncompromising stand against apartheid. By what quirk of logic, what twist of values can we celebrate emancipation and tolerate apartheid? We tarnish and depreciate the memory of Wilberforce so long as slavery South Africa style flaunts its evil and defies our will to curb it, sensing our resolve to be a fragile thing.

Clearly, we must not subside into the comfort of retrospective radicalism, praising the inspiring efforts of the nineteenth century whilst averting our gaze from the evils that have survived or proliferated in the twentieth century. We no longer share the confident optimism of John Stuart Mill who asserted in 1863:

> The entire history of social improvement has been a series of transitions by which one custom or institution after another, from being a supposed primary necessity of social existence, has passed into the rank of a universally stigmatised injustice and tyranny. So it has been with the distinction of slaves and freemen, nobles and serfs, patricians and plebians; and so it will be, in part already is, with the aristocracies of colour, race and sex.[6]

A hundred and twenty years later, they are still on the agenda. The text of these lectures delivered in 1983 is not simply intended as a collective self-congratulatory exercise by people resigned to the defeatist view that Britain has a splendid future behind it. Rather, what follows should be read as a summons to a rededication and reassertion of the liberationist spirit, a determination to fight the good fight abroad and, yes, also at home.

NOTES

1. *The Times*, 13 July 1983, p. 8 and T. W. Bamford, *The University of Hull. The First Fifty Years*, 1978, Oxford University Press, p. 61. Ironically, *The Times* reports on the Hull centenary commemoration (24–26 July) overlapped a serialisation of extracts of the English translation of Hitler's *Mein Kampf*.
2. For a more complete account, see *Wilberforce Anniversary Events in the University of Hull*, University of Hull, 1984.
3. C. L. R. James, *The Black Jacobins*, 1st edn 1938; London, Allison & Busby, 1980 edn.
4. C. L. R. James, *Beyond a Boundary*, London, Hutchinson, 1963.
5. Ivar Oxaal (ed.), *Wilberforce Commemoration International Cricket Match*, Hull, Bermitz, 1983.
6. J. S. Mill, *Utilitarianism*, 1863; Fontana edn, 1962, p. 320.

2

Slavery: the Underside of Freedom

ORLANDO PATTERSON

INTRODUCTION

No one would deny that today freedom stands unchallenged as the supreme value of the Western world. Not only philosophers, but ordinary men and women advocate it as something essential for their very existence as human beings. It is the one value which many people seem prepared to die for, both by their words and their actions. How and why did this situation come about?

To those who hold that freedom is a natural concept, something that all human beings, simply by being human, would naturally want, my problem must seem strange. The truth of the matter, however, is that there is nothing at all self-evident in the idea of freedom. For most of human history, and for many peoples in the non-Western world today, freedom in the sense understood in the West was, and remains, anything but obvious. Other values are to them far more important, values such as the capacity to participate as a full member of society, the sense of belonging, the pursuit of glory and honor for one's self, one's family and one's clan or state. We in the West, of course, value these things too, but we also have the thing we call freedom, and we place it above them all. We even divide the world into two great camps, the free world and the unfree world, and our leaders declare, to public approval, that we are prepared to risk the whole future of mankind in a nuclear holocaust in order to defend our freedom.

From the viewpoint of a comparative historical sociologist, this is an incredible situation. To be specific, I would like answers to three questions: (1) How and why did freedom become a value in the first place? (2) How and why did it become a supreme value? (3) Why did it rise to supremacy only in the Western world?

WHAT IS FREEDOM?

In general intellectual discourse the term freedom is used loosely to refer to three different things. First, we use the term to refer to an independent collective entity, usually a state. This is the sense in which Nicias used the term when, in his address to his dispirited troops at Syracuse he reminded them of their native Athens, 'the freest city' in the world (Thucydides, VII, 69.2). There is nothing peculiarly Western about this use of the term. Nor is it in the least bit problematic. All collective entities everywhere, and in all periods of human history, have desired political autonomy. It bears no relationship to personal, individual freedom; nor, indeed, does it imply in any way a commitment to any general principle of collective freedom. Nicias had gone to Syracuse with imperialist designs on Sicily. The Greeks preferred the term 'autonomy' when speaking of this kind of independence and we should follow their example.

A second way in which the term is used may be called 'organic freedom'. This refers to the capacity of adult members of a community to participate in its life and government. This is the right to what the Greeks understood as citizenship. As Gomme points out, it entails 'at least the minimum: the right to take part in the election and scrutiny of all officers of the state, the voting for laws, and the voting for war and peace and alliance.' This is minimal democracy. It is not, however, the same thing as personal freedom. The two, in fact, can sometimes be incompatible, as the cases of the ancient Spartans and the modern white South Africans demonstrate. Nor, further, is citizenship a peculiarly Western development. I find the ethnocentric claims of Western historians, especially classical scholars, rather tiresome on this subject. Instead of citing evidence to the contrary I merely suggest that the sceptical browse through any anthropology textbook on tribal politics in Asia and Africa.

I come now to the most common meaning of the term freedom, namely personal liberty. This is what I will be talking about, for it is this value which is peculiar to the West; and it is its status as supreme value which is so problematic. I hope to show that there have been two versions of personal freedom in the West, both having their source in a common negation. The version which now prevails is the liberal one, but this is a very recent development, going no further back than the early nineteenth century. By it I mean the belief that an individual, as a 'mere individual' (Plamenatz) independent of any of his social roles, is free from any interference from without. It is the claim that a person can do as he pleases as long as this does not interfere with the capacity of others to do likewise.

Maurice Cranston thinks that this meaning, or something like it, is the only lexicographical one today. He is right in claiming that in conventional usage 'being free to' is not to be confused with 'being able to,' and that 'man does not say he is free to do a thing simply because he possesses the power or faculty to do it ... he says he is free to do it only when he wants to refer to the absence of impediments in the way of doing it.' This is well taken. But as J. H. Loenen has recently argued, the purely lexicographical definition of freedom also includes the idea of 'not being determined from without,' which is not the same thing as 'not being interfered with from without,' since a person who is not being interfered with may well choose passively to be determined. As we shall see, this has been the version of personal freedom which dominated the Western world for most of the history of the idea of freedom. In any case, to define freedom merely as the absence of impediment runs the risk of triviality. All organisms resist constraint. This is a biological imperative. At the very least, in its liberal version, freedom must mean, and has meant, the absence of human restraint on the individual. It has also meant a special kind of restraint.

At the heart of the idea of personal freedom is the notion of a negation of some restraining and endangering power. From this negation, however, it is possible to move in two directions. One is the view that freedom is an inherent desire, a purely human need, so essential that it is a defining part of one's humanness. This leads naturally to what Gibbs terms 'nonprescriptive freedom': 'a man is free if he is able to do, have, or be what is good and pleases him, without being obstructed or threatened by anything or anyone. To set someone free is to take away whatever it is that encumbers or endangers him' (Gibbs, p. 15).

But the negation can be interpreted in another way. It can be seen as coming, not from the individual who of necessity desires and takes it, but from the restraining power which, as an act of pure generosity, bestows it as a gift on the individual who passively and gratefully receives it. This leads to the prescriptive version of personal freedom: 'the idea of exemption from servitude and being allowed to do as one pleases, within certain limits' (Gibbs). Prescriptive personal freedom is the entitlement to do what the law is silent about, but by its very nature it requires the continued existence of the indulging power and its laws, the benign Leviathan.

THE STRANGE CAREER OF FREEDOM

I propose to argue in this preliminary sketch that there were six moments in the socio-historical development of freedom as social value.

(1) *The First Moment: Slavery and the Invention of Freedom*

Who were the first persons to have the unusual idea that being free was not only a value to be cherished but the most important thing that someone could possess? The answer, in a word, is slaves. Freedom began its career as a social value in the desperate yearning of the slave to negate what for him, and for non-slaves, was a peculiarly inhuman condition. Now in saying this I am advocating nothing new. Many historians have pointed out that freedom started as a special legal status. What has not been recognized, however, is the critical fact that the idea of freedom has never been divorced from this, its primordial servile source. Failure to recognize this springs from too great an emphasis on the legal aspects of the status first called freedom. When a slave was freed, however, much more was going on than the simple creation of a new legal status. To understand this requires a better knowledge of the condition called slavery.

Slavery is the permanent, violent and personal domination of natally alienated and generally dishonored persons (see Patterson, 1982). It is, first, a form of personal domination.

Slavery: the Underside of Freedom

One individual is under the direct power of another or his agent. Usually this, in practice, entails the power of life and death over the slave. Second, the slave is always an excommunicated person. He does not belong to the legitimate social or moral community; he is, in other words, natally alienated. Third, the slave is in a perpetual condition of dishonor. What is more, the master parasitically gains honor in degrading his slave.

These three constituent features of the slave condition add up to a generalized conception of slavery as a state of social death. The slave is always conceived of as someone, or the descendent of someone, who should have died, typically as a result of defeat in war, but also as a result of poverty. His physical life was spared in return for his social death and his permanent subjection to the will of another.

Now slavery is a remarkably self-correcting institution. It poses a fundamental problem, but by its very nature provides a novel solution. The problem it poses is that of motivation. Degraded, socially dead, the slave would seem to have no reason or desire to serve his master. The whip was a poor solution, though all masters used it. Few, however, failed to recognize its limitations. Some tried material incentives, but this was rare, the US South being one of those rare cases. Rare because another, far superior solution was presented by the institution. That solution was to hold out the promise of manumission, of freedom, to the slave.

So it was, then, that the idea of freedom as a precious personal value was created. Note with what vile elegance this new value served its purpose. The more the master impresses upon the slave social death, the more he degrades him, the more the latter yearns, desires, hopes for a negation of this terrible state of non-being. The wise master encourages him to hope by permitting him a peculium, that is, he is allowed to save what little he can over and beyond what the master demands. The peculium, of course, legally belongs to the master, but he generously allows the slave to save and to accumulate it through superhuman effort. Then, usually near the end of the slave's life, when he has managed to save the equivalent of his replacement cost, he hands over the peculium to his master as a redemption fee for his freedom. The master's gain is fourfold. The slave has worked excessively hard all his life; the master receives from the slave enough money to buy a brand new slave; he is relieved of any legal responsibility to provide for the slave in his old age; and he now has a free retainer who remains eternally grateful to him for granting him the privilege of buying his freedom.

What on earth, one must ask, does the slave think he is doing? What has he gained? Rarely material security. Rarely, also, complete personal independence for, as with the freedmen of Delphi studied by Keith Hopkins, most freedmen promptly reestablished a relation of dependency with their ex-masters, only now it was a free patron–client relationship. The freedman did not necessarily gain, either, any of the specific powers the master had over him. As Roman jurists noted, the manumission transaction was not a conveyance. Whatever it was the slave gained was not what the master had given up. This presented a real conceptual dilemma, the responses to which I shall return to shortly. First, though, let us answer the question: what did the freedman gain? What the freedman experienced, the essential core of his freedom, was the negation of his generalized condition of social death. Implicit in this was his rebirth. Freedom was the negation which resulted in life. We arrive then at the single most important quality defining freedom, that it exists always in dialectical relation with the horror of social death; that to be meaningful, to have content, it requires the idea of its opposite. Freedom, strictly, makes no sense when viewed in static terms. To define freedom as 'the absence of impediments' and leave the matter at that, as so many modern liberal philosophers do, is to invite confusion or metaphysical drivel. Freedom, the ex-slave knew, so do all ordinary people, is an active thing. To contemplate one's freedom is to think of being freed, being liberated from something. If that liberation is to be generalized, then the thing from which one has been liberated must also be a generalized condition. I am saying that that generalized condition is the state of death. Because of this we think of liberation as a form of rebirth. And further, we think of freedom as life. And that is why, to the man on the proverbial Clapham omnibus, or New York subway, talking about his freedom so naturally runs into talking about his life. And that is why, finally, it is so easy to talk about giving one's life for one's freedom, or being rather physically dead than not having it. So it was with the ex-slave. So it has remained to this day.

Slavery: the Underside of Freedom

I said earlier that the act of freeing the slave presented the master as well as the community of free persons with something of a conceptual dilemma. There were two solutions. One, preferred by all masters, was that freedom could simply not be bought and sold, that it was essentially a gift by the master to the slave. The redemption fee was either a token of gratitude or compensation for services lost. The thing, freedom, the *decision* by the master to permit the redemption, was an act of pure generosity. The master, god-like, gave the slave life, a view explicitly stated in the Koran, and implied in the Christian view that manumission was always an act of piety. The ex-slave, then, was expected to express gratitude, in Roman terms, *obsequium*. As a good client, the slave could expect further gifts and privileges from his ex-master, now his patron or 'father'. These privileges, when they received legal sanction, became rights. Conditional freedom of this sort, then, became the source of what Gibbs calls prescriptive rights. As we have seen, in the primordial ex-slave situation, such rights incurred obligations. Obedience, gratitude, *obsequium* to the law-giving lord were implicit in the transaction. True freedom, so defined, was only possible through obedience to law and authority.

But there was a second interpretation of what freedom meant in social terms, one favored by the ex-slave, though he was rarely in a situation to realize it. The slave could be freed unconditionally. In extreme cases his freedom could even be interpreted as a form of nullification, very much like the Catholic church's treatment of divorce. His enslavement could have been declared null and void because he had been wrongfully enslaved in the first place. He had never really been a slave. Roman law made provision for this, not only in the case of Roman citizens who had managed to escape enslavement in alien lands and returned home, but in rare cases, where the emperor intervened on behalf of some favored slave. Such a freed person had his natality fully restored. He was free to do as he pleased without any regard to the ex-master. Unconditional freedom was obviously a rare occurrence. There was only one circumstance under which large numbers of slaves were so freed: rebellion. Nonetheless it was always held as a model of one version of the freedom which came with the negation of social death. It was, of course, the prototype of what earlier was described as non-prescriptive freedom, the version of freedom which was to triumph, at long last, in the nineteenth century, the liberty which, as J. S. Mill puts it, 'consists in doing what one desires.'

(2) The Second Moment: Ancient Greece

Since slavery existed everywhere at some time, freedom made its appearance among all the peoples of the world. And yet, it is only in the West that it became a dominant value. There are two reasons for this. Partly it is due to the fact that it is mainly in the West that we find large-scale social systems. In most parts of the world where slavery existed, it was of minor significance. The slave population would have been no more than between one and five per cent of the total population; and the freed population rarely above one per cent. For most human populations, then, freedom though known would have remained the eccentric preoccupation of a lowly and demographically insignificant segment of the population. The very fact that this segment of the population celebrated it would have ensured that freedom remained of low status value.

Nonetheless, we know that there were a fair number of cases outside the West in which slavery became structurally important and freedmen came to constitute a not insignificant segment of the total population; certain Islamic societies come to mind, and there was the dramatic, if isolated case of medieval Korea where the slave population was for several centuries as proportionately great as the US South. Why then did freedom not become an important value in these societies? Clearly, a purely socio-economic explanation will not do. The second major reason for the rise of freedom as a supreme value in the West is the fact that the religion which was to dominate and define Western civilization bears a peculiar relationship to freedom as I have defined it above. To these developments which account for the unique relationship between freedom and Western civilization I now turn, starting with ancient Greece.

Ancient Greece was the first group of societies in world history to become dependent on large-scale slavery. By the fourth century BC the slave population of Athens reached approximately thirty per cent of the total. What is more, for the first time slaves were to play a critical role in the economic life of an advanced society. As Moses Finley has shown (Finley,

Slavery: the Underside of Freedom

1960; 1973) slavery became 'a basic element in Greek civilization.' With the exception of politics and the military 'there was no activity, productive or unproductive, public or private, pleasant or unpleasant, which was not performed by slaves at some times and in some places in the Greek world.' He concludes his classic paper on the subject (1960) with the following observation:

> I have already made the point that the more advanced the Greek city-state, the more it will be found to have had true slavery rather than the 'hybrid' types like helotage. More bluntly put, the cities in which individual freedom reached its highest expression — most obviously Athens — were cities in which chattel slavery flourished.

Finley speaks of individual freedom, but it should be noted that there lies behind this assertion a major controversy dating back to a celebrated lecture given by Benjamin Constant in 1819. There he stated that individual liberty did not exist in ancient Greece. Classicists have been arguing the matter ever since. Both sides of the debate, it seems to me, have missed the main point. The proper answer to the question, did personal freedom exist in ancient Greece? is: it depends on what segment of the population you are talking about. If we are talking about the Greek intellectual elite such as Plato and Aristotle, the group we usually think about when we think of Greece, the answer is a definite no. For them, and I suspect for the generality of Greeks, citizenship was to remain the supreme value, and this the Greeks never confused with freedom. For free-born Greeks the term freedom, when not used (and then infrequently) in the sense of collective autonomy, referred to the legal status of freedmen. This they came to define in quite precise terms, actually specifying four elements of freedom: the right of access to the courts; protection from illegal seizure; the ability to go where one wanted; and the right to work where and how one pleased. Now the very schematism of this formulation, so alien to the Greek way of thinking, should raise our suspicions concerning the value which the average Greek, not to mention the aristocratic elite, would place on these freedoms. And when we learn, further, that it was possible for a slave to unbundle this banausic menu of 'freedoms' and, in the ancient equivalent of a down-payment plan (the *paramoné*, on which see Keith Hopkins, 1978) purchase them one at a time, we are left in no doubt about their status. I hope I am not being misunderstood. I am not saying that these things did not matter to the average Greek. I am saying, rather, that he took these 'freedoms' for granted in the same way that he would have taken his right to perform his bodily functions for granted. It would never have occurred to any free-born Greek to celebrate them. To do so would have been to reveal the shame of once having been enslaved. Besides, as I have argued earlier, personal freedom, as it evolved from the experience of slavery, was not a static legal thing; it was an active negation. The four so-called 'freedoms' which were purchased were not identified with liberation even by the ex-slave.

The important fact remains, however, that a substantial proportion of the population of these Greek states would have experienced the negation of death and the rebirth which was freedom. Furthermore, many of these freedmen were literate persons who had not remained immune from the intellectualism of the master class. Thus, in the same way that the ruling class intellectuals took the old idea of participation and both developed and refined it to new levels of sophistication, so must have many of the freedmen of ancient Greece refined the idea of freedom in their reflections. It was among the Stoics that we find philosophical reflections on freedom most developed. To be sure, they thought of personal freedom mainly in terms of spiritual liberation, a major development, for it was to provide the Western tradition with the standard way of circumventing the radical implications of the idea of freedom when large numbers of persons began to interpret it in a non-prescriptive way. Nearly all freedmen in ancient Greece were barbarians; it is perhaps not without significance that Stoicism was the school of Greek thought most influenced by barbarians, beginning with its Semitic founder, Zeno. The large-scale presence of slavery in Greek life did have one important effect on elite thought which was later to influence the Western idea of freedom. I refer to the role of slavery in Plato's thought. Plato not only took slavery for granted but used the master–slave relationship as a model of good government. Gregory Vlastos long ago demonstrated that 'in principle there is no difference in Plato's political theory between the relation of a master to his slave and of a sovereign to his subjects.' He also shows that the slave metaphor is an important key to the understanding of Plato's cosmology. The slave lacks logos, as do the material world and the masses. Left to themselves disorder, hybris, reigns. 'Order is imposed upon them by a benevolent superior: master, guardian, mind, demiurge ... the common title to authority is the possession of logos' (Vlastos, 1960).

Now Plato emphatically did not consider it necessary to distort language by claiming that his ideal society was the repository of freedom. Freedom, if he deigned to consider the concept at all, would have been associated with the 'disorder' of a society without order, reason and justice. Freedom never became, in the Greek world, what Maurice Cranston calls 'a hurrah word'. That, however, would change in the centuries to come.

There was, however, in one area of Greek life an identification of freedom, as we have defined it, with authority. I refer to the system of sacral manumissions widely practiced in Delphi (on which see Boemer; Hopkins). Here the ritual of manumission took the form of a sale to the god Apollo. The slave was not really freed, but re-enslaved to the God who, however, by not exercising his proprietorial rights allowed the ex-slave to go and do as he pleased. This was largely a legal transaction, but behind it was an old religious concept found not only in the Greek, but throughout the ancient Near Eastern world: that true freedom was only possible through re-enslavement to a god since only the gods are free.

Now if we conflate Plato's model of the just state as a form of slavery dictated by reason with this Delphic and Near Eastern idea of freedom as divine re-enslavement, we arrive at a new, startlingly original and thoroughly frightening conception of prescriptive freedom. As we shall see, just such a conflation began with Paul and was to culminate in the Augustinian version of freedom, the version that was to dominate the Western mind for the next 1500 years. But I have anticipated the argument.

(3) *The Third Moment: Rome*

If slavery was an important institution in Greece, in Rome it became *the* all-important institution. By the end of the republic Rome had emerged as a large-scale slave system in which not only its urban economy, but, more important, its rural areas witnessed a massive intrusion of slaves. What is more, this intrusion was accompanied by a major transformation of the traditional mode of production, one in which the small farmer was displaced by large slave-based *latifundi*. For the first two and a half centuries of the empire, the imperial bureaucracy would also be run by slaves and freedmen. Perhaps as much as a third of the entire Roman population were slaves. When we take account of the high rate of manumission in the urban areas, Tenney Frank's estimate that by the first century AD perhaps over two-thirds of the population of the city of Rome were either slaves or descendants of slaves seems not unreasonable.

By the late republic we find a social system, then, which was completely permeated — demographically, socially, culturally — by slaves and slavery. What slaves did and thought really mattered for the entire social order. Roman law, for example, was overwhelmingly influenced by the experience of slavery. As Buckland, perhaps one of the greatest students of Roman law observed, the law of slavery was 'the most characteristic part of the most characteristic intellectual product of Rome' (Buckland, 1908). We do not find in Rome an elitist intellectual culture which stipulated a normative order utterly at variance with socio-political realities. To the pragmatic, essentially anti-intellectual Roman mind, law both reflected and defined the social and normative order. Hence, the legal definition of freedom became the normative and sociologically accepted definition. And that definition, as Buckland points out, was unequivocally the negation of slavery, a condition which the Romans explicitly defined as social or civil death.

It is highly significant that in Rome the freedman was extremely proud of his freedom, so proud indeed that whenever he could possibly afford it he celebrated the fact in monumental inscriptions. These inscriptions were addressed to the general public. Obviously, they were taken seriously, quite the opposite of what we would expect in Greece. In Rome, then, we find for the first time a population, the generality of which took the experience of personal freedom as the negation of social death seriously. Freedom had become, at last, an important social value; and it had done so in the most important empire in the history of the world up to that time. To be sure, it would be some time before it became *the* most important value, but it was in the Roman world that the foundation for such a development was laid down.

What did the Roman elite make of all this? The views of two of its most representative thinkers are worth examining: Cicero and Tacitus. Cicero was an aristocrat who disdained democracy and favored an enlightened form of autocratic rule, one in which there would be harmony and concord between the different classes and parts of society. For him obedience and loyalty were essential prerequisites for constitutional government, one in which we 'are slaves to the laws' so that we might be free. In general, Cicero used the term *libertas* to refer to collective autonomy. But in one of his last speeches we find an interesting conflation of the traditional use of the term in the sense of autonomy with what by then would have been its vulgar meaning as the negation of slavery. Speaking of Antony's defiance of the Senate, he declared:

Matters have been brought to the utmost crisis; the issue is liberty. You must either win victory, Romans, which assuredly you will achieve by your loyalty and unanimity or do anything rather than be slaves. Other nations can endure slavery; the assured possession of the Roman people is liberty. (Cicero, Sixth Philippic)

By Tacitus' time Rome had realized all of Cicero's worst fears. Forced to accommodate to a corrupt and murderous political system he came to a view of freedom which was little short of pathetic. Acquiescence to authority in order to be able to serve one's country well is what he settled for. As Wirszubski has aptly summed up the situation, 'the necessary prerequisite of libertas is the renouncement of self-willed actions; consequently, genuine libertas can be enjoyed under the law only' (Wirszubski, 1950).

(4) *The Fourth Moment: Christianity*

If the socio-political realities of Rome took freedom an important step forward, Christianity, its major cultural heritage, was symbolically to institutionalize this development and, in the process, ensured for one version of personal freedom a permanent place as supreme value in the consciousness of Western peoples.

From the viewpoint of comparative religions, Christianity is a truly strange, even bizarre, creed. It is, of course, the religion of salvation *par excellence*. In this regard, it was not unusual for the times in which it was born. Where Christianity differs, where it is utterly unique among the religions of the world, is in its total reliance on the experience of slavery as its ultimate metaphoric source. In every important respect Christianity is nothing more or less than an elaborate symbolic edifice drawing on slavery not only as a system of signals to make statements about the sacred and the ultimate, but as the sociological *signatum* which is represented and symbolically explained. How is this so?

Let us begin with Maurice Goguel's observation that Christianity is not the religion of Jesus, the simple Palestinian Jewish rebel who preached the healing power of love and fellowship. Christianity is the religion of which Christ was the object, a religion created in the centuries after his death, in the Roman world at the height of its dependence on slavery. Most of the early Christians were not slaves, although many certainly were. It is certain that the vast majority of them were urbanites from the artisan and what today we would call the coping sector of the working class. This much is clear from Paul's letters and the other scraps of evidence available. To know this, however, is to be certain of something else, however circumstantial the evidence: that in all likelihood, a substantial proportion, perhaps the majority of these early Christians who formed the religion were either freedmen or the descendants of freedmen. It should come as no surprise, then, that from the very beginning the idea of freedom was to dominate Christian thought.

It is in Paul, the man whose ideas forged the creed, that we find this in a most pronounced way. Freedom is Paul's central preoccupation, freedom in both senses made possible by the negation of death. As Hans Dieter Betz observes, 'his doctrine of salvation is very clearly and consciously formulated as a doctrine of freedom.' We should expect death, then, to be a vital concept of his dialectics. And so it is. The two experiences Paul most frequently refers to are freedom and death.

For Paul, and for all Christians thereafter, human beings fell into the slavery that is spiritual death as a result of Adam's original sin. 'Therefore as sin came into the world through one man and death through sin, so death spread to all men because all men sinned' (Rom. 5:12). Jesus' sacrifice redeemed mankind, at once atoning for our sins and redeeming us from spiritual death. Thus: 'We know that our old self was crucified with him

Slavery: the Underside of Freedom

so that the sinful body might be destroyed, and we might no longer be enslaved to sin' (Rom. 6:6).

Paul, however, had two radically different interpretations of what Jesus' redemptive negation of death entailed. These two interpretations exactly parallel the two versions of freedom which it is possible to deduce from the secular negation of real slavery. What Goguel calls his ethical dualism actually amounts to a constant shifting between the liberal, non-prescriptive and illiberal prescriptive versions of personal freedom.

In the liberal version, Jesus, the God incarnate, gave his life so as to nullify the original act of enslavement. There was, so to speak, a symbolic return to the primordial moment of Adamic weakness and a sacrificial substitution. By choosing death for mankind, mankind's enslavement was annulled in the most complete form of liberation possible. Death was not just negated, death was destroyed. The slate of history was wiped clean; a fresh start was now possible. And in the same way that death was destroyed, so was eternal life now possible. Unless, of course, mankind chose to sin again and bring death back into the world. The choice, however, was there for mankind who was free to choose death again or endless freedom. It is in his letter to the Galatians that Paul most fully develops this liberal interpretation of personal spiritual freedom. He declares boldly that mankind is no longer justified 'by works of the law' but only by faith in Christ: 'Now that faith has come we are no longer under a custodian; for in Christ Jesus you are all sons of God.' Freedom means not only the removal of the impediment, the custodian of law, but equality: 'There is neither Jew nor Greek, there is neither slave nor free, there is neither male nor female; for you are all one in Christ Jesus' (Gal. 5:28). Freedom also makes possible love and fellowship. The believer is 'called to freedom' to love his neighbor and to express joy, peace, patience, kindness, etc. (Gal. 5:22). In the final analysis freedom means individualism and personal responsibility: 'For each man will have to bear his own load;' what we sow is what we reap (Gal. 6:5–8). There is no more lyrical statement of the liberal version of personal freedom than this in all of Western thought. Not again until Mill's essay on liberty some 1900 years later would anyone in the Western tradition, which is to say in the world, dare to utter so completely radical a statement on the liberal version of freedom.

It is, therefore, with something of a shock that we read Paul's later interpretation of freedom in his letter to the Romans, the letter which the church fathers were to place first in the Bible. Here we find, in equally extreme form, the illiberal version of personal freedom. Sin is still death and freedom its negation. But now we find strongly emphasized the view that the freedom which Christ bought with his sacrificial death is a 'free gift' (Rom. 5:15–16). (Note, significantly, that there is no talk of free gift in Galatians.) It is, furthermore, a 'gift of righteousness.' The sinner has 'been brought from death to life,' but as an '*instrument* of righteousness.' True, he still finds it possible to say that the redeemed person is not 'under law but under grace.' What, however, does this mean? The answer is as startling as it is unequivocal: '... now that you have been set free from sin and have become slaves of God, the return you get is sanctification and its end, eternal life. For the wages of sin is death, but the free gift of God is eternal life in Christ our Lord.'

This is distressing enough. Our distress turns to alarm when, a few paragraphs later, Paul tells how 'the law of the spirit of life in Christ Jesus has set me free from the law of sin and death.' And the extremity of this position approaches the point of perversity when Paul identifies this law of the spirit with a new kind of slavery, and then goes on to declare, almost despotically, that: 'you did not receive the spirit of slavery to fall back into fear, but you have received the spirit of sonship!' The old Delphic view of freedom as re-enslavement to divine authority is now completely assimilated.

It is no wonder that several modern Bible scholars have raised serious doubts about Paul's emotional stability. Paul, however, knew exactly what he was about. For one thing, he saw clearly the common origin of both versions of personal freedom. Second, he realized, shrewdly, how one or other version might appeal to different groups and classes of Christians. The extraordinary pliancy and universal appeal of Christianity would be because of just this dualism in its conception of freedom. It was not accidental that the illiberal version of freedom was addressed to the Roman Christians. Paul, with astonishing foresight, saw in what direction Christianity would have to go if it was to conquer mankind. However appealing the liberal version set out in the letter to the Galatians might be, Paul knew that in

Slavery: the Underside of Freedom

the end Christianity would conquer Rome only by conquering its ruling class. We are slaves to the law so that we might be free. We are free, *cum obsequium*, so that we might serve. The illiberal, elitist views of Cicero and Tacitus were to find their perfect religious counterpart in Paul's view of the freedom which Jesus' negation of death brought about: you have been set free from sin and have become slaves of God.

(5) *The Fifth Moment: The Augustinian Convergence*

It is this harsh version of personal freedom which triumphed in Roman Christianity and, in so doing, rode to supremacy among the values of Western peoples. It remained for Augustine to give it its definitive statement, to weld together on the iron anvil of Platonism the secular and sacred elements of prescriptive personal freedom. As Karl Jaspers remarks, Augustine, 'thanks to his understanding of St Paul' was to concern himself more than any other thinker before him 'with the uncertainty of freedom, the ground of its possibility (and) the question of its meaning' (Jaspers, p. 95).

Like Paul, there is a chronic dualism in Augustine, reinforced by his previous Manichean faith. Unlike Paul, however, Augustine leaves us in no doubt concerning which side to choose. His two cities are, in essence, the two versions of freedom made possible by the negation of death. Evil is the liberal version, the arrogance of self-determination; the Pelagian heresy. It is the freedom of the city of man. Goodness is the freedom which God gives and man by the grace of Christ, passively receives (The City of God, XIV, 28). Liberal freedom is impure, arrogant, anti-social and destructive of the common good. Both forms of freedom are predetermined. God in his 'incomprehensible comprehension' has so determined it. Nonetheless, even though he had once thought that 'no one should be coerced into the unity of Christ' Augustine tells us that others had changed his mind, not by their reasoning 'but by conclusive examples to which they could point' (Przywara, ed., p. 275).

In a brilliant commentary, Jaspers (p. 93) argues that Augustine's views can be summed up in terms of a single antithesis:

The *world of unfree will* is the ought that the will does not obey, the will that does not fulfil its purpose, the good intentions that are dissipated by lust, the will that cannot will; it is the heeding of the ethical injunction which, though it says: thou canst because thou shouldst, is actually an inability that cannot recognize itself as such. The *world of free will* opens up when love has no further need of an ought, but accomplishes without good resolutions and dispels the lusts by its reality. This reality can do what it will, because its loving will is itself a being-able.

Note however, that behind this terrifyingly prescriptive view of freedom lies the core idea of redemption from Adamic slavery and spiritual death. Nowhere is this more evident than in Augustine's view on the role of fear in the attainment of freedom. The Christian serves God in 'fear and trembling.' He distinguishes, however, between two kinds of fear — the servile fear of the slave and the 'chaste' fear of the freedman, the sinner who has been 'adopted' by his loving, generous master, God.

'Thou who art more inward than my inmost self, hast set a law within my heart by Thy Spirit, as it were by thy fingers, that I might not fear it as a slave without love, but might love it with a chaste fear as a son, and fear it with a chaste love' (Augustine, Sermons, 22,6).

This, then, was the version of personal freedom which was to dominate the Western consciousness down to the end of the eighteenth century. Its persistence and dominance, as I have said earlier, was largely due to the Catholic church and, the point must be emphasized, to Protestantism right down to the sectarian revolution at the end of the eighteenth century. However, the socio-political realities of the middle ages and early modern Europe provided the structural framework for such a perpetuation. Slavery, real slavery, remained an important part of the medieval world. The serfs, as they never forgot, or were made never to forget, were the descendants of slaves who had been 'liberated' upward into the status of domiciled bondsmen, and of former freemen who had been 'liberated' from internal and external dangers downward to the status also of domiciled bondsmen. (For an excellent recent analysis of this development see Pierre Dockes, 1979.) The medieval lord had gained his power through military might and by the use of *mafiosi*-type tactics in which free small farmers were made offers that they simply could not refuse: they were 'persuaded' that they needed the protection of the patron from dangers which, as often as not, came from the hit-men of the patrons themselves. The origin of the middle ages, we are just beginning to learn, was a very sordid business.

The presence of slavery as a living institution continued to reinforce the illiberal version of freedom which fitted nicely into this social order. Slavery not only persisted right through the middle ages, but underwent a massive revival in Spain and Italy in the late middle ages. The Venetian Empire was based on large-scale plantation slavery in the Mediterranean islands. These, in turn, were the models for the slave systems of the Iberians in the Atlantic islands, and these, in their turn, were the models for the African-based slave systems of the early New World. There was no break between the slavery of the ancient and the modern world (Verlinden, 1955, 1975; D. B. Davis, 1966). Even in Northern Europe, as Davis has pointed out, 'the continuing prestige of Roman law tended to perpetuate a concept of the slave as a personal possession almost totally subject to his owner's will.'

The main point I want to make in concluding this section is that the Renaissance and the Reformation influenced but in no way fundamentally altered the conception of freedom which triumphed in the late Roman and early medieval world. Their influence must be seen within the context of the development of the absolutist states. These states, as recent scholarship has demonstrated, did not involve any clean break with the feudal past but were, rather, a reform of that order which made possible the continued rule of the feudal nobility: 'Absolutism was essentially just this: a redeployed and recharged apparatus of feudal domination, designed to clamp the peasant masses back into their traditional position — despite and against the gains they had won by the widespread commutation of dues' (Anderson, p. 18).

Complementing this development was the recharging and redeployment of the intellectual and religious life of Europe which we know as the Renaissance and the Reformation. (For an excellent synthesis of recent scholarship on these movements see Gerhard, 1981.) It is now well established that the Reformation, while it had important structural consequences for the absolutist state, involved no major break in Christian thought. Indeed, as far as the central Christian conception of freedom was concerned, it involved a rejection of the fumbling contemplations on the possibilities of the liberal version of freedom which we find in the likes of John of Salisbury and a vigorous restatement of the illiberal Pauline–Augustine version of personal freedom. There is something balefully appropriate in the current rehabilitation and celebration of Martin Luther by the East German authorities.

But Luther was not alone in this business. We all know about Calvin's murderous authoritarianism. Milton, in spite of his political associations, was not much different in his views on freedom. Man 'is free by virtue of a shared belief in the existence of God.' He is not free, however, to do as he pleases. Liberty for Milton meant discipline. Man is free to do only what is good, never what is wrong (see Michael Macklem, 1978).

(6) *The Sixth Moment: Capitalism and the Liberation of the Liberal Version of Freedom*

It was with the rise of industrial capitalism and the ascendancy of the bourgeoisie at the end of the eighteenth and during the nineteenth century that the second, liberal version of freedom finally came to centre-stage in the Western consciousness. How this happened is common knowledge. I will make only a few summary remarks on the process, remarks which will have to be developed elsewhere. There were three interrelated revolts, one political, against the tyranny of the state; the second religious, the sectarian movement, against the tyranny of the Pauline–Augustine–Lutheran tradition of personal spiritual freedom; and the third, moral, against the actual, rampant slavery spawned by capitalism in the New World. The three were closely interrelated. Capitalism required for its proper functioning the personally free individual, unencumbered by ascriptive ties, what Plamenatz calls 'the mere individual.' But it would be gross materialism to suggest that this was all, or even primarily what was involved.

Personal freedom in the liberal sense, even more than its illiberal prescriptive counterpart, requires the menace of an endangering power to be meaningful. Slavery and the dread of social death was once again that menace, both symbolically and realistically. In political terms we find a growing tendency to identify the state with slavery during the late eighteenth and nineteenth centuries. The absolutist state, since it was modelled on the idea of a Platonic harmony of masters and slaves, was easily defined as a form of slavery. In the religious domain, the sectarian

Slavery: the Underside of Freedom

revolution involved a quite self-conscious return to the liberal version of freedom and salvation contained in Paul's letter to the Galatians.

In an exquisite passage, David Brion Davis concludes his discussion of ancient slavery thus: 'For some two thousand years men thought of sin as a kind of slavery. One day they would come to think of slavery as sin.' That moment, as he shows later, came with the humanitarian reforms of the late eighteenth and early nineteenth centuries of which the Abolitionist movement was one critical phase. 'The reformer would achieve freedom from the tyranny of self-interest by merging his soul in a transcendent cause' (Davis, p. 365). This was no doubt quite true, especially for the religious reformers.

But there were many people involved with the Abolition movement who were not religious sectarians, who were quite happy with their self-interest and who had no problems with the state of their souls. What is more, many Abolitionists cared little for the Blacks; were in fact complete racists. Why did they become so intensely involved in this extraordinary movement? The answer, clearly, is that it solved one of the major problems of the liberal version of personal freedom, what may be called the crisis of content. 'The absence of impediment' is simply not enough as a doctrine of freedom. It requires some endangering force, some image of social death which is being negated. Only then does it come alive, does it become liberation and in so doing generate life as its reward. This is what real slavery in the New World provided for those secular Europeans who had lost their Christian faith or at any rate were no longer sufficiently terrified by the idea of spiritual death, and who felt they had gone far enough in the metaphoric definition of the state as a kind of slavery. The Abolitionist movement was for these people not really primarily intended for the Blacks whose freedom was simply a happy by-product of something more important. It was their own freedom which the Abolitionists were experiencing by their actions. The Abolitionists, at any rate the secular among them, did not discover liberal personal freedom first, and then, on principle, feel an urgent moral obligation to abolish slavery. Rather, it was in order to give content to the liberal conception of personal freedom, to discover and experience this freedom that, in a vicarious identification with the real thing, they re-enacted the sense of rebirth that the negation of slavery brings.

I will conclude by reflecting aloud on one point. If the liberal version of personal freedom requires either the experience of social death or its symbolic equivalent, what does it mean today that this version of freedom has triumphed at a time when the idea of social death in both its secular and religious forms has gone or waned? Has the communist world become the new vision of social death? Is it accidental that the president of the United States who most strongly and sincerely believes in the most extreme form of the liberal version of freedom, also believes in 'evil empires.' What does this mean for the peace of the world? Does our concept of personal freedom enslave us to the perpetual re-invention of symbolic substitutes for the social death that was once slavery?

REFERENCES

P. Anderson, *Lineages of the Absolutist State*, London, 1974
St Augustine, *The City of God*, London, 1947
St Augustine, *Sermons*, Westminster, 1952
H. D. Betz, *Paul's Concept of Freedom in the Context of Hellenistic Discussions about Possibilities of Human Freedom*, Berkeley, 1977
F. Boemer, *Untersuchungen über die Religion der Sklaven in Griechenland und Rom*, Wiesbaden, 1960
W. W. Buckland, *The Roman Law of Slavery: The condition of the Slave in Private Law from Augustus to Justinian*, Cambridge, 1908
B. Constant, *Oeuvres politiques*, Paris, 1870, pp. 258–85
M. Cranston, *Freedom*, New York, 1953
D. B. Davis, *The Problem of Slavery in Western Culture*, Ithaca, 1966
P. Dockes, *Medieval Slavery and Liberation*, Chicago, 1982
M. I. Finley, 'Was Greek Civilization Based on Slave Labor?', in Finley (ed.), 1960
M. I. Finley (ed.), *Slavery in Classical Antiquity*, Cambridge, 1960
M. I. Finley, *The Ancient Economy*, Berkeley, 1973
Y. Garlon, *Les Esclaves en Grèce ancienne*, Paris, 1982
D. Gerhard, *Old Europe: A Study in Continuity, 1000–1800*, New York, 1981
B. Gibbs, *Freedom and Liberation*, Sussex, 1976
M. Goguel, *Jésus et les Origines du Christianisme*, Paris, 1932
A. W. Gomme, *More Essays in Greek History and Liberation*, Oxford, 1962
K. Hopkins, *Conquerors and Slaves*, Cambridge, 1978
K. Jaspers, *Plato and Augustine*, New York, 1962
J. H. Loenen, 'The Concept of Freedom in Berlin and Others', *Journal of Value Inquiry*, Winter, 1976, pp. 279–85
M. Macklem, *Liberty and the Holy City. The idea of Freedom in English History*, Ottawa, 1978

- J. S. Mill, *Utilitarianism, Liberty and Representative Government*, London, Everyman, 1910
- O. Patterson, *Slavery and Social Death*, Cambridge, Mass., 1982
- J. Plamenatz, 'Liberalism' in P. P. Wiener (ed.), *Dictionary of the History of Ideas, III*, New York, 1973
- E. Przywara (ed.), *An Augustine Synthesis*, New York, 1958
- C. Verlinden, *L'Esclavage dans l'Europe médiévale*, two vols, Brugge, 1955 and 1976
- G. Vlastos, 'Slavery in Plato's Republic', in M. I. Finley, 1960, pp. 133–49
- C. Wirszubski, *Libertas as a Political Idea in Rome during the Late Republic and Early Empire*, Cambridge, 1950

3

Freeing the Slaves: How Important Was Wilberforce?

JAMES WALVIN

Let me begin by quoting from a slave song of Jamaica in 1816. In that year, almost a decade after the ending of the slave trade to the island and yet a further twenty years before full freedom, slaves themselves were in no doubt as to who were their friends.

> *Oh me good friend Mr Wilberforce make we free*
> *God Almighty thank ye! God Almighty thank ye!*
> *God Almighty, make we free.*

In those slaves' eyes, God and Wilberforce were close allies in breaking the bonds which had tied African and local-born slaves to a lifetime's bondage for almost two centuries past. Nor was this an exceptional view. Time and again, slaves in the early nineteenth century were punished for even mentioning Wilberforce's name. In 1823, seventeen Jamaican slaves were arrested and tried for hurrahing Wilberforce; three of them were transported, the rest dispatched to the local workhouse. The court decided that the event was because of 'reports of what is going on in England'.[1]

Of the many things 'going on in England' one of the most significant was that complexity of events culminating in the abolition of the slave trade in 1807 and the ending of slavery itself in 1838. And at the heart of that series of momentous changes was the person of William Wilberforce; the man who, to many people today, just as to those Jamaican slaves of 1816, not only personified the campaign to free the slaves but was

Freeing the Slaves: How Important Was Wilberforce? 31

also the immediate cause of black freedom. It is worth asking whether such a view remains justifiable.

In some ways it may be felt that this is an open and shut case. Wilberforce was praised by slaves, hated by the planters, immortalised by Parliament and had his memory enshrined in Westminster Abbey, and all for the same reason: his crucial and determining role in the campaign to free the slaves. Yet, as is argued elsewhere in this volume, there are many doubts among modern historians about the role of Wilberforce in the campaign against slavery and the slave trade. What is proposed here is to turn the question round; approaching it, not so much from the standpoint of Parliament but by looking at slavery itself, at the grassroots campaign against it in Britain and, in less detail, at the role played by the slaves themselves.

But let us begin with the slave trade and slavery. From the early sixteenth century onwards, black Africans were intruded into the early settlements and embryonic economies of Iberian America; undertaking work native Indians could or would not do − though often initially working side by side with pioneering white settlers. From this rudimentary beginning, and since Africa seemed able to supply limitless cargoes of black muscle power for whatever European settlements took place in the New World, there evolved the 'triangular trade' (though triangular is too neat a concept accurately to describe what became an increasingly complex web of maritime links) tying together the economies of Europe, West Africa and the colonial settlements of the Americas. The British were relatively late on the scene. But, once attracted to the economic potential of the slave trade, and once having their own settlements from the early seventeenth century onwards to feed with African labour, they were able, because of their dominant maritime power and domestic political conditions, increasingly to dominate and shape the nature and direction of the Atlantic slave trade.[2]

By the mid-eighteenth century the British slave trade was a major economic enterprise; its benefits accruing to the nation's major overseas ports − London, Liverpool, Bristol, Glasgow − and even a host of minor ones. (Who would imagine Whitehaven as a slaving port?) But it also fed and nurtured that complex infrastructure, of banking, insurance, supply and ship building which sustained sectors of the economies of those towns and of their hinterland.

There were few doubts in the minds of the mid-eighteenth-century investors, or dabblers in the slave trade, that it was profitable — or rather that it held out the prospects of profits — though it is true that disaster could strike, in the form of storm, slave disease or revolt. Yet, recent work has suggested the slave trade was not as profitable as earlier historians have claimed. Whereas Eric Williams in *Capitalism and Slavery* imputed to the slave system profits which were so abundant that, in their turn, they laid the basis for the development of late-eighteenth-century industrial capitalism, more recently it seems clear that the profits were actually no greater on average than other forms of overseas trade.[3] Thus, one result of recent research has been to suggest that the direct consequences of the slave trade and slavery on the emergence of modern industrial capitalism — the origins of the industrial revolution — were relatively small. Nonetheless, it has still to be stressed that by, say, the break away of the American colonies in 1776, there were few people who doubted that slave trade's profitability. And it is also clear that few people doubted its morality.

True, there were Quaker denunciations of human bondage which regularly pepper the literature from the 1670s when George Fox himself denounced slavery. But, by and large, even as late as 1776, such voices were echoing in a wilderness. And yet, within a mere generation, this had been utterly transformed. As Fiona Spiers clearly shows elsewhere, by the end of the eighteenth century, it was only accident — contingent factors no one could have predicted — in conjunction with Wilberforce's own political ineptitude — which prevented the slave trade from being abolished before the end of the eighteenth century.

When we consider the undisputed role of the economics of the slaving system, and the unquestioned morality of slavery, this transformation must surely rank as one of the most rapid transmutations of collective political opinion in modern British history. If we compare it, say, to the parallel and contemporary demand for parliamentary reform — to which anti-slavery was in many respects closely related — and which took an eternity to effect — anti-slavery seems swift, effective and clinical. To put the matter simply, within the adult lifetime of Wilberforce (between 1787–1833) not only did Parliament and vast numbers of British people come to view slavery and the slave trade as wrong — and possibly economically irrational — but those institutions themselves were overthrown. Thereafter, the Victorians went to inordinate lengths, using a substantial part of the Royal Navy and the full power of the Foreign Office, to see that the rest of the world adhered to our own newly found morality, by not trading in slaves. Indeed it was characteristic of that cultural imperialism which lay at the heart of the Victorian state that the British went to inordinate lengths to ensure that the rest of the world became as civilised as themselves — by ending the slave trade and slavery. But it is also a sign of British effectiveness, that US slavery was not ended until the disaster of the Civil War — thirty years after the ending of British slavery. And it is also important to remember that even with one-third of the Royal Navy committed to anti-slavery patrols throughout the rest of the nineteenth century, more than one and a half million Africans were nonetheless transported from their homelands and dumped in the Americas, primarily in Cuba and Brazil, in the nineteenth century.[4]

It is not to be a cynic to note that in the USA up to 1863, and in Cuba and Brazil until the 1880s, slavery (and the inevitable slave trading from Africa) thrived *because* the institution was unquestionably economically buoyant. We are then faced once more with a variant of that recurring question which simply will not go away: did the British abolish their own slave system at an earlier date because it was no longer economically worthwhile?

It is helpful to recall that the campaigns against the slave trade and slavery fell into distinct though related stages. Firstly, beginning in 1787 was the campaign against the slave trade; a campaign which had succeeded by 1807. Secondly, in the years between 1815–20, in trying to discover the exact results of abolition, Abolitionists pressed for a slave census — for slave 'registration'. Thirdly, from the mid-1820s through to 1833 there was the campaign to end slavery itself. Fourthly, between 1834–8 there existed the 'apprenticeship' system — a halfway house between slavery and freedom (slaves working free for their former masters for a certain number of hours before being free to work for themselves.) Fifthly and finally, full freedom came in 1838 and the period thereafter, as suggested earlier, witnessed an international campaign against the slave trade. For present purposes, the key episodes in this complex history are the first two, for it was in the campaign against the slave trade and later for slave registration that Wilberforce was most closely involved. As Dr Spiers underlines elsewhere, Wilberforce and his colleagues attached crucial importance to ending the slave trade. They were quite right to do so — but often for reasons they could not have fully grasped at the time.

It was widely felt among the Evangelicals that if the supply of Africans could be cut, slave owners in the West Indies would be forced to treat their slaves better. Since they could no longer buy new Africans, they would have to encourage breeding, by creating better working and social conditions. Thus, through the consequential amelioration after abolition, the slaves would thrive and the slave system would in effect die a natural death. Unfortunately, the arguments pivoted on faulty evidence. The fundamental explanation why slave populations did not thrive had little to do with cruel treatment *per se*; it was largely a matter of demography. The age structure and balance between the sexes on slave plantations was such that no amount of better treatment could have produced a better rate of breeding. In fact, this point has only fully been revealed in recent years by dint of detailed demographic research on slave populations.[5] More recently, however, various historical interpretations have concentrated not so much on what the Abolitionists expected, but rather on what were their motives.

Until the mid-1940s it was widely assumed by historians that the key explanatory determinant of Abolitionist behaviour was religion; that the small band of men led by Wilberforce were convinced that in slavery they saw a monstrous sin, and their efforts were to persuade Parliament of their feeling. Evangelicals undoubtedly saw themselves in this light. But the key question is: does it provide a satisfactory or sufficient explanation for the success of the campaign (as opposed to their motives)? Since World War Two more and more historians have in fact argued that this does not provide a convincing answer. There has in recent years been an irresistible temptation to accept an interpretation of the ending of the slave trade as an economically-determined change in which the humanitarians, led by Wilberforce, played a useful but only incidental role.

Stated crudely, the argument advanced by Eric Williams, and

Freeing the Slaves: How Important Was Wilberforce?

other subsequent historians, is that the slave trade was ended when it had become economically redundant; when other forms of economic activity became more attractive and lured British imperial economic interests *away* from the old protected slaving system. The problem with this interpretation (and inevitably this version is a shortened and crude one by reducing it so drastically) is that it is now challenged by recent economic analysis. It seems very likely that, when the Wilberforce-led campaign against the slave trade reached a peak, in the late 1780s and early 1790s, it did so when the slave trade was economically buoyant. Now if this is so, if the slave trade was profitable and was seen to be so, economic decline cannot provide an explanation. Once more, historians are forced to re-examine the fundamentals of the problem. Could it be, yet again, that we have to turn to Wilberforce and friends, driven by the power of religious conviction, for an explanation of abolition? It is here that the author's own work seems relevant, more especially the degree to which anti-slavery became a *popular* political issue.

The case can be stated boldly and somewhat crudely. The anti-slavery campaign set in train after 1787 rapidly became a national political issue of unprecedented popularity, among all sorts and conditions, among both sexes and to a degree which amazed even the most optimistic Abolitionist. When in 1787–8 Thomas Clarkson made his exhausting lecture tour throughout the country, he was regularly staggered by the crowds packing his lecture rooms. Indeed it is no exaggeration to say, that from 1787 to 1838, the only constraint on the size of anti-slavery audiences was the capacity of the meeting place. If we examine anti-slavery over the whole span of its history, between 1787–1838, it becomes clear that the tactics adopted, in the context of a rapidly changing British society — whose towns and religions were themselves in turmoil — go a long way to explain how anti-slavery became *the* most popular political issue in these years. Abolitionist tactics were responsible for the transformation of the concept of black freedom, from the preserve of a small handful of propertied, educated men of sensibility — Wilberforce and his friends — into the stuff of mass, democratic politics. And it is through this transformation that we can offer an explanation which bypasses the older preoccupation with black freedom as a result, in the main, of a handful of evangelicals.

A crucial factor was the anti-slavery lecture. Between 1787 and 1838 there were literally thousands of lectures delivered on slavery and the slave trade. And in each of the five phases outlined earlier, anti-slavery organisations set out to woo the public through lectures and lecture circuits using men (and in some cases women) renowned for their oratory. The crowds at lectures were huge; thousands at a time, overspill lectures being repeated, professional lecturers travelling on lecture circuits and happily reporting how they took hours to make their points. The evidence shows that the lectures were attended by all social classes. Indeed, efforts were made to arrange lecture times to suit local people – including working men. Furthermore, there was never any trouble finding a suitable meeting place. Town halls, guild halls, music halls, Leeds coloured cloth hall, chapels, churches and so on all provided anti-slavery with a venue. The most conspicuous institutions to house anti-slavery meetings were the churches and chapels. This forms a sharp contrast to the contemporary difficulties faced by parliamentary reformers in securing a meeting place.

In addition to lectures, anti-slavery made extraordinary use of the printed word, which, it may be felt, would only appeal to the minority, educated class. Yet we now know that literacy was much more widespread than we might instinctively have imagined – a fact more than amply illustrated by the phenomenal impact of cheap versions of Tom Paine's *Rights of Man* in the 1790s.[6] Abolitionists fed the voracious public appetite for the printed word. By the last years of the anti-slavery campaign, between 1828–33, the anti-slavery society, based in London, was publishing – quite literally – millions of tracts and pamphlets; some three million in a four-year period, quite apart from the outpourings from local anti-slavery groups.

Yet another skilfully-used Abolitionist tactic was to incorporate women into the anti-slavery campaign. For instance, many dozens of women's anti-slavery societies were established and women were encouraged to raise the matter with their families and children. Indeed, some reflection of the all-pervasiveness of anti-slavery can be seen from the way the issue began to appear even in children's books and magazines in the 1830s. It seems likely that, within anti-slavery, women (admittedly middle and upper class women) were given their first effective role in modern British politics, although always within the strict limits laid down for them by their menfolk. Nonetheless, women proved very effective, never more so than in the canvassing of anti-slavery petitions.

In the fifty years spanning the main history of anti-slavery, public Abolitionist opinion was expressed through the petition to Parliament. Many thousand petitions, most packed with thousands of signatures, were delivered to the House of Commons and Lords. Indeed, in the key phases of anti-slavery, when anti-slavery pressed most persistently at Parliament's doors, the petitions reflected a staggering level of support and organisation. Just a few illustrations will suffice. In 1792, 508 petitions descended on Parliament. The one from Manchester contained 20,000 names – from a total population of *c.* 60,000. In 1814 (when it seemed that France would be allowed to revive her slave trade), 800 petitions were signed by three quarters of a million people. Between 1830–4, more than 4000 petitions went to Parliament. Indeed, it is worth making the point that as a *per capita* reflection of opinion, the anti-slavery petition attracted more names than any other contemporary issue, be it Catholic emancipation, reform of Parliament or even, later, the demands for the Charter.[7]

Of course, all the above points are largely tactical matters. It is when we examine Abolitionist literature, speeches, letters – and artefacts of all kinds – that we begin to edge closer to what the Abolitionists thought and felt about slavery and the slave trade. Above all else, anti-slavery, from first to last, expressed itself most frequently and most stridently in terms of religion. By the 1820s this is understandable, since the very great majority of churches came out openly against slavery. Slavery, by the 1820s, was denounced on all sides as an affront to Christian feelings. Of course, the immediate *riposte* is: why was slavery viewed as unChristian in 1825 but not in 1725? And the answer to this question will take us some way towards an understanding of how anti-slavery was able to build up such reserves of public support. The simple truth is that the churches themselves had changed, more especially with the rapid growth of the nonconformists – especially the Methodists and the Baptists – the former particularly disliked by Wilberforce.

Notwithstanding this religious opposition, there was striking *secular* support for slaves' rights. Throughout the last phase of the campaign for black freedom, from the mid-1820s, Abolitionists regularly refer to the fact that slavery was a denial of the slaves' 'rights of man'. Since the slaves were denied that array of social rights on which so many early-nineteenth-century Britons prided themselves — the right to organise, to free speech, to choice of religion and even the right to a normal family life — it seemed clear, in an age which, after 1789 was concerned at a number of levels with the idea and practice of the rights of man, that the slaves were the most deprived of all social groups. Yet, it was widely assumed that slaves ought to be able to enjoy these rights, whereas in the 1790s the most forceful exponents of those rights were transported for doing little more than arguing the same case — the case for the rights of man in Britain itself.[8]

There remains, however, the troublesome question of economics. What evidence is there, in the profusion of surviving literature, that the attacks on the slave trade and slavery, were inspired or influenced by economic considerations? The truth is, there are few pointers, indeed, to the fact that the great majority of anti-slavery opinion was deeply concerned about economics. Obviously, we would not expect the surviving evidence to divide neatly into types of evidence — some economic, some humanitarian — it is, like any other historical phenomenon, far more complex than that. Nonetheless, there are precious few signs of a real interest in, or even concern about, the economic ramifications of the ending of black slavery. It is true that there were distinct economic interest groups who were opposed to slavery and whose own economic concerns seem to have been best served by ending the slave system. But they were small groups, with no real significant or overweening influence in the conduct of the anti-slavery campaign, inside or outside Parliament. Indeed, having read through much of the anti-slavery literature, what is impressive is how little attention was given to the economics of black freedom. It seems rarely to have been a consideration.

So, if we consider the three modes of expression of anti-slavery dealt with here, the three main conceptual expressions of anti-slavery by the mid-1830s — religion, secular and economic — far and away the most impressive in volume, stridency, persistence and ubiquity, is religion.

Freeing the Slaves: How Important Was Wilberforce? 39

Thus, it may be felt, the ghost of Wilberforce continues to hover over the Abolitionist feast. After all, the Abolitionists of the mid-1820s, when Wilberforce had quit Parliament, and handed over the conduct of affairs to younger men, were saying much the same thing that the young Wilberforce had asserted in the 1780s; that slavery was a deep and abiding sin and wickedness, an affront alike to man and God, and a religious insult which the English would have to remedy to gain collective salvation. Once more, however, the evidence suggests that far from illustrating a victory for Wilberforce and his friends, it reveals the emergence of forces which he himself did not like, could not control and of which he would not have approved. What made the religious attack on slavery by the 1820s so potent was the fact that it was an attack which embraced both the slaves and emergent working class groups in Britain.

Those nonconformist churches which made such deep inroads into new plebeian communities in the Midlands and the North, during and after the lifetime of John Wesley (who was himself a devout Abolitionist), rallied their swelling bands of working people to the side of anti-slavery. Those people who have in the past sought to explain the power of religious objections to slavery, have — almost without exception — ignored the degree to which much of that religious thrust came, not from the privileged religious sensibilities of Wilberforce and his social equals, but from humbler sorts. If we examine carefully where the anti-slavery petitions come from, it is possible to see that a majority came from nonconformist chapels and the very great bulk of those came from humble congregations. There was, it is true, another, contrary tradition best expressed by William Cobbett, of working class hostility to the slaves and to the way they could apparently monopolise the British conscience almost to the exclusion of all other social issues. But, by and large, what is striking, is the degree to which working class communities, organised through the local nonconformist chapel, in the midlands and the north, expressed a fierce anti-slavery sentiment. It is no accident that from those same communities, at much the same time, there was born a complexity of working class and radical organisations — factory act movement, anti-poor law movement, Chartism and the like — which were themselves deeply influenced by the politicising effect, the vocabulary, the tactics and the structure of anti-slavery. Time and again, in working class movements of the years after slavery the language of radicalism seemed to have been borrowed unashamedly from the anti-slavery movement. By the mid-1820s one of the most powerful forces behind anti-slavery was the fact that it had taken root and thrived in newly emergent working class communities.

To repeat an earlier point, what is remarkable about the campaign against slavery was the way it crossed social divides; uniting the nation in an almost unique fashion. Of course, it could also be argued that here was the only opportunity for that to happen; a case of what was later to be called 'telescopic philanthropy'. It was easy to get excited about distant issues and to divert attention from more immediate, closer matters. But as Fiona Spiers shows, the interest in anti-slavery did not take place to the exclusion of other problems. Abolitionists were often involved in other reforming campaigns. The plebeian nature of much of anti-slavery from the 1820s was not new, however, for among those formative working class organisations of the 1790s — the corresponding societies — are to be found denunciations of the slave trade and slavery. Indeed, the Scottish shoemaker, Thomas Hardy, who founded the London Corresponding Society, had as his house guest Equiano, the former slave who, in the 1780s and 1790s, was the most articulate spokesman for the 20,000 or so Blacks who lived in London at the time. And Thomas Hardy, as early as 1792, made the telling point that 'the rights of man are not confined to this small island but are extended to the whole human race, black and white, high or low, rich or poor'.[9]

Thus, to summarise crudely from what is a complex skein of evidence, the most remarkable factor in the emergence of anti-slavery sentiment is not so much its emergence among men of Wilberforce's social station, but among his social inferiors. Anti-slavery intruded itself as a theme in those very radical organisations which Wilberforce actually disliked and feared. And it became a powerful theme within the congregations of the very churches which he disliked. Looking back on his schoolboy flirtation with Methodism, the mature Wilberforce thanked God for steering him away from being 'a bigoted despised Methodist'.[10]

* * *

Freeing the Slaves: How Important Was Wilberforce? 41

There is, however, a further twist to the question of anti-slavery and nonconformity. What made the anti-slavery case so convincing was the personal experience of those Methodist and Baptist missionaries, who were among the first to bring Christianity to West Indian slaves in the 1780s. Indeed, it was a fortuitous accident of timing that the anti-slave trade movement was founded when the first missionaries began to send back to Britain their own eye-witness accounts of the worst details of slave experience. Returning missionaries went on British lecture circuits, telling the chapel congregations of the sufferings of the slaves and of how the planters sought to prevent the conversion of slaves to Methodism and Baptism. It was bad enough to be a slave — but to be prevented from becoming a black Methodist was to add religious insult to secular injury.

This, in its turn, brings me to the question of the slaves themselves — the people who in 1816 so lauded Wilberforce for promoting their freedom. One unfortunate result of the preoccupation with Wilberforce and other humanitarians has been the effective ignoring of the slaves themselves. Practically every historian concerned with black freedom has written as if the slaves were the mere objects — the beneficiaries — of British changing interests. In this case, they were freed because the British changed their mind about the morality or the economics of slavery. But the three quarters of a million slaves in the British West Indies played a much more formative and determining role than that. Indeed, there is a powerful case for arguing that the conduct of the slaves from the late-eighteenth century helped shape and direct the debate about black freedom. In this, there were two paramount, parallel factors, over which Wilberforce and his friends had no control. Firstly, there were the complex and unforeseen ramifications of the ending of the slave trade in 1807; secondly, there was the rapid proliferation of chapels throughout the West Indies. Both of these factors had the effect of radicalising certain slaves, and destablising slave society.

Let us briefly consider the effects of abolition in 1807, effects which Wilberforce could not have predicted. Planters, faced by a shortage of slaves, and unable to buy new Africans, simply reorganised their slave gangs. One consequence of this was that previously privileged slaves — skilled artisans for instance — now found themselves demoted to work in the fields, with a great deal of consequential unrest.[11] And it was among these very same unsettled slaves that the missionaries began to work, luring them off the plantation on Sunday, providing them with an alternative venue, encouraging them to develop oratorical and leadership skills. And all this was in addition to the language of the Bible, prayers and hymns, much of which was readily and obviously transmuted into the stuff of contemporary social and political argument. Crossing the Jordan, seeking the promised land, equality in the eyes of the Maker — these and a myriad other images swiftly entered the vocabulary — secular and divine — of the slaves.[12] The planters were quite right, by their lights, to refuse to help the missionaries. But once the missionaries began to work, the results of their efforts were both predictable and irresistible; it proved the very solvent of slave society. Time and again in the 1820s and early 1830s slave unrest, resistance and, in two spectacular cases, revolt were led by Christian slaves. The greatest revolt of all, at Christmas 1831, was known as 'the Baptist War'. Black Christians were slaughtered in great numbers by a white plantocracy out to preserve what they firmly claimed to be their own civilisation. Mass execution of black Christians, the destruction of chapels, and the hounding of the missionaries — these and countless more grisly stories filtered back to England in 1832, outraging the converted and convincing even the impartial that among slavery's most savage characteristics was the way it debased the Whites. If it were a system which could only be maintained by such levels of violence, it ought to go. Thus, the black Christians who led the revolt, especially of 1831, were indeed instrumental in tipping the scales of British opinion in their direction. It remained but a matter of time before black freedom came. And it is surely significant that when black freedom did indeed come, partially in 1834, and then more substantially in 1838, tens of thousands of slaves celebrated it by packing into the Methodist and the Baptist chapels.

Of course, all this took place 5000 miles from Britain and it needed an institutional framework and personal drive, and contacts, to bring the evidence of slave life before the British public. And that, again is where the nonconformist chapels came in. They provided the skeletal outline for the movement of men and ideas from the Caribbean, bringing, as quickly as

Freeing the Slaves: How Important Was Wilberforce?

contemporary communications allowed, fresh news of the slaves' sufferings.

But this was only one side of the anti-slavery organisation. What is also remarkable is the way the anti-slavery organisation developed as a national network, linking every conceivable urban area with headquarters in London. Simply to describe the numbers of local anti-slavery organisations is to get some feel of the movement. In 1787 there was the single, founding London society (on which Wilberforce did not sit for some time). By 1814 there were about 200 committees throughout the country. By 1825 this had grown to 800; between 1830–4 it was 1300. It was the most complex, national, highly efficient political organisation in those years. It may even have surpassed at any level we choose to examine, other reforming movements.[13]

It was, then, little wonder that the planters and the West Indian interest felt increasingly overwhelmed by the sheer strength of anti-slavery. Wherever they turned, by the mid-1820s, they faced a hostile barrage of anti-slavery opinion. The churches were universally in favour of black freedom. The press had, with some notable exceptions come round to the cause. The people – of all sorts and conditions – took every opportunity to express themselves forcefully against slavery. And, ultimately, most crucial of all, politicians could only stand up in favour of slavery at the risk of losing important electoral support. At the 1826 election in York, one of the candidates said – and all the others agreed with him: 'On the gradual abolition of colonial slavery, I am happy to believe that there are not two opinions in the country'.[14]

In the last resort we have to return to the forum where anti-slavery would be successful or unsuccessful – in Parliament itself. And it was here, of course, where Wilberforce had laboured so hard, especially in the 1780s and 1790s and after 1815, against the slave trade. For all the analysis offered in this paper – that anti-slavery ought now to be seen as a national, popular movement which also embraced black and plebeian elements – black freedom, like the ending of the slave trade, came through an Act of Parliament. And it is the work of the late Professor Anstey that has redirected modern attention back to that fundamental fact.[15]

There is a very strong case for claiming that it was Wilberforce's political ineptitude — his lack of political nous and care for the details of lobbying — which may well have delayed the passing of abolition of the slave trade. By the time the final push for black freedom emerged in the mid-1820s he was too old and sick to play a crucial role and later he was to leave Parliament entirely. What made anti-slavery so potent a force within Parliament were those forces of social and economic transformation which were at work in British society at large. The MPs who came round to anti-slavery were those from English and Welsh urban constituencies, especially those from the bigger cities and shipping towns, more especially those from towns with substantial dissenting congregations. There remains little doubt at all that the pressures exerted by the anti-slavery organisations and the churches were crucially influential in winning over more and more MPs to the side of black freedom.

On the other side, those MPs who stayed faithful to the slave lobby were overwhelmingly from rural constituencies or small towns — areas that were not the strong centres of the anti-slavery movement — or the nonconformist movement.[16] But even they were drastically affected by the reform of Parliament in 1832 which, at a stroke, dramatically reduced the representation of the MPs of the West Indian lobby, many of whom sat for rotten boroughs removed by the reforms. Conversely, the new MPs — or rather MPs from the newer constituencies — were overwhelmingly anti-slavery. Indeed when missionaries in the West Indies heard that Parliament had been reformed, they realised that slavery was doomed.[17]

Even in this, the last phase, the arguments for black freedom were sullied by the question of compensation; eventually the planters managed to extract £20 million from Parliament for the loss of their slaves; a concession to the property status of the slaves which most Abolitionists found little better than slave trading itself. And there followed the four-year twilight period, between 1834–8, when slaves were transmuted into apprentices as a compromise between slavery and full freedom. Finally, on 1 August 1838, at midnight, the three quarters of a million Caribbean slaves were freed, celebrating peacefully in their chapels, and praising the names of their British friends, among whom the name of Wilberforce was pre-eminent. And so we come full circle.

Freeing the Slaves: How Important Was Wilberforce?

Wilberforce died a few days after the granting of partial freedom in 1833. And, from that day to this, his name has been closely associated with the freeing of those slaves. In some respects this is a result of a historical tradition (and until World War Two a historical profession) that tended to seek historical explanations in terms of the 'great men' theory of history. To suggest the greater complexity of this particular story — to argue that freeing the slaves embraced a widely-based popularity, much of it rooted in changing contemporary religions in conjunction with the social transformations of Britain — while also incorporating a powerful and influential role for the slaves, is not deliberately to relegate Wilberforce and his friends to a minor role.

His and their role was crucial. But it was crucial more as a catalyst than anything else. They were the first to appreciate the problems, and to set in train a movement which rapidly moved in directions, and at a speed, they could not have foreseen or controlled. This, after all, is a common historical phenomenon. It is fitting that on the hundred and fiftieth anniversary of his death we should spend time reflecting on the man and his times. But it would be to no real purpose if it is an uncritical celebration of his life. And, yet, it is surely significant that when the slaves were freed it was *Wilberforce* who was praised by the slaves and denounced by the planters for having brought it about. In the last resort, one of the most enduring legacies of the man has been his mythology; over the years it has threatened to take over from reality itself.

NOTES

1. Mary Turner, *Slaves and Missionaries*, Urbana and London, University of Illinois Press, 1982, p. 107; Michael Craton, *Freeing the Slaves*, Cornell University Press, 1983, p. 241.
2. For details of the slave trade, see P. D. Curtin, *The Atlantic Slave Trade: A Census*, Wisconsin, 1969; Herbert Klein, *The Middle Passage*, Princeton University Press, 1978.
3. Eric Williams, *Capitalism and Slavery*, London, 1944; Seymour Drescher, *Econocide, British Slavery in the Era of Slavery*, University of Pittsburgh Press, 1977.
4. Herbert Klein, *Middle Passage*, pp. 16–22.
5. Barry Higman, *Slave Population and Economy in Jamaica 1807–1834*, Cambridge, 1976.

6. James Walvin, 'The Propaganda of Anti-Slavery' in James Walvin (ed.), *Slavery and British Society, 1776–1846*, London, 1982.
7. Seymour Drescher, 'Public Opinion and the Destruction of British Colonial Slavery' in *ibid*.
8. Edward Royle and James Walvin, *English Radicals and Reformers 1760–1848*, Brighton, 1982, chapter 4.
9. British Library, Add. Ms. 27,811,fo9.
10. Robin Furneaux, *William Wilberforce*, London, 1974, p. 9.
11. Barry Higman, *Slave Population*, pp. 2–3.
12. Mary Turner, *Slaves and Missionaries*, pp. 72–3.
13. Seymour Drescher, 'Public Opinion'.
14. *Speeches and Addresses of the Candidates for the Representation of the County of York in the Year 1826*, Leeds, 1826, p. 26.
15. Roger Anstey, *The Atlantic Slave Trade and British Abolition, 1760–1810*, London, 1975.
16. Izhak Gross, 'Parliament and the Abolition of Negro Apprenticeships 1835–1838', *English Historical Review*, July 1981.
17. P. Wright, *Knibb the Notorious*, London, 1973, p. 112.

4

William Wilberforce: 150 Years On

FIONA SPIERS

Anniversary celebrations such as these provide a useful focus and fulfil a need among scholars to concentrate on a series of related problems and to take stock of current trends in research. I am sure everyone in the field of anti-slavery history is glad to have this opportunity and would like to thank the University of Hull for undertaking the organisation necessary to make all this possible. As this is the sesquicentenary not only of the death of Wilberforce but also of the passing of legislation to end slavery within the British Empire, it is perhaps inevitable, if confusing, that the two should have come to be looked at inseparably. Most of the other speakers in this series will be dealing with specialist aspects of slavery and abolition such as extra parliamentary pressures, the economic background and the role played by the slaves themselves, but I have been asked to concentrate on the role and importance of one man, whom many people still consider to be the personification of the struggle to end both slavery and the slave trade. Such an approach is no longer fashionable and, indeed, there is a great risk that by centring the debate on the major characters many of the various complexities and underlying trends become obscured or undervalued. With that caveat, after a very brief overview of the main interpretations of Wilberforce, I shall then consider some of the enduring controversies that surround him and try to demonstrate why his conduct and motives have for so long been simultaneously sources of speculation, inspiration and suspicion.

For the last 150 years studying Wilberforce has been a struggle against geography and finance, as the relevant manuscripts are scattered in approximately 250 different collections throughout the world, and it will be several years more before anyone is able to utilise a comprehensive compilation. This inaccessibility has frustrated all major scholars, and may go some way to explaining the conflicting interpretations. The earliest — and longest — biography was the work of two of his sons, Robert Isaac and Samuel. Appearing in 1838, this work of filial devotion verged on hagiography, and was criticised even on publication for distorting and exaggerating Wilberforce's true contribution. But no subsequent historian has been able to ignore the wealth of almost daily detail revealed in the five volumes, and this has enhanced their importance. The sons were primarily responsible for the traditional view, the simplistic myth of Wilberforce and his Evangelical allies as warriors in a holy crusade against the greatest evil of the times, and whose victory against vested interests, the establishment and the great powers was achieved by the intervention of a benign Providence and the recognition of their intrinsic good.[1] It was an elitist view, given scholarly acceptability in the early twentieth century by Sir Reginald Coupland, who in addition to amplifying the background, presented Wilberforce as a kindly, lovable and immensely popular personality.[2] This is basically the position taken by two more recent biographers — Robin Furneaux, now Lord Birkenhead, and the Rev. John Pollock — both of whom are sympathetic to Wilberforce's religious motivations.[3]

But Wilberforce has never been without critics, of whom the most vitriolic and trenchant among the historians must be Eric Williams, who not only disliked Wilberforce's personality and religion, but who also considered him an incompetent leader, an unforgivable reactionary and a hypocrite, who disguised the national interest in a cloak of sanctimonious morality.[4] Since it appeared thirty-nine years ago, *Capitalism and Slavery* has been a seminal work generating much debate and, although many of the specific conclusions have long since been rejected or disproven, it did demonstrate the importance of economic factors.

Roger Anstey proposed a third interpretation of Wilberforce radically divergent from either the traditionalists or the Williams revisionists. He took into account not only the changed intellectual climate of the late eighteenth century and early nineteenth century, but stressed that as slavery was sanctioned by law, only in Parliament could it be dismantled. Redirecting attention to the political and legislative processes, Anstey tried to balance their relative importance against the force of ideas, religious enthusiasms and the national interest. Standing the Williams thesis on its head, he argued that Wilberforce and his colleagues were in fact forced to use arguments of national interest to conceal their true altruism, and that they were both humanitarian and politically astute.[5] There are many other minor biographies, and Wilberforce is of course examined in most other general works on the period, but this superficial survey would be even more incomplete without reference to the monumental works of David Brion Davis, who examined the intellectual and philosophical roots of anti-slavery ideology. Davis emphasises that for Wilberforce, who accepted traditional notions of deference and paternalism, the Abolition movement was only one skirmish in a vast religious crusade to reform an unregenerate social order. By first infusing government with the spirit of Christian morality, Wilberforce's great dream was a downward diffusion of Evangelical piety, channelled through the existing power and social structures.[6]

Not all these interpretations are mutually exclusive, and most give pride of place to Wilberforce's role in the abolition of the slave trade. And it is here along with his more controversial position on emancipation that we should start our examination of his legacy. The evidence demonstrates that Wilberforce's concern at the horrors of the slave trade predates his religious conversion, and that even as a schoolboy he had been troubled by what he learned.[7] He was reasonably well educated and well read in eighteenth-century secular literature and philosophy before he turned his attention to devotional and religious materials. He was not an innovator or originator of anti-slavery ideology; with his contemporaries, he had matured when the prevalent climate of ideas favoured abolition.[8] By the late eighteenth century the nation was for the most part convinced that slavery and the slave trade were evil. But they also considered them regrettable inevitabilities. Wilberforce's most pressing task was to demonstrate that this need not be so, and to appeal to the humanitarian spirit of the country and the House of Commons, while others dealt with the more mundane chores of marshalling other anti-slavery pressures. After his religious conversion, he began to delve into all the available evidence on the subject, but when he was approached to accept the parliamentary leadership of the crusade against the slave trade, it was not because his record on the issue made him an obvious candidate. His popularity, prestige and position as MP for Yorkshire, his personal wealth and his flowing eloquence made him one of the most influential non-government members, while his reputation for sincerity, integrity and honesty in the application of Christian or moral principles to political problems made him the ideal spokesman. Connection and influence meant he was politically and personally secure, out of reach of the sort of vicious abuse which had hounded the unfortunate James Ramsay to his death.[9] With occasional exceptions, Wilberforce was in little danger of physical martyrdom on account of his espousal of the Abolition cause.[10] He did not face the daily dangers that beset Abolitionists in the United States. He had had political ambition before his religious conversion, but realised the impossibility of holding office after it, so he did not sacrifice a career in government by undertaking the promotion of a non-party issue. In fact, it was because he planned to maintain his independence in the House of Commons and vote according to moral criteria that he was so useful to the Abolition movement.

It is significant that many of Wilberforce's more sympathetic biographers have found it necessary to attempt to prove − sometimes at considerable length − that he was from the outset an Emancipator as well as an Abolitionist. Wilberforce drew a clear and sharp distinction between the abolition of the slave trade and complete freedom for the slaves. He had no doubt that it was the slave trade that was the most monumental evil of the time, a national sin which the nation could only continue to ignore at the risk of retribution. By mutual consent, Wilberforce did not join the London Abolition Committee until 1793, as it was considered that non-affiliation would allow him to operate more effectively. But at first he did not share the commitment of many members to emancipation. He believed that once the slave trade was abolished, necessity would compel the planters to ameliorate living and working conditions on the plantations, ensuring the health and survival of their workforce when easy replacement labour was discontinued.[11] On the other hand,

William Wilberforce: 150 Years On

many members of the Abolition Committee considered slavery itself just as repugnant as the slave trade, but feared that an attempt to curtail both simultaneously would be over ambitious and end in disaster for both ventures. They made a tactical decision to attack the slave trade first, because it could legitimately be considered within parliamentary authority, namely the regulation of commerce. Any assault on slavery itself would have raised legal difficulties concerning property rights and the delicate constitutional issue of interference in colonial legislatures.

Wilberforce had dreamed as he put it, 'of breaking, or at least easing,' the lot of the West Indian slaves as early as 1781,[12] but he had in mind a freedom for the spirit as much as for the body. Wilberforce was convinced that slaves could not discover true salvation in their state of bondage, and he was primarily concerned with their spiritual, not their physical, future. In 1807 he claimed he would have liked to have been able to give the slaves freedom, but that they were not yet ready and would need careful preparation.[13] In later years, Wilberforce was to claim that his intention had always been to complete emancipation of the African race, who would be gradually transmuted into a free peasantry as slavery inevitably withered away. He claimed to have hidden this objective at first, hoping that it would appear to have been brought about as the natural result of these improvements.[14] But there are considerable discrepancies in his writings and his memories. He probably genuinely believed in later years that he had always favoured emancipation but there is evidence to show he would have tolerated a reformed, paternalistic and benevolent system of slavery if it is possible to envisage such a thing. Both he and Clarkson reassured the West Indian planters that they had no intentions of tampering with domestic slavery but sought only to prevent possible slave insurrections.[15] He also asserted that the cessation of the slave trade would double or even treble the value of existing slaves, and would enable British planters to monopolise the West Indian slave market.[16] If one considers this as merely a political ploy to mollify the planters, then Wilberforce's reputation for scrupulous honesty is shattered. On the other hand, if one considers it a true reflection of his beliefs at the time, then one is forced to the conclusion that Wilberforce thought that abolition of the slave trade itself would be sufficient, and that he was only later converted to active emancipation.

It was a profound shock and a bitter disappointment to him that the well-being of the slaves did not substantially improve after the ending of the slave trade.[17] Although he may have wished for freedom for the slaves, he had hoped that there would be no need to interfere further. He had always recognised that the abolition of the slave trade by Great Britain alone would not be enough, and from very early in his campaign he had worked towards an international ban on all trans-Atlantic slave trading. After the passage of the 1806 and 1907 legislation, he concentrated on the struggle to enforce it, and persevered with his international crusade to persuade the rest of Europe to abandon the slave trade.[18] After a further series of disappointments and frustrations, along with the other British Abolitionists he turned his attention in the early 1820s to the full, if gradual, emancipation of the slaves in the West Indies, still believing that the essential blessing of freedom for the slave would be the opportunity to discover true (i.e. Wilberforce's) religion. By the time Abolitionist sentiment revived and coalesced around the issue of emancipation, Wilberforce was old and infirm, and ready to hand on the responsibility of the parliamentary campaign to Thomas Fowell Buxton. His interest never waned and as a matter of courtesy he was informed of the successes and setbacks of the latest struggle, but by this time he was a figurehead, not an activist. It was, however, to his credit, and evidence of his devotion to the slaves, that he endorsed the activities of the Agency Committee, whose populist methods must have horrified him, and whose deportment and tactics were both an implicit and explicit condemnation of the inadequacy of the gradualist strategy favoured and followed by Wilberforce and his supporters for over forty years.[19]

Despite the tremendous energy and industry Wilberforce invested in the Abolition cause, the question really must be considered whether the passage of abolition might have been accelerated in other hands, and whether the eighteen years of setbacks before the eventual triumph were a testament to Wilberforce's persistent dedication or to his incompetence and political mismanagement. It is usually William Pitt who is the subject of controversy as to whether he did enough to speed

William Wilberforce: 150 Years On 53

abolition, and it might sound disrespectful, or even blasphemous, to pose similar questions about Wilberforce. When he first planned to raise the subject of abolition in the House of Commons, Wilberforce was sure that success would be quick and easy.[20] Even when the motion fell after protracted enquiry and debate, he was not unduly downhearted as he was convinced it would be carried in the following session. The traditionalists ascribe the subsequent rejections of his proposals to a retreat from reform and a growing spirit of reaction in the country, which was fostered by a fear of Jacobinism, and a horror of events in the Caribbean. But that misses several important points. Although the West India interest in the Commons in the late 1780s was in disarray, it still had the capacity for successful obstruction. Having been alerted to the situation, it then took the opportunity to regroup and organise. After 1791, Wilberforce had lost the political initiative. The planters strengthened their political and economic arguments, while Wilberforce made a series of political miscalculations.

One of the difficulties in examining Wilberforce's performance is that he seemed to veer from tactical sophistication to almost unbelievable political naivety. Despite his oratorical skills and his ability to charm the House, he seems to have had little instinctive grasp of the workings of Parliament. He introduced bills late in the session, when their chance of passing through all the stages in the time available was at best limited; and in 1793 he introduced his Bill only two weeks after the declaration of war, when the people, the Parliament and the Prime Minister were preoccupied with other issues.[21] He, and his advisers, did not organise the available support consistently, leaving the fate of the Bill, at crucial moments, to the chance factor of who was present in the House. In fact, he was more narrowly defeated in the years 1793-5 than he was in 1791, which hardly indicates a reactionary resurgence.[22] In 1796, having carefully mustered a numerical majority on the second reading, Wilberforce relaxed and squandered that margin at the committee stage, when he failed to rally his supporters, some of whom stayed out of town, while others were at a new opera. He was only defeated 70-74.[23] Perhaps he felt that tight control of his supporters would be ungentlemanly, distasteful or too reminiscent of party, but the fact remains that a House of Commons which was predisposed to a gentle and gradual abolition repeatedly failed to enact Wilberforce's motions. But it was not only in the Commons that these Bills ran into difficulties. The Lords — never known for a willingness to pass major reforms — repeatedly rejected the proposals. Wilberforce admitted in June 1804 (fifteen years after he first launched his struggle) that he had only learned on the previous day how the House of Lords functioned[24] — an extraordinary omission that doomed his measures to failure in the Upper House. Significantly, the 1807 Bill which was eventually enacted into law was introduced first into the Lords not the Commons by Lord Grenville, who personally supervised its passage there.

In addition to these procedural difficulties, Wilberforce did not understand that his dogged insistence on nothing short of complete and immediate abolition alienated the noncommitted majority in Parliament, who were, however, prepared to pass a gradualist measure. This would have set a fixed date for abolition, giving the planters a short breathing space to prepare the necessary improvements. Henry Dundas's 1792 proposals were approved by a substantial majority. They envisaged co-operation between the British government and the colonial legislature that would have led to a complete, but not to a financially punitive, abolition by 1800. Furthermore, the slave trade to foreign colonies would have ended in 1793 not 1806.[25] Wilberforce was a major factor in the frustration of these intentions. By his insistence on an early date for abolition regardless of the planters' readiness to adjust to it, he antagonised Dundas and offended many sympathetic if noncommitted MPs. This inflexibility contributed to the successive defeats of the 1790s and arguably postponed the final passage of abolition.

Wilberforce had assumed parliamentary leadership and, therefore, it is not unreasonable that he should shoulder at least some of the responsibility for so many parliamentary inadequacies. Despite repeated disappointment in his old friend, Wilberforce was content to delegate to Pitt the task of creating favourable political conditions, whilst he cultivated his moral leadership. It was this insistence on moral rectitude that prevented Wilberforce ever contemplating co-operation with the planters in an attempt to work out a compromise satisfactory to both. Historians like Porter have pointed out the further irony that when Wilberforce had little or nothing to do with Abolitionist measures they passed relatively easily. In fact, all the abolition legislation of the period 1788 to 1807 was passed without Wilberforce's direct leadership. Dolben's Regulating Act of 1788 was adopted by peripheral Abolitionists during Wilberforce's absence through very serious illness. Ellis's Address to the King of 1797 had nothing to do with Wilberforce. The major legislation of 1806 and 1807 was put through Parliament by Fox and Grenville, without the conspicuous leadership of Wilberforce.[26] Admittedly Grenville carried on a long and detailed correspondence with Wilberforce, seeking his opinion and advice in a manner unusually deferential for him, but Wilberforce himself played little personal role in the piloting of the Bills.

If Wilberforce's exertions and commitment were not reflected in actual effectiveness, the question arises as to how he has come to be regarded as the personification of the struggle, why the House of Commons rose to give him an unprecedented personal ovation after the tribute to Sir Samuel Romilly in 1807,[27] and why many people still perceive him as 'the man who freed the slaves'. There is little doubt that his repeated attempts to introduce legislation — virtually on an annual basis — identified him permanently with the cause of the slaves, whether in the slave ships or on the plantations. This very persistence kept the idea alive at a time of grave national crisis. It was generally agreed that there were serious, fundamental problems in West Indian agriculture and Wilberforce can be credited with narrowing the range of options under regular consideration to the Abolitionists' solution. But when the Act eventually passed, by whatever convergence of political and economic circumstances made it possible, it appears that a great many people both in Parliament and throughout the country wanted to believe that they had made a great humanitarian gesture. Of course Wilberforce had been involved with the routine collection of signatures for petitions, the setting up of corresponding committees and the organisation of public meetings, but although he liked to claim an emphatic popular mandate, he preferred to work through friends and influence, rather than entrust his cause to popular fervour. He gathered and sifted the evidence for the parliamentary committee hearings, but not on the scale of Thomas

Clarkson, Zachary Macaulay or earlier Granville Sharp, and those strategic initiatives which were eventually successful usually originated from James Stephen at the Colonial Office. However, none of the others, who may have done more of the dangerous investigating or the tedious administrative chores, or who perceived the political, social and economic nuances more astutely, had the personal prestige and popularity necessary for the leader of such a movement.

Wilberforce may not have been a great leader, but he was the most suitable figurehead available. The evangelicals, and even others who did not share their faith, hailed Wilberforce as God's instrument, whose apparent disinterested virtue gave him an inner reward far greater than any transient temporal successes. As Professor Davis has shown, when Napoleon was enslaving Europe and America was hostile to most things British, abolition in general and Wilberforce in particular lifted Britain's self-image and morale, as self-congratulation and relief at the erasing of an awesome guilt swept the nation.[28] Other Abolitionists worked as hard, or even harder than Wilberforce, and their behind-the-scenes contributions were vital to the final triumph. Despite the tactical failing of Wilberforce's contribution, many people believed that he had guided and inspired the nation to a humanitarian act unequalled in British history, which mitigated their complicity in one of the greatest atrocities of all time. Wilberforce appears to have filled a need — almost a longing — for uplift and rectitude at a time when the country lacked self-confidence. The burden that this perception placed on Wilberforce, was that henceforth, as many biographers have remarked, he came to be regarded as the 'keeper of the national conscience'.[29] He was invested with a moral authority, in which many people placed high expectations. Conversely the disappointment of those whose views he did not endorse was often disproportionately bitter.

One interesting aspect of this purported moral victory is that Wilberforce had not in fact based all his arguments on humanitarian principles, but rather on a mixture of policy and religion. In his writings and speeches, he argued that abolition would not damage the West Indian economy, but would rather compel a rise in living standards bringing about a larger and more efficient labour force; that Liverpool and other cities would not be paralysed; that the merchant marine would not be curtailed, as a new African trade on orthodox commercial principles would flourish; and that British interests would not be sacrificed to the French. However, he did insist that the iniquity of the slave trade was unaffected by whether or not the French followed the British example. He also argued that the slave trade had not christianised Africa but rather had made it more barbarous, and the harrowing conditions of the Middle Passage resulted in terrible loss of life among British seamen as well as the slaves, negating the argument that the slave trade was a naval nursery.[30] Over the years he elaborated and updated his basic arguments, but it seems he was renowned for his style and oratory rather than the substance of his speeches. Economic and political points were debated for two decades, yet Wilberforce is mainly remembered for his overriding contention that the slave trade violated the divine authority of the ten commandments, and contradicted the principles of justice and the laws of God. Wilberforce warned that such conduct could not continue indefinitely with impunity, and that retribution would fall not just on those directly involved, but on the whole nation which shared the guilt by tolerating, regulating and even encouraging such enormous wickedness.[31] Wilberforce worked long and hard on the policy implications, yet he was associated even in his own day with the triumph of moral and religious rectitude. But the image of Wilberforce has become as important as the reality, for he was a symbol to the slaves themselves and to later generations of Abolitionists. To the former he was proof that there were white men willing to take risks to espouse their cause, and to the latter he was the embodiment of the possibility of morality in political action which was reflected in their outlook, their tactics and their faith in a legislative solution to the problems of slavery.

One of the most important and lasting arguments Wilberforce stressed in his speeches and writings, which if it seems obvious and self-evident today was not so at the turn of the nineteenth century, was the emphasis on the full humanity of the slaves. Instinctively and intellectually, Wilberforce repudiated any assumptions of black inferiority, especially as a justification of slavery. He grasped the significance of this prejudice in the defence of slavery very early, and realised that if both public opinion and West Indian law regarded black people as inferior, then many forms of bestial treatment could be tolerated.[32] As Abolitionists revealed the harsh realities, the planters responded by claiming they treated Blacks 'as well as was necessary'. This gave Wilberforce the opening to stress the 'common nature' between black and white.[33] There are numerous examples of his repudiation of the notion of racial inferiority, and it is possibly for this that he really ought to be honoured.

We have noted already that the climate of opinion favoured the Abolitionists, and many proofs of racial equality were being forwarded. As was the case with so many other ideas, Wilberforce was not the originator of these doctrines, but he gave them a wider currency and respectability than they might otherwise have enjoyed. Wilberforce brought the concepts of racial equality and the intrinsic humanity of the African races into the most influential social and political circles in the country, ensuring that they were no longer the prerogative of intellectuals or religious minorities. The racial arguments he brought into circulation were to be central to the slavery debate on both sides of the Atlantic, and were endorsed by both black and white Abolitionists. Wilberforce also realised that it was unjust to draw any conclusions about black capabilities and potential based on observation of the slaves, so he set about to discover all he could about life in Africa, before the brutalising experience of enslavement.[34] He was among the first to argue that slavery would brutalise and deprave the victim of whatever race, citing as evidence the character changes in white slaves held by Arabs and concluding that the effects of such trauma should not be interpreted as innate and unchangeable racial characteristics.[35] He wanted 'damning proof' that the slave trade was neither humane nor beneficial to Africans, so that no reasonable person would be able to resist the force of the argument, and he required data to refute the notion that the African race was incapable of civilisation, but that on the contrary it sought the teachings of the Christian church.[36] It can be argued that he dealt in stereotypes, meeting the racist argument within its own terms of reference by merely substituting the image. But the importance of the positive portrayal of Blacks should not be underestimated, and Wilberforce's approach was adopted and developed by Abolitionists both British and American, at least until 1863.

In 1804 Wilberforce confided in Lord Muncaster.[37] He was worried that the emphasis on abolition might divert too much attention away from conditions in Africa to the miseries of the West Indies. His studies of pre-slavery West Africa and the deportment of free Blacks, both in Sierra Leone and later in Trinidad, where black soldiers had been released to freedom, did not modify the implicit assumption underlying his refutation of racial inferiority, that all other races would nevertheless be improved by being christianised and anglicised. He was well aware of the cultural and artistic achievements of West Africa and the progress and political stability of Sierra Leone, but he still believed that, although all races were spiritually equal, that is to say equally capable of salvation, Blacks were only potentially equal in terms of what he considered civilisation. He had no doubt that British ways, rights and political institutions were superior to all others, and his religious preoccupation focused his concern on individuals rather than slave society. He believed that the slaves would benefit by adopting his outlook and religion, and was convinced that this is what they would like to do if offered the opportunity. He had limited respect for and no wish to preserve their cultural heritage, political systems or religious beliefs. Such paternalism and cultural imperialism seem offensive today, but at the time were advanced not only by the Evangelicals and the other Abolitionists but by most of the Blacks with whom they came into contact. If their black allies did not challenge and always shared such notions, there was little or no stimulus to question or reassess these assumptions. Wilberforce has frequently been criticised on this score, but it is unrealistic to expect a more liberal approach to other cultures from him, and to acknowledge the paternalism in the argument from a contemporary perspective should not diminish his repeated emphasis on the common humanity of all races.

Wilberforce's racial attitudes were not confined to Africans, and his outlook on cultural issues affected his responses to the Indians and the Irish. Wilberforce's views on the latter were determined by his extreme distrust of Roman Catholicism, which he barely tolerated and to which he ascribed all of Ireland's troubles.[38] A reluctant supporter of Pitt's attempt to combine Catholic Emancipation with Irish Union, he did acknowledge that religious persecution was not only wicked but foolish.[39] His decision to support Catholic Emancipation was taken on grounds of expediency rather than justice, but afterwards his religious attitudes mellowed until in 1831 he even conceded that the doctrines of true Christianity were not inconsistent with Roman Catholicism and that there was no longer a continuing threat from Catholic propaganda.[40]

The Indians, on the other hand, were not favoured with similar grudging tolerance. Wilberforce was appalled by what he was told of the current practices of Hinduism and other native religions, and also by the behaviour of officials of the East India Company. After the slave trade he considered the policy of the exclusion of missionaries from India as the greatest of our national sins. Furneaux claims that at times he even gave the saving of these millions of doomed souls precedence over abolition itself, and was not prepared to leave their future to the unaided efforts of Providence.[41] Wilberforce refused to accept that the mutiny of the sepoys at Vellore had had anything to do with their fear of a forcible conversion to Christianity, and determined that he knew what was in the Indians' best interests.[42] He even feared the Methodists and other dissenters might mobilise before he could stir the Church of England into action.[43] He knew he had taken on a strong and powerful opponent in the East India Company, and that he was likely to be obstructed in the House of Commons itself. In 1813, therefore, when the company's charter was due for review in Parliament, he decided to organise a demonstration of public support, using the petitions which had been so useful in the Abolition campaign. The Evangelicals managed to raise 837 petitions – which was sufficiently impressive to persuade the government to endorse the measure.[44] Relying on Dr Claudius Buchanan for briefing, background information and detailed planning, and choosing to ignore the warnings of Warren Hastings and the Anglo-Indians on the hazards of enforcing conversion, Wilberforce became convinced that only Parliament stood between the Indians and salvation.[45]

His speeches on the subject are preserved almost in their entirety with his vituperative and abusive descriptions of the prevailing practices of Hinduism. Although he did reject the concept of compulsory conversion, he contrasted the beauty of

Hindu philosophy with practices such as infanticide, geronticide, polygamy, child marriage and suttee — the burning of widows on their husband's funeral pyre. He characterised the caste system, an integral part of the religion, as more evil than slavery itself.[46] There is little evidence that he pleaded for Indians with the same sympathy as he had for Africans. He refused to acknowledge that there was any morality worth mentioning among the Indians, dismissing those who feared that conversion would be dangerous or superfluous as influenced by the French sceptical philosophers, who had attempted to discredit Christianity by showing that in non-Christian countries people could behave peacefully, amiably and morally.[47] Wilberforce simply would not countenance such a suggestion. So convinced was he of the superiority of his own faith and its necessity in bringing about an acceptable society, that he regarded adherents of all other religions as debased, depraved and dwelling in the grossest moral darkness. Never imagining that this kind of language might be offensive, he used it repeatedly, and in the 1813 debates he was not afraid to flaunt his beliefs in the House of Commons, where usually such an approach would have doomed his cause.[48] Wilberforce refused to acknowledge the possibility of political or legal redress of the practices he wished to eradicate. For him that would not be sufficient, as he believed the problems of India demanded a religious and moral solution. Everyone had to decide for him or herself whether such actions stemmed from cultural and religious arrogance or an honest and fervent sense of Christian duty. It should also be noted, however, that Wilberforce was careful to emphasise that Indians were fellow subjects of the British Empire, and as such ought to be judged by a standard set of morals, principles and feelings.[49]

He also desired that the 'official' or standard religion of the empire should be Christianity. Wilberforce calculated that conversion would make India more secure, both internally and as part of the empire, would guarantee lasting gratitude from the converts and establish order under the patronage of English law and institutions. He did, however, stress that the government of India depended on the affections of the subjects and that Britain had responsibilities there as well as opportunities.[50] In addition to missions, he encouraged funding for education in the subcontinent, both of which, despite the motives, marked at least a partial move away from plunder towards paternalism in the attitude of the East India Company.[51] Coupland describes this as 'a doctrine of mutual goodwill' which became the principle by which India was governed in the nineteenth century,[52] and notes that despite the denunciation of Indian morals Wilberforce, at least, did help to sow the seeds of an ideal of responsibility towards native populations within the British Empire, which may have prevented or mitigated some of the worst abuses of imperial power.

Although these lectures focus mainly on the wider issues of slavery and abolition, when dealing with Wilberforce it is necessary to devote a little time to domestic issues. With other Abolitionists, he has been accused of using slavery as a 'screening device' — to divert attention away from white wage slaves and the miserable conditions of English labourers. This allegation was first circulated by the West Indian interest, then adopted by the Radicals and has persisted ever since. Wilberforce was aware of it, and did his best to refute it. In fact, he even wondered if it was wise to urge the grievances of the slaves in competition with those of the English workers.[53] There is further suspicion about Wilberforce's political attitudes, as he feared the growth of trade unionism and the actions of the mob (which he considered qualitatively very different from the mass support he had enlisted for his Abolitionist and missionary causes). He maintained he was an Independent, but in upbringing and outlook he was a Tory, or at least a Pittite, and voted that way on most occasions. Having failed to win his support, the Radicals questioned the sincerity of this independence. This was part of the burden of the moral authority invested in him. Unlike many other reformers, Wilberforce had not seen abolition as a radical act, although he had had support from almost all the Radicals. In fact, he was a great disappointment to the latter, who expected his sympathy for their causes, after his defence of other races, and this left them with a bitter feeling of having been betrayed. But far from having a double standard, Wilberforce brought his consistent philanthropic and humanitarian response to domestic social and economic problems; the difficulty was that he did not fully understand them. He seriously miscalculated the effects of the Corn Laws, for which he had voted, underestimating the hunger that they would bring. He never investigated industrial problems as he had slavery, and so was unfamiliar with the hardships of the Industrial Revolution, for he held an idealised and outdated view of manual workers. He was mystified when demobilisation and other post-war difficulties created unrest. He feared revolution, and voted for the Sedition Acts, the suspension of Habeas Corpus, the Six Acts and other repressive measures.[54]

But having been returned with the assistance of the Yorkshire Association, in 1784 Wilberforce described himself as a hearty and zealous well wisher to parliamentary reform.[55] By this he meant very moderate improvements. Rather than the limited franchise, the rotten boroughs or the old electoral boundaries which left the new industrial centres massively under-represented, Wilberforce considered that the worst evils of the old system were drunkenness and bribery. As he aged and gave his backing to repressive measures, Wilberforce continued to assert his political independence. Although he favoured reform, his innate conservatism prevented his acceptance of the radical version. By the 1830s, he thought that the electoral qualifications proposed by Lord John Russell should have been stiffer, but he was gratified by the additional county representation. He admitted that he was now less optimistic about great political reforms, but eventually he gave the 1832 measures his general support, believing that they would inhibit bribery and vice, and benefit the West Indian slaves.[56] By then his political influence was negligible, as he had retired in 1825, and his health was very poor. He admitted that he could only get really excited about slavery questions – he simply did not have the strength for any other issue.[57] His political attitudes need explanation if only to put criticism in perspective. He could never have agreed with the Radicals on account of their attacks on Christianity, but he tried to bring about moderate reform and alleviate the hardships of the working poor wherever possible. He believed the moral condition of the poor – not their political rights – was of paramount importance, and so his solution to their grievances, political, social or economic was to aid a wide variety of social and reformist causes in his own paternalistic style.

He only had a finite amount of time and energy, for he never enjoyed good health, but despite his physical handicaps he was actively involved in a staggering number of religious and humanitarian activities. He contributed to sixty-nine of these, was patron of one, vice president of twenty-nine, treasurer of one, governor of five and on the committee of a further five, in addition to membership of many auxiliary and branch associations.[58] In addition to this, for the various subscriptions and dues came to a considerable amount, he made many anonymous donations to other charities, and was unfailingly generous to a wide range of individual supplicants. His friends tried to curtail this generosity, for both they and he knew he was sometimes deceived by the dishonest, but Wilberforce replied that he preferred to give several times over to such people than miss a single case which really deserved his charity.[59]

All this is evidence of the consistency of his approach to both wage and chattel slaves, in that Wilberforce wanted to alleviate hardship wherever it existed, not to change the social order, but more especially he wanted to propagate his faith. He supported the Peels in their efforts on behalf of factory children, and helped to found a society for the relief of the manufacturing poor.[60] He encouraged welfare schemes such as inoculation against smallpox and the growing of potatoes.[61] He was interested in prison reform, supported Jeremy Bentham's schemes and Elizabeth Fry's prison visiting and he argued for the restriction of capital punishment to only the most serious offences. He visited prisons himself, comforted condemned prisoners and helped their families.[62] He campaigned for the protection of climbing boys (chimney sweeps) and interested himself in naval conditions. He supported every effort to improve the treatment of animals, culminating in the foundation of the Society for the Prevention of Cruelty to Animals. He was concerned to stop the brutal sadism in many common practices towards animals, and to stamp out the depravity of both perpetrators and spectators which 'sports' such as bull-baiting encouraged.[63] He considered most of these as questions of humanity, and this enabled him to reconcile his conservatism with his philanthropy. For example, he did not regard measures such as the Factory Acts or the Chimney Sweeps Bill as contrary to the accepted economic doctrines of *laissez-faire*, or interventions in worker/employer relationships. To Wilberforce they merely rectified abuses.

Wilberforce certainly did not ignore the sufferings of his own countrymen, but despite the caring he does seem to have had a blind spot to the effects on them of coercive legislation. Either he did not see how repressive some measures were, or else he understood but considered it of little importance. Wilberforce believed that all agitation menaced Christianity and that this was sufficient justification to suppress it, for he regarded the constitution and its civil and religious establishment as indivisible. The overriding importance of his religion caused him to provide bibles, churches and education for the poor, who would probably have been more appreciative of something to eat. On the other hand, he also provided them with more food and practical relief than most of his critics. He accepted the class structure of his day, even if he cared little about acquiring social rank or honours for himself. Similarly, he expected the poor to accept the social strata assigned to them by God, which was only temporary, and to take comfort in the knowledge that soon all human souls would be equal. He did not regard social position as a non-commutable life sentence. He favoured a meritocracy where the worthy and deserving would triumph over social handicaps, and he mixed with people from a variety of social backgrounds, rejecting snobbery, social ambition and the offer of a peerage.[64]

This concern for the spiritual rather than the temporal condition of the poor was reflected in his support for missionary movements at home as well as abroad. He overcame his fear that an educated populace could equally be exposed to blasphemy and sedition as to the Bible, and supported many advanced teaching methods and educational experiments although his cash donations were all to religious rather than to secular schools. He was active in the Church Missionary Society and the British and Foreign Bible Society, and in attempts to impose the Evangelical Sunday on the rest of the country.[65] He had founded the Proclamation Society, which later became the Society for the Suppression of Vice, whose object was to enforce existing laws against vice and immorality, as decreed in the Royal Proclamation of 1797. The unwholesome forms of behaviour to be curtailed included Sabbath-breaking, duelling, lotteries, drunkenness, unlicensed entertainment, blasphemy and obscenity.[66] It did not occur to Wilberforce that many would find his concept of self-righteous, self-appointed moral guardianship quite odious, for it was an integral and fundamental aspect of his desire to be 'useful'. The reformation of national morality was as much a motivation for Wilberforce as his desire to abolish the slave trade, and the Proclamation Society, despite the abuse and controversy it provoked, is indicative of Wilberforce's outlook, and as much a part of his historical legacy as his fight for abolition.

To sum up briefly, it seems that Wilberforce was neither simply a saint nor a sanctimonious hypocrite. He was extremely popular, unstintingly generous and caring, and despite his persistent attempts to save the souls of all around him, his manner seems to have endeared him to those he sought to convert, not to have antagonised them. His direct role in the bringing of black freedom may have been overstated for the last century and a half, but his importance as a symbol should not be underestimated. There are paradoxes in many of his positions, most notably his insistence on immediate abolition but his patience in accepting gradual emancipation; his warmth towards Africa but his repugnance towards many things Indian; his protestations on Christianity yet his unconcealed dislike of all other denominations, most especially non-conformists and Catholics, and his genuine concern for English labourers but his inability to grasp the limitations of his piecemeal philanthropy. He was a spokesman and figurehead, not a strategic planner or a profound analyst. The single factor which brings a consistency to these various contradictions is his sincere devotion and overriding commitment to Evangelical Christianity. He assessed each new issue from that perspective, then responded accordingly. The motivating force of this religious fervour sustained and encouraged him against criticism, and explains his narrow and blinkered focus, but also his tenacity and his involvement with all the major social and moral issues of his day.

NOTES

1. Robert Isaac Wilberforce and Samuel Wilberforce, *The Life of Wilberforce*, five vols, London, 1838, hereafter referred to as *Life*.
2. R. Coupland, *Wilberforce*, London, 1923; revised 1945.
3. Robin Furneaux, *William Wilberforce*, London, 1974; John Pollock, *Wilberforce*, London, 1977.

4. Eric Williams, *Capitalism and Slavery*, Durham, NC, 1944, pp. 181–2.
5. R. Anstey, *The Atlantic Slave Trade and British Abolition, 1760–1810*, London, 1975; R. Anstey, 'A Reinterpretation of the Abolition of the British Slave Trade, 1806–1807', *English Historical Review*, LXXXVII, 1972, pp. 304–32.
6. David Brion Davis, *The Problem of Slavery in the Age of Revolution*, Ithaca, NY, 1975, p. 427.
7. *Life*, I, p. 9.
8. Anstey, 'A Reinterpretation ...', p. 311.
9. *Life*, I, p. 235.
10. For anti-slavery reasons, he was threatened in 1788 and 1792; *Life*, I, pp. 354–6.
11. W. Wilberforce, *An Appeal to the Religion, Justice, and Humanity of the Inhabitants of the British Empire, in behalf of the Negro Slaves in the West Indies*, London, 1823, pp. 5–6; *Parliamentary History*, vol. XXVIII, 1789, p. 52.
12. *Life*, IV, p. 306.
13. W. Wilberforce, *A Letter on the Abolition of the Slave Trade Addressed to the Freeholders and other Inhabitants of Yorkshire*, London, 1807, pp. 258–9; *Parliamentary Debates*, vol. IX, 1807, pp. 143–4.
14. Wilberforce to J. J. Gurney, 21 February 1818, quoted in Pollock, *op. cit.*, p. 71.
15. *Parl. Hist.*, vol. XXIX, 1791, pp. 274–5.
16. *Parl. Hist.*, vol. XXVIII, 1789, pp. 53–4; vol. XXIX, 1791, p. 261.
17. *An Appeal ... in behalf of the Negro Slaves*, pp. 4–5.
18. Betty Fladeland, 'Abolitionist Pressures on the Concert of Europe, 1814–1822', *Journal of Modern History*, vol. XXXVIII, 1966, pp. 355–7.
19. Furneaux, *op. cit.*, p. 445; Coupland, *op. cit.*, pp. 418–19.
20. Wilberforce to Sir William Eden, 18 Jan. 1788, BM add mss 34427, f. 403; *Parl. Hist.*, vol. XXIX, 1791, pp. 250–78.
21. Dale H. Porter, *The Abolition of the Slave Trade in England, 1784–1807*, Hamden, Conn., 1970, p. 91.
22. *Ibid.*, p. 95.
23. *Life*, II, pp. 141–2.
24. Wilberforce to Lord Grenville, 27 June 1804, in *Life*, III, p. 179.
25. Porter, *op. cit.*, p. 141.
26. *Parl. Hist.*, vol. XXVII, 1797, p. 573; *Parliamentary Debates*, vol. VI, 1806, pp. 597–9, 917–9, 1021–5; vol. VII, 1806, pp. 227–36, 580–603, 1143; vol. VIII, 1807, pp. 257–9, 431–2, 563–4, 601, 612–18, 657–72, 677–83, 691–3, 701–3, 717–22, 940–95, 1040–53; vol. IX, 1807, pp. 59–62, 114–46, 168–70.
27. Coupland, *op. cit.*, p. 341; *Parl. Debates*, vol. VIII, 1807, pp. 977–9.
28. Davis, *op. cit.*, pp. 448–9.
29. Coupland, *op. cit.*, p. 284.
30. *Parl. Hist.*, vol. XXVIII, 1789–91, pp. 41–67, 307–14; vol. XXIX, 1791, pp. 250–78.
31. *Parl. Hist.*, vol. XXVIII, 1789, p. 42.
32. William Wilberforce, *A Letter to his Excellency the Prince of Talleyrand Perigord, on the Subject of the Slave Trade*, London, 1814, p. 22.
33. *Life*, II, p. 140.
34. *Life*, II, p. 149.
35. *An Appeal in behalf of the Negro Slaves*, p. 47.
36. Wilberforce to Zachary Macaulay, 23 Aug. 1793, *Life*, II, pp. 409–12.
37. Wilberforce to Lord Muncaster, 18 Dec. 1804, *Life*, III, pp. 199–203.
38. *Life*, III, p. 363.
39. *Parl. Debates*, vol. IV, new series, 16 March 1821, pp. 1290–8.
40. A. M. Wilberforce (ed.), *The Private Papers of William Wilberforce*, London, 1897, pp. 275–6, hereafter, *Private Papers*.

41. Furneaux, *op. cit.*, p. 322.
42. *The Speeches of William Wilberforce Esq., on the Clause in the East India Bill for Promoting the Religious Instruction and Moral Improvement of the Natives in the British Dominions — in India, on the 22 June, and the 1st and 12th of July, 1813*, London, 1813, pp. 88–94.
43. Wilberforce to Joseph Butterworth, 15 Feb. 1812, *Life*, IV, pp. 10–12.
44. Furneaux, *op. cit.*, p. 330.
45. *Ibid.*, p. 325.
46. *The Speeches of William Wilberforce ... (on) the East India Bill*, pp. 70–1.
47. *Ibid.*, p. 54.
48. *Ibid.*, p. 67.
49. *Ibid.*, p. 76.
50. *Ibid.*, pp. 101–4.
51. Furneaux, *op. cit.*, p. 331.
52. Coupland, *op. cit.*, p. 321.
53. Pollock, *op. cit.*, p. 255.
54. *Parl. Hist.*, vol. XXXI, 1794, p. 1129; vol. XXXII, 1795, pp. 292–5; vol. XXXIV, 1798–1800, pp. 122–3, 129 and 1471.
55. *Parl. Hist.*, vol. XXIV, 1784, p. 1004.
56. Wilberforce to Thomas Babington, 14 March 1831 in *Private Papers*, p. 266.
57. Wilberforce to Thomas Fowell Buxton, 21 April 1831, in Anti-Slavery Society Papers, Rhodes House Library, Oxford.
58. Furneaux, *op. cit.*, p. 217.
59. *Life*, II, pp. 304–5.
60. Pollock, *op. cit.*, p. 256.
61. *Cobbett's Weekly Political Register*, vol. III, p. 96.
62. *Life*, II, pp. 321–3; IV, p. 370.
63. *Life*, II, p. 366; *Parl. Debates*, vol. XXXVI, 1802, pp. 845–8.
64. *Life*, V, p. 229.
65. *Life*, II, pp. 271–2.
66. *Life*, I, pp. 130–8, 393.

5

Wilberforce the Saint

IAN BRADLEY

'Who, Carruthers, was William Wilberforce?'
'The man who freed the slaves, sir.'
And yet the answer to the schoolmaster's question might equally well be the man who called his countrymen to repentance, the leading exponent and the leading lay theologian of the Evangelical Revival, the politician who dedicated himself to improving a nation's morals or simply, as so many of his contemporaries saw him, the saint, a man whose public and private life provides one of the most shining and inspiring examples of the principles and practice of Christianity.

Our secular age remembers and celebrates Wilberforce the Emancipator, perhaps Wilberforce the high-minded and somewhat puritanical politician who sought to curb the amusements and recreations of the people, and enforce the drab dullness of the Evangelical Sabbath and who so staunchly supported the repressive measures introduced by William Pitt and Lord Liverpool to stifle popular protest in the aftermath of the French Revolution and the Napoleonic Wars. Yet this — which is the version still largely contained in the textbooks and in the popular view of Wilberforce — is to recall only one aspect of the man, and the one which he himself would regard as the least important. For him his Christian faith, conceived in the familiar language of Evangelicalism as a 'vital religion', was the central feature of his existence, and the application of that faith in his relations with his family, his friends and in his public career was the great task of his life. It is with that side of Wilberforce, the man whose death 150 years ago we are here to commemorate, that I want to deal in this essay.

Wilberforce himself would have had little hesitation, I think, in identifying the most important period in his life. It would not, as we might imagine, be those early months of 1807 when the Bill to abolish the British slave trade — the task on which he had laboured for twenty years — finally went through both houses of Parliament and secured the royal assent. Nor, would it have been that last week of his earthly existence when his life's work was crowned with the successful passage of the measure ending all slavery in the British Empire. No, he would himself, I think, unhesitatingly have picked on the autumn of 1785 when, tortured and agonised, he went through the 'great change' that was the hallmark of conversion from nominal Christianity to Evangelical religion. A consideration of that conversion and what it meant must be the starting point for any examination of William Wilberforce, the 'Saint'.

Before the great change, William Wilberforce was hardly the great reprobate and example of degenerate and fallen humanity that he later felt himself to have been, but rather a cheerfully light-hearted and carefree young man, enjoying but not to excess the pleasures of London society and with a keen but perfectly proper political ambition. He had as a boy come under the influence of the vital Evangelical religion which had first been preached in England by John Wesley and George Whitefield in the third decade of the eighteenth century. The uncle and aunt with whom he lived in London after the death of his father were devout Methodists and the young William came under their influence. His mother was appalled by this influence and took the eleven year old boy away from London and brought him back to Yorkshire and to Pocklington School. There all traces of his early religious enthusiasm were gradually removed, and by the time he went up to Cambridge William seems to have thrown off all signs of Methodism.

Wilberforce's time at Cambridge and his early years in Parliament, as MP first for Hull and then for Yorkshire, showed no sign of the seriousness that was to mark his later life. He was not a great sinner but he was certainly not a saint either. Ambitious, able and popular, he enjoyed the clubs of the West End and attended the races and balls of Yorkshire. In the autumn of 1784, newly elected for Yorkshire and the confidant of William Pitt, a glittering political career seemed to be open to him. Yet just eighteen months later he was to write to Pitt telling him that he was withdrawing from public life, and that he had undergone a great change which must fundamentally alter his life and transform their relations.

The religious conversion which Wilberforce underwent between October 1784 and December 1785 was a long drawn out affair, less instantaneous and concentrated than that experienced by many of his Evangelical contemporaries, but it followed a pattern which is familiar in the lives of many of those who espoused vital religion in that turbulent and troubled period of English history which began with the loss of the American colonies and continued through the shock waves of the French Revolution and the threat of invasion across the Channel. Like his fellow Saints, Wilberforce's conversion took the form of an intense sense of his own sin and inadequacies, leading to a period of almost manic depression which was alleviated by a sense of God's grace and the purchase of his salvation by the atoning death of Christ on the cross. Like others also, Wilberforce's conversion was effected through the agency of an Evangelical friend and through the reading of an Evangelical book.

It was, in fact, coincidence that threw William into the company of the Rev. Isaac Milner, former usher at Hull Grammar School and fellow of Queen's College, Cambridge, and leading Evangelical divine. Seeking a male companion to accompany himself, his mother and sister and two ailing female cousins on a continental tour, he had originally asked an apparently unregenerate friend William Burgh. It was only when Burgh declined that William turned to his old Hull tutor, Milner. It was a decision that was to have momentous consequences.

As the party journeyed to Nice in October 1784 the conversation turned to religious subjects. On the whole, Wilberforce met Milner's remarks with flippancy and banter. Then, just after leaving Nice in February 1785, Wilberforce picked up a book belonging to one of his travelling companions, Doddridge's *Rise and Progress of Religion* and asked Milner if it was worth reading. 'It is one of the best books ever written', the ecclesiastic replied, 'Let us take it with us and read it on our journey.'

The reading of Doddridge does not seem to have had an immediate impact on Wilberforce. When he got back to London in April he seems to have resumed his usual life although his diary does betray increasing signs of uneasiness at the lax and frivolous diversions of his friends. In the summer he was off again with Milner to rejoin the ladies in Genoa and travel from there to Geneva. This time, on Milner's suggestion, they read the New Testament in Greek. On the way back to England Wilberforce became more and more introspective and serious. By the time he got back to London in November 1785 he was in a state of deep depression, overwhelmed by feelings of guilt and hopelessness.

In his despair Wilberforce turned to another Evangelical divine, the Rev. John Newton, remembered chiefly today as author of such hymns as 'How Sweet the Name of Jesus Sounds' and 'Glorious Things of Thee are Spoken'. Newton was in fact one of the strangest figures of the Evangelical Revival — a former slave trader who was converted to Christianity reading Thomas à Kempis' *Imitation of Christ* while on his ship in the mid-Atlantic. Newton, who was a rough, harsh uncompromising Calvinist in his beliefs, seems to have given Wilberforce some peace of mind in telling him that Christ had indeed died to save such unregenerate souls as his and by the end of 1785 Wilberforce, although still subject to depressions, had come through the agonies of his conversion and undergone the great change.

What was the religion which Wilberforce had espoused and which was to be his driving force and inspiration for the remaining forty-eight years of his life? There is, in fact, no better guide to the theology of the Evangelical Revival than the pages of the book which he wrote in 1797. This work, indeed, became the handbook of Evangelicalism. It sold 7500 copies within six months and by 1826 had gone through fifteen editions, and twenty-five in the United States. It itself brought about many conversions to vital religion. From several points of view, then, it is worth examining, not least because it gives an insight into the mind of Wilberforce the Saint.

The full title of Wilberforce's work is very significant: *A Practical View of the Prevailing Religious System of Professed Christians of the Higher and Middle Classes in this Country*

Wilberforce the Saint

contrasted with real Christianity. The great theme of the book, as indeed of the Evangelical Revival, was the worldliness and torpor of the general level of Christian belief and practice in the eighteenth century. As Wilberforce put it:

> It seems in our days to be the commonly received opinion, that provided a man admit in general terms the truth of Christianity, though he neither know of nor consider much concerning the particulars of the system; and if he be not habitually guilty of any of the grosser vices against his fellow-creatures, we have no great reason to be dissatisfied with him, or to question the validity of his claim to the name and privileges of a Christian.[2]

It was against this vague, undemanding concept of Christianity which pushed God and his commandments far into the background of man's consciousness that Wilberforce and the Evangelicals rebelled.

The first chapter of his book was entitled 'Inadequate Conceptions of the Importance of Christianity'. Its purpose quite simply was to pluck religion from the peripheral position which it occupied for most people in the eighteenth century and put it right at the centre of human life. The second chapter, pursuing the same theme, was titled: 'Inadequate Conceptions of the Corruption of Human Nature'. At the root of the Christian faith of Wilberforce and his fellow saints lay their belief in man's utter sinfulness. 'Man is an apostate creature', Wilberforce wrote, 'fallen from his high original, degraded in his nature and depraved in his faculties; indisposed to good and disposed to evil; prone to vice, it is natural and easy to him; disinclined to virtue, it is difficult and laborious; he is tainted with sin, not slightly or superficially, but radically and to the very core'.[3]

Now although this overpowering sense of original sin characterised the Evangelicals, it did not make them all gloomy misanthropes. Its corollary was, of course, an equally overwhelming sense of the goodness and mercy of God, who through his grace and specifically through his Son's death on the cross had taken away the sins of all those who truly believed in him and given them everlasting life. If Wilberforce felt that his contemporaries had an inadequate conception of man's sinfulness then he equally believed them to have an inadequate conception of the saving power of God's grace and Christ's death. His third chapter was entitled: 'Chief Defects of the Religious System of the Bulk of Professed Christians in what regards our Lord Jesus Christ and the Holy Spirit — with a Dissertation concerning the Use of the Passions in Religion'. That last clause is important incidentally in reminding us that the Evangelicalism preached and practised by Wilberforce and his friends was, unlike the deism of many of his contemporaries, a religion of the heart rather than the head, a matter of emotion and feeling rather than reason and intellect. In this chapter Wilberforce summed up the essence of his faith:

Christianity is a scheme for justifying the ungodly, by Christ's dying for them when yet Sinners, a scheme for reconciling us to God when enemies and for making the fruits of holiness the effects, not the cause, of our being justified and reconciled: that, in short, it opens freely the door of mercy, to the greatest and vilest of penitent sinners who obeying the blessed impulse of the grace of God, whereby they had been awakened from the sleep of death, and moved to seek for pardon, may enter in, and through the regenerating influence of the Holy Spirit be enabled to bring forth the fruits of Righteousness.[4]

It might be thought in the Evangelical scheme of salvation that once the repentant sinner had accepted Christ's death for himself and through his faith purchased salvation through the saviour's blood, his passport to heaven was assured and he needed to do no more on earth. This extreme position held by some Calvinists and others was totally rejected by Wilberforce. He intensely disliked the idea of the converted sinner's compact with his saviour being seen as a contract motivated by self-interest. Rather it arose out of a sense of love and gratitude and those same feelings naturally led the believing Christian on to strive to walk ever more closely in the ways of the Lord, following his commandments, modelling himself on his example and seeking to please him in all ways. For Wilberforce and his fellow saints, then, conversion to Evangelical religion did not lead to quietism, retreating from the world and resting on your laurels. Rather it introduced a new, demanding, active practical Christianity. The Calvinist doctrine of sanctification was invoked. The converted soul might be saved by faith alone but it was commanded to perfect holiness, to go on unto perfection.

The fourth chapter of Wilberforce's 'Practical View' was entitled: 'On the Prevailing Inadequate Conceptions concerning the Nature and Strictness of Practical Christianity'. In it he wrote:

Wilberforce the Saint

> I apprehend the essential practical characteristic of true Christians to be this: that relying on the promises to repenting sinners of acceptance through the Redeemer, they have renounced and abjured all other masters, and have cordially and unreservedly devoted themselves to God.
>
> ... It is the fixed desire of their hearts to improve in all holiness. The example of Christ is their pattern, the word of God is their rule, there they read, that 'without holiness no man shall see the Lord'. It is the description of real Christians, that 'they are gradually changed into the image of their Divine Master' and they dare not allow themselves to believe their title sure, except so far as they can discern in themselves the growing traces of this blessed resemblance.
>
> It is not merely however by the fear of misery, and the desire of happiness, that they are actuated in their endeavours to excel in all holiness; they love it for its own sake: nor is it solely by the sense of self-interest that they are influenced in their determination to obey the will of God and to cultivate his favour. This determination has its foundations indeed in a deep and humiliating sense of his exalted Majesty and infinite power.[5]

For Wilberforce, then, it was emphatically not enough if you were a Christian merely to eschew vice and lead a relatively straightforward and comfortable life. Nor was it right to retreat from the world, however much you might be a pilgrim and a stranger in it. That was the sphere of action in which you had to work: in converting other sinners, in doing good, in forwarding the Lord's work in a million different ways. 'Christianity', he wrote, 'calls her professors to a state of diligent watchfulness and active services.'[6]

Wilberforce's eschewing of the temptation to retreat from the world after his conversion undoubtedly owed something to the entreaties of his old friend Pitt. After receiving Wilberforce's letter telling him of his conversion and intimating that he might withdraw from public life, Pitt wrote back asking,

> You confess that the character of religion is not a gloomy one ... But why then this preparation of solitude, which can hardly avoid tincturing the mind either with melancholy or superstition? If a Christian may act in the several relations of life, must he seclude himself from them all to become so? Surely the principles as well as the practice of Christianity are simple, and lead not to meditation only but to action.[7]

John Newton gave Wilberforce the same advice. In fact Wilberforce's hesitation about continuing in his political and public career after conversion was momentary. He was never beset with the same agonising doubts that Mr Gladstone had about whether he should not rather be a clergyman. The strong notion of Providence which he, like other Evangelicals, had was an important factor in this. 'My walk, I am sensible, is a public one', he wrote in 1788: 'My business is in the world; and I must mix in assemblies of men, or quit the post which Providence seems to have assigned me.'[8] In fact, of course, few careers have embraced more active participation in affairs and public causes. He himself reflected not long after his conversion: 'My shame is not occasioned by my thinking that I am too studiously diligent in the business of life; on the contrary, I then feel that I am serving God best when from proper motives I am most actively engaged in it.'[9]

How then did Wilberforce's conversion change his life and how did his religion affect him? Perhaps the most noticeable and striking difference between Wilberforce the Sinner and Wilberforce the Saint, if thus we can describe him before and after conversion, was that in the latter incarnation he had an almost obsessional urge for self-examination, accounting for every single moment of the day and constantly finding fault with himself. One of his first actions after conversion was to begin a daily spiritual journal which meticulously examined his faults and recorded how he had spent every unforgiving minute. This was a characteristic shared by many Evangelicals, terrifyingly conscious as they were of the dreadful day of judgement when they would be required by the all-seeing eye to give an account of how they had used their talents and how they had passed their time on earth.

The unremitting self-examination and self-chastisement which fills Wilberforce's journal jars on the modern reader. There is, predictably, an enormous amount of harping on his own sinfulness. From January 1794 to May 1800 he wrote at the top of each page headings of the various faults to which he considered himself prone: 'Volatility, wandering in prayer, Christianity forgetting, Holy Spirit forgetting, regulation of company and conversation, friends' spiritual good, truth erring, humility and self-denial'. Every lapse from the highest standards of gospel Christianity was recorded, ready for that final reckoning at the judgement seat.

Wilberforce the Saint

This sense of accountability gave the Evangelicals a determination not to waste a moment in idleness. For many years after his conversion in 1785, and whenever in later life he felt himself to be slipping, Wilberforce noted in his journal at the end of every week a precise account of how he had spent the past seven days, listing in tabular form the number of hours devoted to the following occupations: serious devotion, major application – study, serious reading and writing; minor application – study, reading with no great attention, family letters; House of Commons and business; requisite company and visits; dressing; relaxation *sua causa* and meals – 'the more this head can be reduced the better'; squandered and bed.

Like all his fellow Saints, Wilberforce began the day early rising at 6 or 7 a.m. and spending most of the next three hours in prayer and meditation. Lying in bed late was an unpardonable sin in Evangelical eyes. Wilberforce told his son Samuel 'a decline in religion generally began in this way as it led to a hurrying over of the morning devotions; he had seen many instances of it when from lying in bed late private prayers would be neglected and the soul had always suffered in consequence'.[10]

Wilberforce's daily routine followed a fairly standard pattern. The first hour of the day was spent in private devotions. Then for the next three-quarters of an hour one of his children read to him while he dressed. Breakfast at 9 a.m. was followed by morning prayers – of which more anon. The rest of the morning was taken up with answering correspondence and other work. Dinner was taken at midday and in the afternoon, if Parliament was not sitting, he took a two-hour walk. There was another hour of devotion in the evening, followed by more family prayers, supper and bed by 11 p.m.

Wilberforce's lifestyle changed considerably after his conversion. There was not just the large amount of time devoted to prayer and meditation, but also the conscious abstention from many pleasures and pastimes he had previously enjoyed. He took his name off all the five clubs to which he had belonged. Card games, idle gossip and singing over the wine and into the small hours were banished. So were dancing and visits to the theatre and the races. He continued to read novels, but not without a certain sense of guilt. He once chided himself for bestowing on Scott's *Heart of Midlothian* precious eyesight and time that could have been better employed. He did not altogether cut himself off from social engagements and functions but these now became a duty rather than a pleasure, opportunities for securing conversions or for forwarding serious causes rather than frivolous diversions. The temptations of the table featured constantly in Wilberforce's journal. 'No dessert – no tastings' reads one typical entry: 'Never more than six glasses of wine, my common allowance 2 or 3' – a generous enough limit one might feel but modest, I suppose, when compared to the couple of bottles regularly put away by some late eighteenth-century politicians and parsons.

Wilberforce's Evangelicalism also expressed itself in a strong desire to convert other people to his own vital if demanding creed. He took his duties as a missionary to polite society very seriously, preparing 'launchers' as he called them which were conversational gambits designed to introduce a serious theme in light social gatherings. In 1815 he wintered in Brighton specifically it seems for the purpose of attempting to convert the Prince Regent, later George IV. He failed, despite several attempts. His own book was written very much as a tract, and 6000 copies of it were distributed by agents of the Religious Tract Society in the more respectable residential areas of London where it is said to have been instrumental in securing several conversions. Like all Evangelicals, Wilberforce was ever keen to see signs of the great change in friends and family and not least in his own children. The main thrust of the letter which he sent to Sam on his ninth birthday was 'Above all, my dearest Samuel, I am anxious to see decisive marks of your having begun to undergo the great change'.[11]

Yet for all this, Wilberforce was not a gloomy or puritanical person. As we have seen, he did not totally abstain from the pleasures of the flesh although there is a trace of asceticism in his habit of sometimes putting a pebble in his shoe to serve as a reminder that his mind should always be on higher things. He was strict in his own observance of the commandments and in his insistence that others should observe them as well. His views on the evils of the theatre seem excessively harsh to us now and he was a rigid Sabbatarian, believing that 'Sunday is intended for strengthening our impression of invisible and eternal things; and as such people can only innocently recreate themselves on that day by attending to their religious duties'.[12]

But contrary to the view of some historians, Wilberforce was not a humourless killjoy. He remained a gay and joyful personality, never happier than when he was laughing and singing with his family, playing blind man's bluff or walking in the Lake District. He was always careful to keep a check on his pleasures to prevent them turning into indulgences. When he was asked by one of his children why, given his love of the Lakes, he didn't buy a house for the family there he replied coldly: 'I should enjoy it as much as anyone, my dear, but we must remember we are not sent into the world merely to admire prospects and enjoy scenery.'[13] But in general he enjoyed life and, within his somewhat narrow views of what constituted innocent recreation, he wanted others to enjoy it too.

One other aspect of Wilberforce's life was profoundly changed by his conversion and is often overlooked. He became an enormous giver to charitable causes. Until his marriage he regularly gave away more than a quarter of his income to charity and the figure was still considerable when he had a family to support. Much of this went to the poor and destitute as well as to the various Evangelical missionary and moral welfare agencies. It is something that should be borne in mind when Wilberforce's attitude to the social and economic problems of his time is considered. His response was the personal and emotional one of digging directly into his own pocket to relieve distress rather than the collectivist and more intellectual one of changing prevailing social conditions and providing government money to help those in need.

How did Wilberforce's religion affect his public life? Fundamentally is the answer. It established the agenda for his political career and determined the campaigns to which he was to devote nearly all his energies during the forty years between his conversion and his retirement from Parliament in 1825. At the top of that list of campaigns were of course the two which he alluded to in his famous entry in his journal in October 1787: 'God Almighty has set before me two great objects, the suppression of the slave trade and the reformation of manners'. Of his life long campaign against the slave trade and then slavery you will read in other contributions to this book and I will say no more about this best known aspect of Wilberforce's life, except to remind you — if reminder were needed — that the drive to take up this issue was an Evangelical one: concern for the thousands of souls who were kept in spiritual darkness through the iniquities of the terrible traffic in human lives.

Wilberforce's campaigns in the fields of public and private morality are also well known and I do not intend to dwell long on them here. He was, of course, a leading figure in the formation of the Society for the Suppression of Vice, later the Vice Society, which spearheaded the Evangelicals' assault on the dissolute manners and practices of the eighteenth century and whose members acted as moral policemen, bringing prosecutions, often under long forgotten statutes, against anyone they caught offending their rigorous code. Wilberforce was as active as any in securing these prosecutions. He is remembered particularly for his rather callous treatment of Thomas Williams, a bookseller prosecuted by the Vice Society for selling Tom Paine's *The Age of Reason* and who was sentenced to a long period in prison.

Those Evangelicals who sat in Parliament were, of course, particularly useful in the crusade to reform the nation's morals as initiators of legislation. Wilberforce introduced and sponsored Bills to outlaw the sports of bull and bear baiting, punish those who swore profane oaths and ban Sunday newspapers. William Pitt supported this last measure until it was pointed out to him that most of the papers in question supported his administration. Wilberforce organised a successful campaign to abolish state lotteries in Britain and maintained a constant watch for any new legislation which would promote immorality or vice. He intervened, typically, during the second reading of the River Thames Bathing Bill in 1815, for example, to protest that the measure 'would go to sanction the indecency frequently committed on the banks of the Thames, and would be a declaration of Parliament that it was expedient that persons should expose their bodies on the banks of the river'.[14]

There is no doubt that there was a side to Wilberforce which made him see his duty as a Christian in public life as being to seek to impose on the country the kind of repressive, puritanical regime which had last been attempted by Oliver Cromwell and his associates. It was this side of Wilberforce which made him so staunch a supporter of the illiberal and repressive measures introduced first by Pitt and then by Lord Liverpool in the face of social unrest and political agitation during and after the wars with revolutionary France: the suspension of Habeas Corpus, and the Acts gagging the press and free assembly which he justified with Pauline theology about the need to obey the potentates and powers of this world and with his association of political radicalism with irreligion.

Yet this was only one side of Wilberforce the Christian politician. The other is his great concern and charity, which showed itself in public as well as in private ways; in his championship of prison and factory reform which laid the basis for the great work of later Evangelicals like Lord Shaftesbury and the Victorian paternalists. Wilberforce was also charitable and liberal in his attitude to the great political questions of the day: on parliamentary reform, on the repeal of the Test and Corporation Acts which discriminated against the nonconformists, and perhaps more surprisingly on Catholic Emancipation he voted consistently with the Whigs rather than the Tories from whose ranks he had sprung. Unlike those Evangelicals who went into politics later in the nineteenth century, Wilberforce and his fellow Saints were not the friends of conservatism and reaction.

It is not the purpose of this essay to consider the composition and achievements of that little band of Evangelical MPs who gathered around Wilberforce and followed his lead on many political issues. Nor is it within my scope to assess the career of Wilberforce the politician.[15] Yet it is very much within the province of this essay, I think, to consider the particular contribution which Wilberforce the Christian statesman made to English public life, and in my concluding reflections on the enduring legacy of Wilberforce's Saintliness I would like to begin with that aspect.

A Christian statesman – that is the phrase I have just used. It is the way Wilberforce himself was seen by many of his contemporaries. It was in many ways a very novel concept in the age in which he lived. Politicians in the eighteenth century had been largely poorly regarded, with a good deal of justice in many cases, and certainly had not been seen as possessing the characteristic Christian virtues. Indeed, those virtues did not seem very appropriate or necessary for those who went into politics. It was a grubby, corrupt profession, if indeed profession it could be called. Most of the business of Parliament was, after all, the necessarily rather sordid horse trading involved in creating and keeping majorities and the promulgation of a limited amount of legislation to forward the narrow interests of the landed classes.

The presence of the Saints and especially of William Wilberforce in the House of Commons changed both the public conception of politicians and the idea of what Parliament should be about. There is no doubt that the Evangelicals played an important role in two of the most important changes which took place in British politics in the first half of the nineteenth century – the transformation of Parliament from a gentleman's club primarily concerned with the private interests of its members, to a national assembly legislating for the public good, and the development of political leaders whose support was based on principles and policies rather than ties of family connection or personal interest.

Evangelical MPs, and Wilberforce pre-eminently, were among the first to introduce into the House of Commons the discussion of serious issues of principle and appeals based on moral considerations rather than self-interest. Into an assembly which had hitherto spent most of its time discussing game laws, enclosures and other matters of narrow concern to the landed interest, Wilberforce introduced debates on slavery, the condition of factory workers and prisoners. His campaigns and his example widened the perspective of Parliament and gave it a greater concern in questions of morality and principle. Reflecting on the successful outcome of the Saints' campaign in 1813 to get the East India Company to allow missionaries to go with its merchants into India, Wilberforce noted: 'When I consider what was the state of the House of Commons 25 years ago, and how little it would then have borne with patience what it heard not only with patience but acceptance during these last discussions, I cannot but draw a favourable augury for the welfare of our country.'[16] On the eve of his departure from the Commons, after forty-five years as a member, a fellow Saint wrote: 'It must be a satisfaction to have observed that the moral tone of the House of Commons, as well as of the nation at large, is much

Wilberforce the Saint

higher than when you first entered public life; and there can be no doubt that God has made you the honoured instrument of contributing much to this great improvement.'[17]

The fact was that in being a Christian statesman Wilberforce had not only helped to change the tone of politics — he had also established a new style of political leadership, and one which was clearly popular with an increasingly serious public. It is no coincidence that his life spans the period when the age of Fox gave way to the age of Peel. The Evangelicals established politics as a serious calling and vocation. They carefully developed a cult of the Christian statesman — two features of their legacy to the Victorians which reached their apogee in the career and the popularity of W. E. Gladstone. It is the subject of a chapter in my book on the Evangelical impact on the Victorians, *The Call to Seriousness*. Let it just be noted that Wilberforce was in many ways the original and the exemplar of the Christian statesman — a public man holding fast to high principles and living in the fear of God, and admired and respected as such by his countrymen.

If this public example was one of the main legacies of Wilberforce the Saint, then the other was surely the essentially private example which he gave in his family life. Evangelicalism had much to do with establishing that primacy of the home and the family unit which characterises the Victorian age, and in this as in so much Wilberforce was perhaps the outstanding exemplar and model. He himself was utterly devoted to his family — he shunned boarding schools for his children's education, preferring them to be taught at home, and agreeing with John Bowdler that 'public school was inadmissible from its probable effect on eternal state'.[18] He gave up the representation of Yorkshire in 1812 so he could devote more time to them, noting 'As to my plan in life, I conceive that my chief objects should be — first my children; secondly — Parliament; thirdly — when I can spare time, my pen to be employed in religious writing.'

His long letters to his children — displaying a mixture of love and affection, exhortation and rebuke and earnest concern for their spiritual state — show Wilberforce to be the very model of the Victorian paterfamilias. His sons were, of course, to depart far from their father's Evangelical creed: William, the eldest, into financial profligacy and general dissoluteness, Samuel into high churchmanship and both Henry and Robert Isaac, like so many other children of the Saints, into Roman Catholicism. Yet, as David Newsome has pointed out in his splendid book *The Parting of Friends*, in many ways these last three did not really depart from the religion of their father. For Wilberforce Christianity had never been a party matter – he never saw himself as an Evangelical in that narrow, party sense which characterised low churchmen later in the nineteenth century. For him vital religion was a call to lead a holy life and in that it had much in common with the Oxford movement and the Catholic revival. It was not unnatural that the second generation Wilberforces should take those different roads in their search for the same goal as their father.

I want to leave you with a picture of Wilberforce at his most characteristic, taking family prayers, that peculiarly Evangelical institution which became – not least through his example – a feature of every self-respecting Victorian household. There is an often quoted description of prayers in the Wilberforce home by Marianne Thornton which I think conveys the essence of Wilberforce's saintliness – his deep, simple, emotional faith and piety, his enthusiasm, his love of humanity and his infectious warmth and charm. Here it is:

The scene at prayers is a most curious one. There is a bell which rings when Mr. Wilberforce begins to dress; another when he finishes dressing; upon which Mr. Barningham begins to play a hymn on the organ and to sing a solo, and by degrees the family comes down to the entrance hall where the psalmody goes on; first one joins in and then another; Lizzy calling out 'Don't go near dear Mama, she sings so dreadfully out of tune, dear', and William, 'Don't look at Papa, he does make such dreadful faces'. So he does, waving his arms about, and occasionally pulling leaves off the geraniums and smelling them, singing out louder and louder in a tone of hilarity. 'Trust Him, praise Him, trust Him, praise Him, praise Him ever more.' Sometimes he exclaims 'Astonishing! How very affecting! Only think of Abraham, a fine old man, just a kind of man one should naturally pull off one's hat to, with long grey hairs, and looking like an old aloe – but you don't know what an aloe is perhaps: It's a tree – no a plant which flowers ...' and he wanders off into a dissertation about plants and flowers.[19]

So how should we remember William Wilberforce? As the liberator of the slaves, as the Mary Whitehouse of his age who

Wilberforce the Saint

battled to improve the moral standards of his countrymen, as the model Christian statesman, the father of Victorian family life or simply, as Hugh Price Hughes described Mr Gladstone, as a man who said his prayers? As all of these and more besides, Wilberforce the Saint has been the title of my talk and I think its subject has every right to a place in that blessed company. He walked close to God without being over pious or sanctimonious. He threw himself into 101 campaigns to improve the lot of suffering humanity in this world without ever losing sight of the transitoriness of man's earthly existence and the central importance of the world to come. Above all, perhaps, he displayed in his character the joy that comes from living faith in Christ.

NOTES

1. Quoted in R. Furneaux, *William Wilberforce*, London, 1974, p. 34.
2. W. Wilberforce, *A Practical View ...*, 7th edn, London, 1798, p. 91.
3. *Ibid.*, p. 18.
4. *Ibid.*, p. 79.
5. *Ibid.*, pp. 97-8.
6. *Ibid.*, p. 108.
7. Quoted in Furneaux, *op. cit.*, p. 48.
8. R. I. and S. Wilberforce, *The Life of William Wilberforce*, London, 1838, I, p. 196.
9. *Ibid.*, I, p. 106.
10. Wilberforce manuscripts in Bodleian Library, Oxford, e. 11, f. 27.
11. D. Newsome, *The Parting of Friends*, London, 1966, p. 49.
12. *The Correspondence of William Wilberforce*, R. I. and S. Wilberforce (eds), London, 1840, I, p. 373.
13. R. I. and S. Wilberforce, *op. cit.*, IV, p. 389.
14. *Hansard*, 1815, XXXI, p. 615.
15. For a full consideration of the role of Evangelical MPs in the period 1784 to 1832 see my unpublished Oxford D.Phil. thesis 'Evangelicals in Parliament, 1784-1833'. See also E. M. Howse, *Saints in Politics, the Clapham Sect and the Growth of Freedom*, London, 1952.
16. R. I. and S. Wilberforce, *op. cit.*, IV, p. 125.
17. *Ibid.*, V, p. 240.
18. *Ibid.*, III, p. 348.
19. E. M. Forster, *Marianne Thornton, 1797-1887, A Domestic Biography*, London, 1956, pp. 137-8.

6

Abolition and the National Interest

HOWARD TEMPERLEY

Britain's involvement with the institution of modern slavery spans a period of roughly three hundred years, from the late sixteenth century when Elizabethan seadogs first began dabbling in the slave trade to the later nineteenth when, in conjunction with other powers, she finally succeeded in eradicating all but the last vestiges of it. So far as the earlier period is concerned, that is to say the years up to the 1770s, no great effort of the historical imagination is required to understand why the British acted as they did. The enormous potential of the newly discovered lands across the seas together with the lack of native labour with which to exploit them led the British, like other Europeans, to turn to the one source of labour which was available, namely Africa. As a leading sea power, and in due course as a coloniser, Britain naturally played a prominent part in these developments. What is a good deal harder to explain is why, having so actively participated in building up this system she should then, with no less diligence, have set about dismantling it.

At first sight the reasons may seem obvious enough. After all, nothing could be more averse to our present-day ways of thinking than the slave trade and chattel slavery. However one regards them, whether in terms of Christian ethics, natural law or simple human rights, they represent an implicit denial of what we have come to regard as basic moral principles. But then we are very much the intellectual heirs of the Abolitionists. Certainly this is not how most contemporaries viewed the matter. One only has to dip into the work of Defoe to realise that he

Abolition and the National Interest 87

was writing for an audience which took slavery pretty much for granted.¹ Nor, initially at least, did readers take kindly to the strictures of Abolitionists, as is indicated by James Boswell's squib

> Go W[ilberforce], with narrow *scull,*
> Go home, and preach away at Hull,
> No longer to the Senate cackle,
> In strains which suit the Tabernacle.²

As late as 1814, in *Mansfield Park*, Jane Austen has her heroine's uncle, Sir Thomas Bertram, go off to manage the family's estates in Antigua. Sir Thomas is shown as a kindly man, and so far as the novel's plot is concerned all that is required is his temporary absence from the Bertram household. Yet the author has him go off to run what, although we are never specifically told, could only have been slave plantations without apparently having any qualms about the impression this might make upon the minds of her readers concerning Sir Thomas's character, or the legitimacy of the enterprise upon which his family's fortunes were based.³

The fact is that until the 1780s most people in Western society regarded slavery with no particular repugnance. It did not conjure up, as it was to do for later generations, a sense of moral outrage. It was simply a way of organising labour, not perhaps in their own societies but in those newly developing regions where non-slave labour was unavailable. It had its seamier side, but then so too did other labour systems. Its principal justification – indeed the only justification it required so far as most people were concerned – was its ability to produce goods which could not otherwise have been obtained, or at least not in such quantities or so cheaply. And if slavery could be justified on these grounds, so also, of course, could the trade which maintained and nourished it.

Yet in a remarkably short time, as we all know, opinion on these matters underwent a sea change as first the slave trade and then slavery itself came under attack. Like most revolutions, it began in men's minds. What seemed self-evident to the men of the 1770s no longer seemed so to their children, still less to their grandchildren. And, once opinion began to shift, practical consequences followed. Slavery in the Northern states of the

American Union had largely disappeared by 1810. In Santo Domingo it had ended quite abruptly — although admittedly in rather exceptional circumstances — in the 1790s. The United States and Great Britain both abolished — or, more accurately, withdrew from — the slave trade in 1808. Britain abolished slavery in her West Indian colonies in the 1830s. Other European countries followed suit, most notably Denmark, Sweden, France and Holland. Slavery in the United States ended as a result of the Civil War. Eventually Spain and Portugal fell into line. The last New World country to abolish slavery was Brazil in 1888. Thus chattel slavery, which in the 1770s had been legally recognised throughout the hemisphere from Hudson's Bay in the north to Tierra del Fuego in the south, had by 1890 vanished from the Americas and, one might add, from most of the rest of the world too. It was a remarkable achievement and one which not only Abolitionists but also historians, who for the most part have shared the Abolitionists' principles, have rightly celebrated.

What is notably lacking from this catalogue, however, is any indication of what brought it all about. In short, what was it in the late eighteenth and early nineteenth centuries that made men turn against an institution which, so far as they could see, had up to that time served them well? Did something suddenly happen to make them think that they had been mistaken? Or was the purely pragmatic justification for slavery outweighed by other considerations?

These are questions to which modern historiography provides no clear-cut answers. Broadly speaking the accounts given by historians take two forms. First, there are those which stress the moral and religious impulse which lay behind the anti-slavery crusade.[4] This, of course, was very much how the Abolitionists themselves saw the matter. For them the triumph of abolition represented the victory of right thinking over error, of the forces of light over the forces of darkness. It had been a long struggle but in the end truth had prevailed. The problem with this approach, which until a generation ago was also the approach of virtually all historians, is that it assigns primacy to developments in the realm of ideas without adequately explaining what it was that gave rise to those ideas. This is not to deny that ideas often develop according to an inner logic and thus achieve a momentum of their own. Most important ideas have long pedigrees and tracing them may well help to illuminate an issue. Yet the very length of the pedigrees — and in the case of abolition they were very long indeed — points up the difficulty of explaining why certain events occurred at one time rather than another. What was it, in other words, that made these particular ideas come to fruition at the time they did?

The second type of explanation given by historians for these events may, at first sight anyway, appear more plausible in that it does at least face up to the problem of timing. According to this account, the abolition of the slave trade and slavery was the result not of moral but of economic pressures.[5] What has impressed writers of this persuasion is that the attack on slavery coincided with what economic history textbooks call the Industrial Revolution — with all that that entailed. What exactly it *did* entail is, of course, something about which no two historians agree and as a result different terms are used. Eric Williams talks of the shift from mercantilism to mature capitalism. Karl Polanyi speaks of 'the great transformation'.[6] But what all these historians do agree on is that in the latter part of the eighteenth century something quite unprecedented in human affairs began to happen. And what impressed those who looked for some connection between this and the abolition of slavery was not simply that the two revolutions proceeded in parallel, but that it was the same nations and, indeed, to a large degree the same groups within those nations, which were at the forefront of both movements.

It is, thus, tempting to assume that what we are observing is not two revolutions but one, and that the shift to new modes of production in the commercial and manufacturing centres required a corresponding shift away from slave labour in those dependent economies which provided them with raw materials. This would not, of course, rule out the arguments of those who claim that moral and religious beliefs played an important part in the process. The evidence that they did is simply too overwhelming to be ignored. All the same, if it could be shown that abolition in some way served the national interest, or at least the interests of powerful groups within the nation, the evidence might well be used to explain not only why it triumphed but why the beliefs associated with it gained a more ready acceptance than they had done up to that time.

One way of throwing light on these matters is to examine the arguments advanced by the two sides and then to consider what, in practice, the consequences of abolition were from the point of view of the national interest. National interest is not, of course, an easy concept to define. But let us begin by looking at it in strictly economic terms, which, as anyone who dips into the parliamentary debates of the later eighteenth and early nineteenth centuries will soon see, is how most contemporaries regarded it. The British Empire was still in those days very much a ledger-book affair, and whatever was done by way of regulating it needed to be justified in terms of profit and loss to the mother country.

And here we must appropriately start with the debates over the slave trade. In choosing to attack the trade the Abolitionists were undoubtedly hitting the institution at its most vulnerable point. Whatever the injustices of slavery, they scarcely compared with the horrors of the African traffic. Moreover, to regulate trade was a normal parliamentary function in a way that interfering with colonial slavery, involving as it did rights to private property and the competing claims of colonial assemblies, was not. That abolition of the trade would have an effect on the viability of slavery in the colonies was, of course, a point which the traders did not overlook. Indeed, many of them talked as if what the Abolitionists were proposing was, in fact, the destruction of colonial slavery. In the debates of 1788–9 successive speakers reminded Parliament of the enormous capital tied up in the colonies. Most of this was private capital, a good deal of it in the form of mortgages advanced by London finance houses. According to Lord Penrhyn there were mortgages in the West Indies to the amount of seventy millions.[7] If the government were ever so unwise as to abolish the slave trade, Mr Alderman Newnham informed the Commons, 'he was persuaded it would render the City of London a scene of bankruptcy and ruin'.[8]

One must, of course, make allowance for oratorical hyperbole. There was also much alarmist talk of the loss of Britain's mercantile pre-eminence and the danger, if the agitation continued, of slave rebellions in the colonies. All the same, it is plain that the defenders of the trade had a case. If Britain gave up the traffic there was no guarantee that other powers would follow. In these circumstances, finding their labour force static or actually declining, British planters would be hard pressed to compete with planters elsewhere, as they would need to do if they wanted to go on selling their produce on the world market. By altering the rules, Britain would not only be cutting herself off from a profitable branch of commerce; she would also be putting obstacles in the way of the future development of her colonies and jeopardising the fortunes of those who, under the old rules, had been encouraged to invest their capital there.

What is striking about the case presented by the defenders of the trade is that, apart from stressing this supposed commitment to defending the rights of her own merchants and planters, no attempt was made to defend the traffic on ethical grounds. Admittedly this would not have been easy, although not, one might suppose, beyond the bounds of human ingenuity. In later years the American planters developed a highly sophisticated argument in defence of their peculiar institution. No such sophistication, however, is evident in the arguments presented by British defenders of the trade. One may put this down to simple lack of imagination but also, one suspects, it reflected a traditional belief – as James Boswell's attack on Wilberforce indicates – that such issues were not the proper concern of Parliament. In any case, as the spokesmen for the trade saw it, ethical considerations were irrelevant since if Britain were to withdraw from the traffic others would hasten to fill her place. Whatever happened it was clear that the Negroes would not gain, although it was only too likely that, if the Abolitionists went on agitating the issue, and certainly if Parliament were so ill-advised as to heed their counsel, Britain herself would be the loser.[9]

The Abolitionists' case, by contrast, was a good deal more subtle, as in a sense it needed to be. It was not easy to show, at least not in the 1780s or in balance-sheet terms, that doing away with the slave trade would actually promote the national interest. The most that could be claimed, at least with any degree of plausibility, was that some of the traders' assertions – for example with regard to the trade as a nursery for seamen – were ill-founded and that the energies currently devoted to the trade would readily find an outlet in other, more legitimate, forms of commerce. The Abolitionists' main concern, however, was with the morality of the trade. The danger here was that they would overreach themselves. It was no secret that those who disapproved of the trade also disapproved of slavery. Privately they regarded the removal of the one as a first step towards the destruction of the other. There were good reasons, however, for not saying this in public. The success of their campaign depended on a piecemeal approach. The decision to concentrate their attack on the trade was essentially a matter of tactics. Enforcing this discipline on their supporters was not, however, easy. In the 1788 debate speakers did not hesitate to dwell on the iniquities of slavery in general. According to Edmund Burke 'the state of slavery, however mitigated, was a state so improper, so degrading, and so ruinous to the feelings and capacities of human nature, that it ought not to be suffered to exist'.[10] Such statements, though they doubtless stirred the consciences of some, played into the hands of the opposition by conjuring up alarming pictures of what the Abolitionists were intent on achieving.

What would have happened had the war with France not broken out there is no way of telling. According to the traditional view, the events across the Channel, the onset of war, and the subsequent slave rebellion in Santo Domingo, set back abolition by at least a decade. Certainly they strengthened the forces of conservatism and thereby weakened the appeal of measures based explicitly on notions of justice, humanity and religion. On the other hand, as Roger Anstey has shown,[11] the disruption of normal patterns of trade and the conquest of new territories favoured the adoption of measures the cumulative effect of which was to cut back significantly on the traffic. In each case these restrictions were adopted largely, if not wholly, as a means of protecting the national interest in wartime. The most notable of these measures was the 1806 Act which, by cutting off the traffic to the recently-conquered territories, effectively reduced the trade by two-thirds.

These developments cast doubt on Charles James Fox's earlier judgment that 'the question of the abolition of the slave trade was a question between humanity on the one side and interest on the other'.[12] But then, in politics, issues are seldom so clear cut. The 1807 Act, it is true, was supported on traditional humanitarian grounds, but by that time the Abolitionists could argue that what they were talking about were only the last vestiges of a traffic which had already been largely eliminated. But what one can say, looking back over these events as a whole, is that the Abolitionists had shown themselves shrewd tacticians by exploiting the vicissitudes of war to carry through legislation which, in normal circumstances, would almost certainly have been subject to closer scrutiny.

One result of this was that no clear picture emerged as to what the likely long-term effects of these measures would be. The political disposition of forces in the postwar world remained very much in doubt. The supporters of the trade, outmanoeuvred and often divided among themselves, were less effective than formerly in spelling out the dire consequences of such policies. The Abolitionists, for their part, were reluctant to say anything in public that linked the trade and slavery, although privately they hoped that the need to conserve labour would lead, by a process of gradual amelioration, to ultimate freedom. Meanwhile, operating through the newly established African Institution, they turned their attention to encouraging legitimate commerce with Africa, seeing that the laws against the slave trade were effectively enforced and persuading other nations to follow Britain's example by withdrawing from the traffic.[13]

When, however, the effects of abolition on the West Indies became evident, they provided few grounds for satisfaction. The cutting off of the trade had not led to any significant improvement in the treatment of those slaves already held. This was what caused most concern to the Abolitionists and resulted, in 1823, in the launching of a new campaign, this time directed towards, first the amelioration, and later the eradication, of slavery itself. What most immediately concerned the planters, however, was the fact that the economic consequences of the ending of the trade almost exactly corresponded to the predictions of those who, thirty years earlier, had warned Parliament against such a measure. Up to 1807 the West Indian economies had been expanding. New, virgin territories were being acquired. The West Indians' share of exports to and imports from Britain was increasing. So also was their share of world sugar and coffee production. Despite the perennial complaints of the planters, the evidence suggests that, economically speaking, the British

West Indies were doing very well.[14] The result of the ending of the trade, however, was to deny the planters the labour they needed in order to go on expanding their production. In this respect it is worth noting that the United States was exceptional – indeed, one can say unique among New World slave societies – in having a labour force that grew by natural increase. Elsewhere, expanding the labour force – or even preventing it from diminishing – depended on the trade. Thus, in the case of the British West Indies, the result of cutting off the trade and, no less important, the decision to forbid the transfer of slaves from one colony to another, was to prevent the newer colonies – the most notable of these being Trinidad and British Guiana – from acquiring the labour force they needed to develop their resources. It was as if, to use an American analogy, there had been no internal slave trade, in other words as if slaves could not have been moved from Virginia and South Carolina to Mississippi and Louisiana. Not surprisingly, therefore, the British West Indies, as compared with Cuba and Brazil, which had no inhibitions about importing slaves or moving them about, went into relative decline.

These developments were the subject of successive parliamentary committees of enquiry which, although sympathetic, could see no way of getting the planters out of their predicament. To reopen the slave trade was unthinkable. Whatever the reasons for abolishing it, there was no going back. Particularly revealing of the way the planters regarded the matter is the 1832 'Report of the Select Committee Appointed to Inquire into the Commercial State of the West India Colonies' which considered in detail a paper submitted by the West Indian proprietors showing what they believed were the additional costs borne by the planters as a result of British philanthropy. According to these calculations, the amount added to the cost of each hundredweight of sugar exported amounted to 17s 3d and consisted of 1s 5d for 'superior treatment' occasioned by Parliament's attempts to ameliorate slavery, 4s 10d for the relatively smaller number of efficient workers in a labour force dependent on self-propagation, and 11s for the additional cost of raising slaves. This latter figure was arrived at by comparing the cost of rearing a slave up to the age of fourteen as compared with the cost of buying one in Cuba. Not surprisingly, the members of the

Abolition and the National Interest 95

committee regarded these figures with some scepticism although they had 'no hesitation in submitting to The House their opinion, first, That some loss, and consequently some part of the present distress of the Colonists is occasioned by [Britain's humanitarian measures]; and, secondly, That such loss constitutes a fair ground of claim for compensation'. Since private investors were no longer prepared to put capital into the colonies it was suggested that the government might consider advancing money from the Treasury.[15]

One reason why no one was prepared to lend money to West Indian proprietors was, of course, the growing strength of the campaign for the abolition of slavery itself which, by 1832, was moving into its final stages. The Abolitionists themselves were divided over whether the planters should be offered compensation. But whether they were compensated or not it seemed to the planters that to abolish slavery meant ruination so far as the sugar colonies were concerned. The problem, as they never tired of explaining, was not whether free labourers could produce sugar, but whether they could produce it as cheaply and effectively as the slave labourers with whom they would inevitably be obliged to compete on the world market. The ending of the slave trade had already brought the colonies to a state of near collapse, the abolition of slavery itself would simply complete the process. It was all very well to say, as Buxton did in response to a challenge by the Colonial Secretary, 'that if justice were incompatible with the cultivation of sugar, he should prefer justice to sugar'.[16] No one, including Buxton, expected British consumers and manufacturers to do without sugar. The question was who would produce it, Britain's own colonies which had been developed by British capital and enterprise, or the colonies of other powers which, if Parliament accepted the measures that were being proposed, would henceforward reap the benefits of the trade? With remarkable foresight, the Duke of Wellington outlined what the consequences of abolition would be: 'If the West India trade were abandoned, whence would we get our sugar? Only from slave colonies which were at this moment carrying on the slave trade ...' In consequence, Britain would not only be abandoning her own planters but her Negroes as well and also providing an incentive for carrying on a traffic in slaves to the suppression of which she was already committed.[17]

Up to this time, the one example of practical abolition in a genuine slave society was in Santo Domingo which in the 1780s had been expanding rapidly as a sugar producer but which, as a result of abolition, effectively dropped out of the world economy. This was a source of much embarrassment to Abolitionists. Yet it could be argued — and this was their first line of defence — that circumstances there were so exceptional (the French Revolution, the war with Britain and Spain, the fact that it had all happened in such a haphazard way) that no general conclusions could be drawn, certainly no conclusions that would have any bearing on what might be expected to happen if abolition were handled responsibly with proper planning and adequate finance.

Yet now that, moving with all due deliberations and assisted by a grant of twenty million pounds to distribute by way of compensation, Britain began dismantling slavery in her colonies, the results, economically speaking, were not very reassuring either. That the Duke of Wellington's predictions would be borne out was not, of course, immediately evident. What had been foreseen, even by many of those who supported it, was that abolition would hasten the process of colonial economic decline. The reasons are entirely understandable and have nothing to do with 'reversion of African barbarism' or any of the other horrors predicted by the planters. Quite simply the ex-slaves chose to exercise their newly acquired freedom either by quitting the plantations entirely or by working shorter hours. The extent to which this occurred differed from colony to colony, depending on the alternative opportunities available and the attitude of the planters, but overall the loss of sugar production comparing 1823–33 and 1839–46 was 36 per cent.[18]

One consequence of this was that, for the first time in more than a century, Britain had a genuine sugar shortage. In theory, of course, the West Indians had long enjoyed a monopoly of the British market by virtue of paying lower tariffs than other producers, but in practice this had meant little since they produced more than the British domestic market could absorb and the remainder had to be sold abroad at world prices. Thus, it was the world price which had hitherto determined how much they obtained for their produce. But now that production fell below domestic needs, they had a genuine monopoly and prices

Abolition and the National Interest 97

soared to more than double the world level. By the early 1840s, therefore, the government was under pressure to scrap the monopoly by granting entry to foreign sugar. Foreign sugar, of course, meant slave-grown sugar and understandably enough Abolitionists campaigned against its acceptance on the grounds that it would weaken the West Indian economies, strengthen those of their rivals and boost the African slave trade. Yet, despite this, the government in 1846 gave way with precisely those consequences which the Abolitionists had predicted.[19]

A second consequence of abolition was to increase the demand for alternative forms of labour. Trinidad and British Guiana had long wished for coolie labour with which to develop their plantations. Now they were joined by Jamaica and the other colonies which felt the need to compensate for the loss of labour occasioned by abolition. Once again the Abolitionists campaigned against the proposals, this time on the grounds that indentured labour was not genuinely free labour and that the new system would be subject to many of the same abuses as the old. Nevertheless, they were overruled, although once again events were to prove that they had been right.[20]

The West Indian example is particularly interesting not only because it was the most fully discussed and carefully planned of all the New World experiments in emancipation, but also because it anticipated the experiences of other colonial powers which also found that abolition resulted in the withdrawal of labour and attempted to compensate for this by recourse to indentures, differential taxes, vagrancy acts and other similar expedients. In the case of the French colonies the planters began purchasing so-called 'free' labourers from Africa — the *emigré* system — which differed from the old system scarcely at all.[21] And in every one of these countries Abolitionists' voices were raised against what they saw as attempts to circumvent the law by subterfuge. Sometimes their protests were listened to and from time to time governments stepped in to end blatant abuses, as the British government did in 1853 when it was revealed that West African tribes had gone to war in order to obtain 'free' labourers to sell to British vessels for transportation to the West Indies.[22] And, of course, for the planters themselves life had become more complicated. They now had to make do with various kinds of labour — that provided by their former slaves, that provided by coolies newly imported from India or elsewhere and that provided by coolies who had opted against repatriation and agreed to sign on for second or third terms. It was all very difficult. But what is absolutely clear is that abolition had not created, overnight as it were, a free market in labour. As often as not, the labour force upon which these colonies depended for the production of their export staples were semi-free and as such subject to many of the same disabilities and abuses as before.

How far this was true of the United States is a matter which can be debated. As was the case in Santo Domingo, abolition in the United States was exceptional in the sense that it was the result of civil war, so that it is not easy, in the early phases particularly, to distinguish the effects of the one from the other. The United States, as already indicated, was exceptional in another respect too, namely in that its Negro population grew by natural increase. This went on happening after emancipation. It would also appear that, despite its size, there were restraints — although what exactly these were, and why they did not operate in the same way elsewhere, is not entirely clear — which prevented the freedmen from quitting the plantation system in the way they did in other New World societies. Nevertheless, there is substantial evidence that emancipation resulted in a significant withdrawal of labour, particularly in the case of women and children. One way of expressing this is to say that in the South, and elsewhere, the freedmen were paying themselves in the form of more leisure. But in addition to this it is evident that freedom resulted in an improvement in the economic conditions of the labour force, always bearing in mind that both are relative terms, that the amount of each accorded to the ex-slaves was not large, and that it did not increase significantly in the years that followed. In 1900 southern blacks were scarcely better off than they had been in 1870.[23]

But if a transfer of wealth did occur — and the evidence, as I say, suggests that it did — the question arises as to where it was transferred from? The answer would seem to be from Southern Whites, because the cotton and tobacco producers of the South were not able to pass on additional costs to consumers in the way that, for example, British West Indian producers did in the early 1840s by virtue of their monopoly position. They were competing in a world market — in the case of cotton newly enlarged by the advent, during the Civil War, of Egypt and India as major producers — which, since supply generally outran demand, effectively ensured that profit margins remained low. For this reason, northerners were saved the necessity of having to pay for their philanthropy as, for a time, the British did.

What is peculiarly striking in both cases, however — and the same goes for the other post-emancipation societies — is their poor economic performance generally. So far as the production of export staples was concerned, free labour simply could not compete with slave labour, as the British implicitly conceded when they turned to Cuba and Brazil for their sugar. Nor were the shortfalls in this respect made up by gains elsewhere, except insofar as the ex-slaves turned to village or subsistence agriculture. But so far as economic development in general was concerned, the results were disappointing and in some cases catastrophic. Nowhere do we find anything to match the astonishing performance of the free-labour societies of Europe and the Northern states. As often as not what emancipation left in its path were husks, drained of whatever economic vitality they had once possessed, struggling to survive in markets increasingly dominated by low-cost peasant societies, and obliged to use labour which, although no longer strictly speaking servile, was nevertheless far from being free. If the Abolitionists' aim was not simply to get rid of slavery but, as they often claimed, to secure for the ex-slaves the full privileges of freedom, then it is plain that their triumph was far from complete.

This is not to suggest that the Abolitionists were at fault, although in some cases they may have been a little over-optimistic. Many of the problems faced by the post-emancipation societies are still with us and known euphemistically as underdevelopment. Many of them, too, may be detected in earlier slave societies from which, as a result of changes in the market, capital and labour was withdrawn, as happened in the tobacco states when cotton became the main staple, although to some degree this was offset by the reverse flow of capital obtained by selling slaves. But with emancipation there was no reverse flow and capital was desperately short. So also were skilled manpower and entrepreneurship, both of which depended upon qualities which the former regimes, because of their concentration on export monoculture, had done little to encourage. In short, the problems of the ex-slave societies were not of the Abolitionists' making and even if Abolitionists had fully understood them it is hard to see what could have been done.

Nevertheless, the fact that these societies were economically so ill-prepared for the changes they were being compelled to make — and in practice performed so lamentably — raises questions about the motives for these actions. The principal justification for slavery, as I have indicated, was that it worked. The problem with emancipation, economically speaking, was that it did not work, at least not so well. It could not be claimed that this was unforeseen. The planters had used it as their main line of argument. It is true that they had used a good many other arguments which were more dubious. But whatever they might say, it was plain that they were not philanthropists. And it was also clear that, if sugar, tobacco and cotton could have been more cheaply produced in some other way, they, or someone else, would have done so. For proof that slavery worked, one need look no further than the slave markets of Kingston, Havana and New Orleans.

So who stood to profit? The slaves certainly. Planters in those slave societies which managed to stave off emancipation. East Indian and Egyptian producers who, until the Civil War, had scarcely managed to get a toe-hold in the market and might well not have managed to survive subsequently had not slavery been abolished. Who else? Certainly not consumers in the importing countries; nor any of the middlemen, the traders, bankers and manufacturers who looked to the plantation economies for business and raw materials, although they could usually pass on the extra cost to their customers in the form of higher prices. Nor did the exporters profit since they depended for their trade on the purchasing power of their customers which in most cases declined.

For these reasons it is extremely difficult to construct a national interest argument for the abolition of slavery. The twenty millions paid out of public funds to compensate the planters was no small amount. To pay out that sum for a *diminished* supply of labour and then attempt to make up the shortfall by importing workers from ten thousand miles away

Abolition and the National Interest

made no sort of sense at all. In the case of the United States the agitation of the slavery issue had altogether more catastrophic consequences. It could, of course, be argued that there were those behind the scenes who manipulated events in their own interests. But who were these hard-faced men who stood to profit? One can find them on the other side — the Liverpool and New York merchants, for example. But where are the capitalists who supported the Abolitionists out of interest? Their absence from the historical record is striking. If they existed they would seem to have had a singularly mistaken view of where their interests lay.

If, on the other hand, we turn history around, it is only too easy to imagine a set of policies which would have been entirely reconcilable with notions of national interest, that is to say national interest in the narrow sense in which we have defined it. Let us suppose that Wilberforce and Buxton, and Garrison and Weld had never existed, in short that there had never been a campaign against slavery. In these circumstances, Britain would have gone on supplying slaves not only to her own colonies but to the rest of the world. We now know that the profits deriving from this traffic were not so great as its critics, associating wickedness with mammon, often alleged.[24] Nevertheless, there were profits to be made and these, we may presume, would have gone to British rather than French or Spanish or Portuguese merchants or the entrepreneurs of indeterminate nationality who flourished during the later phases of the traffic. We may also suppose that a significant proportion of these new slaves would have gone to British colonies, in particular to the hitherto undeveloped territories of Trinidad and British Guiana, while probably fewer would have gone to Brazil and Cuba. Britain's West Indian planters, while no doubt continuing to complain that they were on the point of bankruptcy, would have gone on enlarging their share of the world's sugar market. The United States would presumably have imported more slaves too, if only because they were relatively so cheap, and, in due course, have found new ways of employing them.

One could go on and imagine whole new industries manned by slave labourers. But like all exercises in counterfactual history this one becomes progressively less plausible. This is not because slave labour was intrinsically unskilled or unadaptable. There is plenty of evidence that slaves could, when required, perform complex tasks. One already sees this happening to a degree in the American South.[25] What makes this particular foray into counterfactual history implausible is that it presupposes a kind of society totally at odds with the sort of societies we actually see emerging in Britain and the United States and, indeed, in the developing world generally. These were societies in process of rapid transformation. Economically they were growing at a remarkable rate. What is most striking, at least in the present context, is that they were societies dedicated to principles which explicitly rejected everything which slavery stood for. It is simply unrealistic to imagine that these societies, busily engaged in exploiting the potentialities of a free labour market, could at the same time have supported an expanding slave labour segment with all the restrictions that would have required. The problem with maintaining such a dual system, as we know from those slave societies which did exist, was that it raised issues which had important implications so far as the operation of the free sector was concerned. Quite apart from the physical difficulty of policing such a system, there was the added problem of controlling thought and expression within the free society. To suppose that the economically expanding and intellectually open societies of Western Europe and North America would have been prepared to lumber themselves with such burdens flies in the face of reason.

This, of course, is to look at the issue with the benefit of hindsight. The Abolitionists who pioneered the attack on slavery had no such advantage. All the same, one finds in their arguments, even in the earliest days, a belief that slavery was not only wrong from an ethical point of view but also that it was, economically speaking, an anachronism. It was not possible for them to match their opponents by providing precise figures showing profit and loss. Often they tried to bypass the issue. When they did face up to it, what they had to say frequently looked like wishful thinking. Nevertheless, they did have an argument which, at least by the 1820s (when, of course, the issue was no longer the trade but slavery itself) had come to seem at least as plausible as those advanced by the planters.

So far, as you will have been aware, I have been defining national interest in the narrowest of senses, meaning, in effect, guaranteed profit to the mother country. But if one alters the definition just slightly so as to include people's *perceptions* of where the national interest lay, a whole new range of possibilities opens up. And perhaps this is how we should approach the matter. After all, what determines political behaviour are not the hard facts of history but men's perception of them and these perceptions are influenced by the beliefs of those who do the perceiving.

To understand what, in the case of the Abolitionists, these beliefs were, we may most appropriately begin with the works of the political economists. The term political economy was not invented by Adam Smith but it became common currency largely through his writings and was employed by his successors for a century and more thereafter. As Smith himself saw it, its purpose was to provide statesmen and legislators with the means

first, to provide a plentiful revenue or subsistence for the people, or more properly to enable them to provide such a revenue or subsistence for themselves; and secondly to supply the state or commonwealth with a revenue sufficient for the public services.[26]

In short, its object was to redefine for the benefit of a new and more enlightened generation the principles by means of which the national interest was to be promoted. In this way, according to Smith, 'it proposes to enrich both the people and the sovereign'.[27] Yet it was also, and this he and his successors continually emphasised, a science, a system of principles based on empirical observation and logical reasoning, and, as such, quite independent of politics. It was, as one of his successors, John Elliot Cairnes put it in his *Character and Logical Method of Political Economy*, 'a science in the same sense in which Astronomy, Dynamics, Chemistry, Physiology are sciences'.[28] Politicians might pay attention to it or they might not, but in either case the empirical data and the conclusions to be drawn from it were available for their instruction.

What is also clear, however, is that, then as now, the advice given by economists was in practice rather less neutral than these protestations imply. For what we see when we look back over the history of this 'science' is that despite its claim to objectivity it has also operated as a supporting faith. Indeed, the political economists themselves continually talked of morals in that they saw it as being the task of statesmen and moralists to spread the knowledge of true morals, in the sense that wisely circumscribed self-interest would harness the energies of individuals in ways that would promote the interests of the community at large. Exactly how self-interest should be circumscribed was, of course, a matter that could be debated, although in general they agreed that the greater the economic liberty that was accorded to individuals the larger would be the yield, in terms of economic prosperity, to society. In short, what we have, masquerading as a science, is a faith in a divinely ordained harmony of egoistic and altruistic impulses in man.

There are four further points which should perhaps be made. One is that it was an entirely appropriate faith for societies undergoing changes, such as those which we see occurring in Western Europe and the Northern United States. By this I do not mean that it occasioned those changes but rather that it was a reflection, a rationalisation if you like, of developments that were already occurring. This is not to impugn the originality of the political economists but merely to suggest that, as has so often happened since, originality in economics consisted of bringing theory into line with practice, or at least with practice as observed in the commercial and industrial centres. The second point is that what they proposed on the basis of this obviously limited experience were universal laws, that is to say laws such as the laws of physics and chemistry, the effects of which were to be observed in all societies everywhere. The third point is that these laws were implicitly hostile to slavery. It is easy to see why. After all, if greater liberty, the unleashing of individual self-interest, led to greater prosperity, then it was difficult to justify keeping any group in total subjection; for if exceptions were made with respect to one group why not in the case of another? To make *any* exceptions was therefore to destroy the harmony of the system as a whole.

It might be instructive to go through the works of the political economists, American and British, to see what they have to say about slavery. In fact, what they say is virtually the same in volume after volume and scarcely changed, even down to the form of words used, in the course of a century. Adam Smith had said that 'The experience of all ages and nations ... demonstrates that the work done by slaves, though it appears

Abolition and the National Interest

to cost only their maintenance, is in the end the dearest of any.'[29] Similarly, we have Dr Thomas Cooper, President of South Carolina College, saying in his *Lectures on the Elements of Political Economy* (1829) 'Slave labour is undoubtedly the dearest kind of labour; it is all forced ...'[30] And so on down through John Stuart Mill, John Elliot Cairnes to John Lancelot Shadwell who in 1877 was still saying more or less what Smith had said a century before.[31] No wonder George Fitzhugh advised his fellow Southerners to 'throw Adam Smith, Say, Ricardo and Co. in the fire'.[32]

But let me again make clear that I am not suggesting that people read these books and were thereby stirred to anti-slavery fervour. Very few Americans, for example, read Adam Smith — astonishingly few if one looks at the years up to 1820. But then 1776 was not a good year in which to publish, at least not for British authors seeking an American market! More important, however, was the fact that, in a sense, the Americans had it all already. It was mostly there in the Declaration of Independence and in Thomas Paine's *Common Sense*. My point is not that people read the political economists, although a good many, including Wilberforce, did, but that what the political economists said was indicative of a set of mind, an attitude towards the world — an ideology if you wish — which permeated western society, even, if we may judge from Cooper and Fitzhugh, the Old South, where, of course, it met countervailing forces of a very practical kind. But that was not the case elsewhere. There, it accorded very precisely with what men and women — or, at all events, middle class men and women — saw happening about them. And, of course, it directly contradicted what they had hitherto taken for granted, namely that slavery was an economic necessity, for if the experts were right it was nothing of the sort.

My fourth point is that these beliefs were propounded with a degree of didacticism and an air of superiority which infuriated the planters who felt, and often with justification, that those in the free-labour societies had failed to grasp the special problems which slave holders faced. Replying to just such a protest, Viscount Goderich, the British Colonial Secretary, explained to the governors of the Crown Colonies in 1831 that:

If the Colonists know much of which others are ignorant, they are also inevitably ignorant of much which others know. They have few opportunities of studying the progress of public opinion throughout society at large. They unavoidably live in a contracted circle, which is agitated by petty feuds and pecuniary embarrassments. In those colonies neither learned leisure, nor literary and scientific intercourse, nor even the more liberal recreations, are commonly to be found.[33]

This is precisely what many Northerners believed about the South. Enmeshed in their day-to-day problems, saddled with an uneconomic labour system, cut off from the mainstream of enlightened opinion, Southerners were no longer competent judges even of their own situation.

The burden of my argument has been to suggest that what threatened the slave societies were not the economic interests of the newly emerging world order but the economic and social assumptions it had conjured up. That these were wrong, or at all events less universal in their application than had been supposed, is irrelevant. The important point is that they were believed, the obvious corollary of this belief being that the free-labour societies, whose achievements, real and potential, so mesmerised contemporaries, should serve as a model for all societies. When Emerson sang the praises of West Indian emancipation he seems actually to have supposed that those sadly ill-provided colonies had suddenly become like New England.[34]

I am not, of course, saying that this *explains* abolition. I have said nothing about religion and very little about the moral case against slavery upon which the Abolitionists laid so much stress. I could, I suppose, be tendentious and suggest that religion and the moral fervour associated with it were merely epiphenomena. They were not, particularly if one looks at the United States, confined to one side of the argument. If men of strong religious principles and high moral aspirations were among the chief critics of slavery, they were also, it must be remembered, among its chief defenders.[35] It was the Southern clergy who led the way in constructing and elaborating the intellectual justification for slavery. For the most part, they belonged to the same denominations and subscribed to the same religious tenets as their opposite numbers in the North. That there were fewer of them, one might argue, merely reflects the relative strength of the opposing forces.

But this is to go far beyond my present brief which is to consider abolition from the point of view of national interest. All that need be noted in the present context is that the moral and religious views of the Abolitionists were much more in phase with the needs of the developing free-labour societies, which to some degree no doubt they reflected, than they were with the needs of the slave economies. Even so, it would have been impossible to carry the day on the basis of moral argument alone, particularly when their opponents were able to show, often in very specific terms, how much slavery contributed to the national wealth. What the Abolitionists needed was an alternative concept of the national interest and this they found, partly in the writings of the political economists, but principally in their own perceptions of what it was that made their own societies work. In the event this proved a more persuasive concept than the ledger-book calculations of their opponents in that it drew on the strength, dynamism, inventiveness and idealism of those societies which, for historical reasons, had never adopted slavery, and which now, finding themselves in the ascendant, were reaching out to remake the world in their own image.

NOTES

1. C. Duncan Rice, 'Literary Sources and the Revolution in British Attitudes to Slavery', in Christine Bolt and Seymour Drescher (eds), *Anti-Slavery, Religion, and Reform: Essays in Memory of Roger Anstey*, Folkestone, Kent, and Hamden, Connecticut, Dawson/Archon, 1980, pp. 322–5.
2. James Boswell, *No Abolition of Slavery, or, the Universal Empire of Love: A Poem*, London, 1791, quoted in C. Duncan Rice, *The Scots Abolitionists, 1833–1861*, Baton Rouge, Louisiana State University Press, 1981, p. 21.
3. Jane Austen, *Mansfield Park*, chapters 2 and 3.
4. This is the approach adopted in Thomas Clarkson's *A History of the Rise, Progress and Accomplishment of the Abolition of the African Slave Trade*, two vols, London, 1808, which is notable for being the first attempt to provide a comprehensive account of the origins of the anti-slavery movement. More recent examples include F. J. Klingberg, *The Anti-Slavery Movement in England*, New Haven, Yale University Press, 1926; Dwight L. Dumond, *Anti-Slavery: The Crusade for Freedom in America*, Ann Arbor, University of Michigan Press, 1961, and David Brion Davis, *The Problem of Slavery in Western Culture*, Ithaca, Cornell University Press, 1966.
5. The classic example of this approach is Eric Williams's *Capitalism and Slavery*, Chapel Hill, University of North Carolina Press, 1944. Such arguments are

less readily adapted to fit the American experience although occasionally such attempts have been made. See C. A. and M. R. Beard, *The Rise of American Civilization*, two vols, New York, 1927, vol. 2, pp. 6–7.
6. Karl Polanyi, *The Great Transformation: The Political and Economic Origins of Our Time*, first published 1944; Boston, Beacon Press, 1957.
7. William Cobbett, *The Parliamentary History of England*, vol. 28, 12 May 1789, p. 78.
8. *Ibid.*, p. 76.
9. *Ibid.*, vol. 27, pp. 499–506, 579, 595–9, 639–47; vol. 28, pp. 41–100; vol. 29, pp. 250–72.
10. *Ibid.*, vol. 27, 9 May 1788, p. 502.
11. Roger Anstey, *The Atlantic Slave Trade and British Abolition, 1760–1810*, London, Macmillan, 1975, pp. 343–90, 408–9.
12. Cobbett, *Parliamentary History*, vol. 28, 23 June 1789, p. 100.
13. There is still no adequate modern study of the work of this organisation. Accounts of its many activities will, however, be found in its *Reports*, twenty-seven volumes, London, 1807–27.
14. The continued expansion of British West Indian production up to 1807 and its subsequent decline is brilliantly described and analysed in Seymour Drescher, *Econocide: British Slavery in the Era of Abolition*, Pittsburgh, University of Pittsburgh Press, 1977. This account supersedes the earlier accounts by Lowell J. Ragatz and Eric Williams.
15. 'Report of the Select Committee Appointed to Inquire into the Commercial State of the West India Colonies', *Parliamentary Papers, 1831–32* (381), vol. 20, pp. 139–57.
16. *Hansard's Parliamentary Debates, 3rd Series*, vol. 18, 10 June 1833, p. 538.
17. *Ibid.*, vol. 17, 2 May 1833, p. 838.
18. Howard Temperley, *British Antislavery, 1833–1870*, Harlow, Longman, 1972, pp. 111–36.
19. *Ibid.*, pp. 137–67.
20. *Ibid.*, pp. 124–35. For a general account of the Indian indentured labour traffic see Hugh Tinker, *A New System of Slavery: The Export of Indian Labour Overseas, 1830–1920*, Oxford, Oxford University Press, 1974.
21. James Duffy, *Portugal in Africa*, Harmondsworth, Penguin Books, 1962, p. 97.
22. Temperley, pp. 133–4; F. H. Hitchins, *The Colonial Land and Emigration Commission*, Philadelphia, University of Pennsylvania Press, 1931, p. 248.
23. Roger L. Ransom and Richard Sutch, *One Kind of Freedom: The Economic Consequences of Emancipation*, Cambridge, Cambridge University Press, 1977, pp. 1–13.
24. Anstey, *The Atlantic Slave Trade*, pp. 38–57.
25. Robert S. Starobin, *Industrial Slavery in the Old South*, New York, Oxford University Press, 1970.
26. Adam Smith, *An Inquiry into the Nature and Causes of the Wealth of Nations*, 1776; reprint of the Methuen 1904 edition, University of Chicago Press 1976, p. 499.
27. *Ibid.*
28. John Elliot Cairnes, *The Character and Logical Method of Political Economy*, 3rd edn, London, Macmillan, 1888, p. 34. Cairnes attempted to apply his theories to American slavery in *The Slave Power: Its Character, Career and Probable Designs*, London, 1862; 2nd enlarged edn, London, Macmillan, 1863. Although he knew very little about this subject his views are highly revealing so far as his logical method is concerned. See Howard Temperley, 'Capitalism, Slavery and Ideology', *Past and Present* no. 75, May, 1977, pp. 111–13.

29. Adam Smith, p. 411.
30. Thomas Cooper, *Lectures on the Elements of Political Economy*, 2nd edn, Columbia, SC, McMorris and Wilson, 1829, p. 106.
31. John Lancelot Shadwell, *A System of Political Economy*, London, Trubner and Co., 1877, pp. 180–1.
32. George Fitzhugh, *Cannibals All!: or Slaves Without Masters*, Richmond, Va., A. Morris, 1859, p. 175.
33. Circular Dispatch from Viscount Goderich, 5 Nov. 1831, *Parliamentary Papers 1831–32*, vol. 46, p. 69.
34. Ralph Waldo Emerson, *Address Delivered in the Courthouse in Concord, Massachusetts, on the 1st August, 1844, on the Anniversary of the Emancipation of the Negroes in the British West Indies*, Boston, J. Munroe, 1844.
35. H. Shelton Smith, *In His Image But ...: Racism in Southern Religion, 1780–1910*, Durham, NC, Duke University Press, 1972, especially pp. 129–65.

7

Emancipation from below? The Role of the British West Indian Slaves in the Emancipation Movement, 1816−34

MICHAEL CRATON

On 22 March 1816, Matthew Gregory 'Monk' Lewis, gothick novelist and absentee planter on his first visit to his Jamaican estates, recorded in his diary a kind of proto-calypso or revolutionary hymn, said to have been sung by some Ibo slaves plotting a rebellion under cover of a funeral in the neighbouring parish of St Elizabeth. Allegedly, there were 'above a thousand persons ... engaged in the plot, three hundred of whom had been regularly sworn to assist in it with all the usual accompanying ceremonies of drinking human blood, eating earth from graves, &c'. Among the would-be rebels were said to be 'a *black* ascertained to have stolen into the island from St Domingo, and a *brown* Anabaptist missionary'. The latter was perhaps the author of the hymn, but the singing was led by the elected 'King of the Eboes':

> Oh me good friend, Mr. Wilberforce, make we free!
> God Almighty thank ye! God Almighty thank ye!
> God Almighty, make we free!
> Buckra in this country no make we free:
> What Negro for to do? What Negro for to do?
> Take force by force! Take force by force![1]

What are we to make of this subversive ditty, which, significantly, was not published until 1834, after the Emancipation

Emancipation from below?

Act had come into effect, sixteen years after Lewis's own death by yellow fever, and a year after the death of Wilberforce himself? Provided that we are certain of its authenticity,[2] it seems to indicate that the St Elizabeth plotters believed that God had the power, and perhaps the will, to free them, that they could call upon certain godly allies in England – the chief of them being the chief of the Evangelical Saints – that, with or without external aid, the time was ripe for making a move, and that since they could not expect their immediate oppressors ever to relent, they had every justification and right to resort to armed rebellion.

I believe it to be axiomatic that all slaves wanted their freedom – that is, freedom to make a life of their own – and that all slaves resisted slavery in the ways best open to them, actually rebelling, if rarely, when they could or had to. In rebelling, they seized the weapons that were to hand and used the aid of whatever allies they could find. Perhaps, then, the Lewis ditty accurately reflected the resistant spirit of the British West Indian slaves when it was sung; their ideology of resistance.[3]

Between the year that Lewis recorded the Ibo song and the year of its publication, not only did the emancipation movement come to fruition, but there was also a crescendo of slave unrest in the British West Indies, with highlights in three of the largest ever slave rebellions, in Barbados in April 1816, in Demerara in August and September 1823 and in Jamaica between December 1831 and February 1832. What this paper aims to do is to examine each of these major outbreaks, briefly describing the sequence of events, the causes alleged at the time and what I take to be the truer causes, and the outcome, both in the colonies and, even more important, in the metropole. It will try to establish the relative parts the principal actors played in the drama of British slave emancipation, which was enacted barely a year after the suppression of the Jamaican rebellion; the avowed Emancipationists, the British legislators, the West Indian planters, the missionaries and, above all, the British West Indian slaves themselves. My main purpose is to test the conclusions by Eric Williams, in 1944, that 'the alternatives were clear: emancipation from above or emancipation from below', and of Richard Hart, in 1980, that British West Indian blacks were 'slaves who abolished slavery'.[4]

The Barbados revolt began with thrilling suddenness on Easter Sunday night, 14 April 1816, at a time when the slaves were free from work and had ample opportunities to organise under the cover of the permitted festivities. What made the outbreak all the more shocking to the planters was that there had never been an actual slave rebellion in Barbados, and not even a plot had been uncovered to ruffle their complacency for 115 years. Indeed, so convinced were the Barbadian planters of their physical and psychological control over their slaves that they were certain that a rebellion could only have been generated by outside forces, namely the English Emancipationists, and fomented by local agents other than slaves, specifically a cabal of disaffected free coloureds under the leadership of one Joseph Pitt Washington Franklin, 'a person of loose morals and abandoned habits, but superior to those with whom he intimately associated'.[5]

Some 20,000 slaves were involved, from more than seventy-five estates, and within a few hours they had taken control of the whole south-eastern quarter of the island. They fired the cane-trash houses as beacons and drove most of the Whites into Town, but did not commit widespread destruction or kill any of the hundreds of Whites virtually at their mercy. Having reached within sight of Bridgetown, they set up defensive positions, hoping and expecting the regime to negotiate.

They were soon disabused. Martial law was declared by the Acting Governor and the military commandant, Colonel Codd, was placed at the head of a punitive column. This consisted of regular troops, including the black First West India Regiment, and the much less disciplined and more vindictive white parochial militiamen. Codd encouraged the killing of all slaves who resisted and authorised the burning of houses and destruction of gardens, but still had to report that 'Under the irritation of the Moment and exasperated at the atrocity of the Insurgents, some of the Militia of the Parishes in Insurrection were induced to use their Arms rather too indiscriminately in pursuit of the Fugitives'.[6] Whereas one white civilian and one black soldier were killed, at least fifty slaves died in the fighting and seventy more were summarily executed in the field. Another 300 were carried to Bridgetown for more leisurely trial, of whom 144 were in due course put to death and 132 deported.[7]

Emancipation from below?

Once the revolt was suppressed, the regime was at pains to exculpate itself. Whites asserted that slaves never gave bad treatment as a cause of revolt, and masters were eager to demonstrate, against their metropolitan critics, that Barbadian slaves were well fed, clothed and housed, were not cruelly punished, received good medical treatment and had opportunities to grow their own provisions and raise livestock, even to sell their surpluses. The official Assembly Report, not published until 1818, echoed the statement made by Colonel Codd as early as 25 April 1816: 'The general opinion which has persuaded the minds of these misguided people since the proposed Introduction of the Registry Bill [is] that their Emancipation was decreed by the British Parliament. And the idea seems to have been conveyed by mischievous persons, and the indiscreet conversation of Individuals.'[8]

However, such a spontaneous rebellion could not have occurred without widespread disaffection, organisation and leadership among the slaves themselves, and concerted, if unrealistic, aims. The local equivalent of the authors of the subversive ditty from St Elizabeth, Jamaica, seems to have been a remarkable woman called Nanny Grigg, a literate domestic from Simmons's estate. Nanny had been telling her fellow slaves during 1815 that they were to be freed on New Year's Day. She claimed to have read this in the newspapers and said that her master and the other planters were 'very uneasy' about it. Accordingly, she urged strike action, telling the other slaves 'that they were all damned fools to work, for that she would not, as freedom they were sure to get'. When the New Year came and went without emancipation, Nanny's advice became more militant. 'About a fortnight after New-year's Day', reported another slave, 'she said the negroes were to be freed on Easter-Monday, and the only way to get it was to fight for it, otherwise they would not get it; and the way they were to do, was to set fire, as that was the way they did in Saint Domingo.'[9]

Yet Nanny Grigg was no more than a firebrand. The real leaders and organisers of the slaves were tightly-knit groups, cells, of elite creole slaves led by rangers – that is, slave drivers, chosen by the Whites for apparent reliability, with much more freedom of movement than most of their fellows. Chief of all these was Bussa, the ranger of Bailey's estate, after whom the revolt has always been popularly known. What motivated Bussa and his lieutenants, it seems, was a hatred of slavery made intolerable by even worse than average conditions, coupled with a misguided sense that because the plantocracy now had enemies in England the time was opportune to rise up and dictate the terms under which the Blacks would continue to work on the sugar plantations.

What makes Bussa's revolt all the more poignant is the evidence that the rebels felt that they had the right to negotiate because they, even more than the Whites, were now true Barbadians. As Colonel Codd put it, 'they maintained to me that the island belonged to them, and not to white Men'.[10] In their attempts at mobilisation, the Barbadian rebels marched under certain banners or standards, carried by such persons as 'Johnny the *standard bearer*' who came from Bussa's estate. One of these banners, since, unfortunately, lost, was forwarded to London. Reports of it differ. Some locals claimed that it depicted 'the Union of a Black Man with a white Female', an accurate configuration of the planters' Freudian fears, while another account simply discerned that it showed a black Barbadian on terms of equality with a white. Perhaps even more significant was the fact that when the rebels took as their first objective the St Philip's militia armoury, besides muskets they took away the standard of the parochial militia regiment, which they carried forward into the skirmish at Lowther's yard on Easter Monday. Thus, it could be maintained, the slaves saw themselves not as simple rebels but as the authentic black militia of their native parish.[11]

The chief miscalculations of the Barbadian rebels lay in underestimating the power of the local regime, in vainly presuming that the imperial troops would not be used against them (particularly the black West India Regiment), and in overestimating the support they might get from metropolitan liberals. In fact, even those in the metropolis who blamed the white Barbadians for bringing the rebellion on themselves by complacency and loose talk — calling slave registration but the thin end of a wedge leading to slave emancipation, and talking of imperial dictation over a Registry Act as tyranny worthy of rebellion in the style of the Americans in 1776 — were horrified by the slave uprising. Not a single white person anywhere, it seems, reckoned the deaths of 264 rebel slaves as overkill.

Wilberforce's own role was critical. Although he had supported the Corn Law in 1815 ostensibly in return for government support of the Slave Registry Bill, he was already wavering over the Bill before news of Bussa's revolt reached London at the end of May 1816.[12] The news, though, seems to have convinced him that the Emancipationists had best 'rest on their oars' for the moment. He did not oppose the address to the Prince Regent deploring the insurrection, and on 19 June made a speech so defensive and self-exculpatory that he came close to a rift with his brother-in-law, James Stephen.[13] Clearly, Wilberforce was terrified by the thought that he might be held responsible for the Barbados slave revolt, and he may well have been influenced by none other than Monk Lewis himself, with whom he dined between Lewis's arrival in England on 5 June and his speech in the House on 19 June.[14] Wilberforce's diary merely records that he and Lewis met 'to talk over Jamaica', and discussed Lewis's plans 'to secure the happiness of his slaves after his death', but it is inconceivable that Lewis did not tell Wilberforce of the St Elizabeth plot less than three months before, including the fact that the plotters had so memorably invoked Wilberforce's name. The idea of popular insurrection was anathema to Wilberforce, in England even more so than in the West Indies. In the period 1817–19, indeed, he spent almost as much effort in supporting the government's repressive measures at home, as he did on the West Indian cause.[15]

Just as Bussa's revolt came in conjunction with the dissensions over the Slave Registry Bill, so the Demerara rebellion of August 1823 followed close on the heels of the next great wave of Emancipationist activity: T. F. Buxton's assumption of the leadership from the ailing William Wilberforce, the founding of the new Anti-Slavery Society in January 1823, Buxton's unsuccessful motion for gradual emancipation and Canning's canny substitution of an ameliorationist policy in May, and the Colonial Secretary, Lord Bathurst's first amelioration circular, which reached Georgetown on 7 July 1823.[16] As happened in Barbados, the Guiana plantocracy angrily complained of imperial interference and dragged its feet over the implementation of the Bathurst circular. What further provoked the planters was that in British Guiana, unlike Barbados in 1816, nonconformist missionaries were already active and rapidly gaining converts, the most effective being the Rev. John Smith of the London Missionary Society, pastor of Bethel chapel on Le Resouvenir estate.

When the revolt was found to have been preceded by exaggerated rumours of impending changes decreed from London, seemed to focus on Le Resouvenir and the adjacent Success estate (owned by the father of William Ewart Gladstone), and to have been inspired by Smith's chief deacon, Quamina, the planters naturally claimed that the Emancipationists, misguided imperial statesmen and meddling missionaries were chiefly to blame. A more careful analysis, however, shows that the causes were, at least, more complex and, maybe, basically other.

Despite the planters' disclaimers, the Demerara slaves had even more cause to rebel than the Barbados slaves in 1816. Sugar monoculture had intensified and the slaves were worked harder and punished cruelly, callously shifted around with family ties ignored. Quamina, for example, on the day that Peggy, his wife of thirty years, lay dying, was refused leave to return to his house before sundown, when he found Peggy dead.[17] For Christian slaves, the refusal of the planters to grant more than Sunday free from estate labour was particularly irksome, since it led to a conflict between the will to worship in chapel and the need to work provision grounds and go to market.

Christianity undoubtedly provided solace for many slaves, but less encouragement for rebellion. The missionaries, including Smith, were scrupulous in following their instructions to spurn political issues and counsel hard work and obedience. Bethel chapel was undoubtedly an important meeting place for slaves from the entire East Coast of Demerara, but subversive discussions occurred outside rather than inside the building. Likewise, Quamina, though a revered figure, seems to have been drawn into the rebellion rather than leading it, carrying no arms and being absent from the fighting. A far more dangerous type of rebel was his son, Jack Gladstone, a backslider in chapel but an ardent and wily agitator who was later to give evidence against Parson Smith and got off with deportation to St Lucia.[18]

As far as the Whites were concerned, the revolt broke out with shocking suddenness on Monday 18 August. Nearly all the 30,000 slaves on the sixty estates over a thirty-mile stretch east of

Emancipation from below?

Georgetown were involved. Again, by a concerted policy, there was little property damage, and the Whites held captive were merely placed in the slave punishment stocks. Governor Murray, himself a planter, on the first morning confronted a party of rebels and asked them what they wanted. 'Our rights', he was told. When Murray told them of the forthcoming Bathurst reforms, the rebels replied, in Murray's account, that 'these things ... were no comfort to them. God had made them of the same flesh and blood as the whites, that they were tired of being Slaves to them, that their good King had sent Orders that they should be free and they would not work any more'.[19] Murray then said that he would only negotiate once the rebels laid down their arms, at which the crowd grew ugly. Murray thereupon turned tail, galloped into Georgetown and ordered a general mobilisation.

The slaves were no match for the forces of the regime under Colonel Leahy, which, contrary to the slaves' wishful expectation, included well-drilled regulars, black and white, and Amerindians, as well as the local white militia. The only serious clash was at Bachelor's Adventure plantation, halfway down the coast, on 20 August, where 2000 slaves met with Leahy's 300 redcoats. 'Some of the insurgents called out that they wanted lands and three days in the week for themselves, besides Sunday, and that they would not give up their arms till they were satisfied,' wrote a militia rifleman. 'They then said that they wanted their freedom,' went another account, 'that the King had sent it out − and that they *would* be free.'[20] Leahy did give the rebels three chances to lay down their arms, but when their leaders announced that 'the negroes were determined to have nothing more or less than their freedom,' and one prominent rebel waved a cutlass and dared the troops 'to come on', Leahy gave the order to fire. The first volley scattered the rebels and in the ensuing orgy of hunting and shooting, particularly enjoyed by the militia, between 100 and 150 rebels were killed or wounded, at the cost of two wounded soldiers.[21] The rest of the campaign was simply mopping up.

Besides the slaves killed in resistance, Leahy himself admitted that some sixty were shot out of hand, while an equal number were more ceremonially executed after military trials, a total of 250 slaves killed in all, compared with three Whites killed and a handful wounded. Quamina was hunted down and shot by Amerindians on 16 September, his body being hung in chains close to Bethel chapel, where it was left for months. Parson Smith was arrested and charged with complicity and incitement, tried under martial law, found guilty and condemned to death – with a recommendation for mercy – on 19 November. Suffering from galloping consumption, he died in his prison cell on 6 February 1824, a week before King George IV signed a reprieve with an order for deportation.[22]

When the news of the Demerara revolt reached England in early October, it was a great disappointment for the Emancipationists but provided fresh ammunition for the pro-slavery lobby. Both sides were initially convinced that it was the timing of the Bathurst circular which had triggered the revolt, and even Zachary Macaulay went so far in attempting to reassure Buxton and Wilberforce as to maintain that the insurrection was 'the work of Canning, Bathurst and Co. and not of your firm'.[23] Canning and the government duly reneged on their promise to impose the amelioration measures, except in Trinidad, and when Buxton opposed this in Parliament he felt himself to be 'the most unpopular man in the House'.[24]

No one dared to defend in public the actions of the slaves. However, as the details of Smith's trial reached England, along with the news of the concurrent wrecking of Shrewsbury's Methodist chapel in Barbados and the Jamaican planters' over-reaction to a threatened revolt in Hanover parish, a more effective line of attack presented itself to the Emancipationists. Clearly, the West Indian Whites could be held chiefly to blame; not just for agitating the slaves by their repressions, resistance to reform and loose talk of secession, but, even more, for their lawless godlessness in attacking the Christian church and its adherents. Lord Brougham, in a four-hour attack on the colonial plantocracies on 1 June 1824, virtually, in Charles Buxton's phrase 'changed the current of public opinion'.[25] John Smith, rather than any of the 250 dead rebels, was styled 'the Demerara Martyr'; not just because of what was described as his Christ-like forbearance and fate, but because his teaching had actually prevented the slaves from greater excesses. In perhaps the most telling passage of his marathon speech, Brougham quoted the Rev. W. S. Austin, the Anglican rector of Georgetown who had been deported for daring to defend Smith at his trial, that 'he

Emancipation from below?

shuddered to write that the planters were seeking the life of the man whose teaching had saved theirs'.[26] A fortnight later, in his last ever speech before Parliament, Wilberforce castigated the government for believing that such a body as the Guianese planters would ever reform itself, and helped wrest the minor concession that the Bathurst measures would be imposed on Demerara and St Lucia as well as Trinidad.[27]

The period between 1824 and 1832 saw a steadily widening gulf between the metropolis − Colonial Office, public and even Parliament − on the one hand, and the colonial plantocracies on the other. The Emancipationists, gaining confidence, made the crucial transition from gradualism to immediatism in May 1830, while, for their part, the colonial slaves increasingly took advantage of developing conditions.[28] Slave unrest was widespread, almost endemic. Even in a non-plantation colony like the Bahamas, where the slaves were healthier, less hard worked and less supervised than elsewhere, dissatisfactions with slavery fed on rumours of imperial change. For example, the largest holding of Bahamian slaves, Lord Rolle's in Exuma Island, fearing a transfer to Trinidad and loss of their lifestyle, rose up early in 1830. A group of forty-four led by one Pompey, seized their master's boat and sailed to Nassau to lay their case before a governor, Carmichael Smyth, who enjoyed an exaggerated reputation for favouring slaves over their masters − being flogged for their rebellion but at least ensuring that they would not be moved from their island home.[29]

Fittingly, though, it was in Jamaica − the richest and most populous plantation colony, with the harshest regime and most turbulent history of slave resistance − that the climactic and largest ever British slave revolt erupted around Christmas 1831. Jamaica was also the colony in which Christianity had most firmly taken root, a development that the planters regarded as chancy at best, highly dangerous at worst. Cautious proselytising by the established church or by the more 'respectable' and regime-supporting sects − such as Moravians or Methodists − might usefully socialise the slaves. Yet the most ardent converts were the followers of 'Native Baptist' preachers, who had originally come to Jamaica with the Loyalists in the 1780s, more than twenty-five years before the first white Baptist missionaries arrived in the colony. Obviously, the 'brown Anabaptist priest' mentioned by Monk Lewis in 1816 was such a person. Another was Sam Sharpe, the pre-eminent leader of the 1831 rebellion, though he, like most of his kind, had more or less been subsumed into a white missionary's chapel as a deacon.[30]

So many black deacons and their followers were to be involved in the Christmas rebellion that it was popularly known as the Baptist War — a fact that was initially a great embarrassment and only retrospectively useful to the white ministers who, like John Smith in 1823, were largely ignorant of what went on beyond their notice or understanding. From an extreme point of view, the preferred kind of 'native' Christianity was quasi-millenarian, and thus politically explosive. Evidence garnered after the rebellion described 'the rebel churchgoers' emphasis on membership and leadership, their fervent secret meetings, their use of dream, trance and oaths, their almost cabalistic reverence for the Holy Bible, [and] their choice of biblical texts stressing redemption, regeneration and apocalypse'.[31] Undoubtedly there was intrinsic tinder in the Native Baptist style, but a careful examination of the actions and aims of Sam Sharpe and his coterie of leaders suggests a close affinity to those of the vanguard led by Bussa in Barbados — who were, of course, not Christians — and that which included Jack Gladstone, Sandy and Telemachus in Demerara. The slaves' more or less authorised Sunday activities and the chapels provided cover for organisation and planning, chapel services contributed to rebel rhetoric and contact with missionaries even provided a sense that the slaves were linked with sympathetic allies overseas. But Christianity was not essential to the slaves' resistance.

Consider the best evidence of Sam Sharpe's activities in the latter part of 1831. Though he was a slave and based in Montego Bay, Sharpe was practically free to roam far inland on the pretext of preaching. A favourite meeting place was the home of a senior slave called Johnson (later to die at the head of an armed body of slaves some have called the Black Regiment), on Retrieve estate, a dozen miles up the Great River valley. One condemned rebel called Hylton later described how the charismatic Sharpe

referred to the manifold evils and injustices of slavery: asserted the natural equality of man with regard to freedom ... that because the King had made them free, or resolved upon it, the whites ... were holding secret meetings

Emancipation from below? 121

with the doors shut close ... and had determined ... to kill all the black men, and save all the women and children and keep them in slavery; and if the black men did not stand up for themselves, and take their freedom, the whites would put them at the muzzles of their guns and shoot them like pigeons.[32]

The slaves, said Sharpe, should be ready to fight, but merely threaten force while engaging in strike action, binding 'themselves by oath not to work after Christmas as slaves, but to assert their claim to freedom, and to be faithful to each other'. A rebel slave called Rose testified that Sharpe asked him to take the oath. 'I said Yes. The oath was if we should agree to sit down & I said Yes & so did every body in the house say Yes. Must not trouble anybody or raise any rebellion.' Another rebel called Barrett testified that, 'Sharpe said that we must sit down. We are free. Must not work again unless we got half pay. He took a Bible out of his pocket. Made me swear that I would not work again until we got half pay.'[33]

The Whites had some premonition of the drift of events as early as 15 December but largely ignored the signs, so that the uprising that began with the refusal of thousands of slaves to go back to work after the Christmas holiday ended on Tuesday 27 December, and the firing of Kensington estate high above Montego Bay that night, was a stunning shock. Almost immediately, the revolt spread over an area of 750 square miles centred on the Great River valley, involving more than 200 estates and perhaps 60,000 slaves. The Whites, including a militia regiment defeated at a skirmish at Montpelier on 29 December, were driven into the coastal towns, and the rebels controlled the western interior of the island for nearly three weeks. Their hopes of bringing the regime to terms, with the imperial government as mediator and the imperial troops standing aside, turned out (as in 1816 and 1823) to be a cruel delusion. The Governor, Lord Belmore, promptly declared martial law, the military commander, General Sir Willoughby Cotton, acted with ruthless efficiency, while the white militia exacted savage retribution for their earlier setback.

This time, however, the regime's response was undoubtedly overkill. Though the planters later claimed damages of over a million pounds (including the valuation of the slaves and the crops they had lost), no one computed the damage to the slaves whose huts and provision grounds were burned. Some 200 slaves were killed in the fighting (for less than a dozen killed by them), while no less than 340 were executed, including more than a hundred after civil trials once martial law was lifted on 5 February 1832.[34] Beyond this, the local Whites, largely under the aegis of an Anglican organisation called the Colonial Church Union, carried out a veritable pogrom against the nonconformist missionaries and their congregations, burning down virtually every chapel in Western Jamaica. Sam Sharpe himself was one of the last to die, being hanged in Montego Bay on 23 May 1832; his last statement being, in the words of an admiring Methodist missionary, 'I would rather die on yonder gallows than live in slavery'.[35]

Had Sam Sharpe known what had already happened in England, and what was about to happen, he might have died happier. When the first news of the Jamaican rebellion reached England in mid-February, it found the country in the throes of the complex political ferment that accompanied the reform of Parliament itself — the last phase of which saw the reckless obstructionism of the House of Lords, mobs stoning the houses of unpopular Tories, radical working men's associations arming and drilling, and, in early May, that famous petty bourgeois slogan recorded by Francis Place: 'To stop the Duke, go for gold'.[36]

The response of the pro-slavery forces to the Jamaican news was to mount a propaganda campaign to match that of the Agency Committee, to call public meetings that as late as 5 April could draw 6000 people, and to persuade the Lords to set up a committee of inquiry designed to bury the whole question of emancipation. Even the anti-slavery lobby faltered, with those terrified of insurrection at home and abroad fading away, while others, convinced of the involvement in the rebellion of nonconformist converts, retreating back into gradualism.[37]

But T. F. Buxton chose a bolder, and in the event far wiser, line of campaign. As early as 7 March, he threatened the Commons that unless 'the question respecting the West Indies was not speedily settled ... it would settle itself in an alarming way, and the only way it could be settled was by the extinction of slavery'.[38] In a debate on the sugar duties on 23 March, buttressed by reports from Jamaica about the Whites' attacks upon slave Christians and their loose talk about revolt and

Emancipation from below? 123

secession from the empire, he blamed slave unrest and rebellion squarely upon the regime.[39]

Throughout April, further news about the rebellion and its aftermath crossed the Atlantic, including Governor Belmore's despatch about the destruction of chapels, and in early May the first missionary refugees arrived in England. This was at the peak of the crisis over the Great Reform Bill – what Cobbett called 'The Days of May'. When the annual meeting of the Anti-Slavery Society was held on 12 May, the Whigs had just resigned over the obduracy of the Lords and the king's refusal to create reformist peers. Driven forward by the exhortations of James Stephen – the person best placed to know what was happening in the colonies – and by Buxton's statement that it was now 'unquestionable that only by the interposition of Parliament any hope can be entertained of peacefully terminating [slavery's] unnumbered evils, or any security afforded against the recurrence of those bloody and calamitous scenes that have recently affected Jamaica,' the Anti-Slavery Society resolved that Parliament be pressed to fulfil its earlier pledge to end slavery, without delay.[40]

Wellington failed in his attempt to form a government and the Whigs returned to power on 19 May. Less than a week later, and the very day after Sam Sharpe's execution in distant Jamaica, Buxton made his crucial speech in the Commons pressing for the appointment of a select committee, not just a committee of inquiry like that of the Lords, but one that would 'consider and report upon the Measures which it may be expedient to adopt for the purpose of effecting the Extinction of Slavery throughout the British Dominions, at the earliest period compatible with the safety of all Classes in the Colonies'.[41] Buxton's motion was defeated, by 136 to 90, but a committee was appointed, although with a mandate far short of discussing the means of emancipation. And the evidence that the committee heard over the next six months, in conjunction with the rising wave of anti-slavery agitation throughout the country, made it inevitable that the Whig government would be bound to pass an Emancipation Act within eighteen months. Key actors in this phase were the refugee missionaries, especially William Knibb (who, on hearing as his ship came up the Channel that the Reform Bill had passed, is alleged to have said, 'Thank God!

Now I will have slavery down!');[42] though another important witness was the same Rev. W. S. Austin who had been deported from Demerara eight years before.

Even the English public, it seems, was far more easily stirred up by the evidence of the persecution of white missionaries than by the slaughter of slave rebels — and in this sense the missionaries, as in 1823, stole the martyrs' crown. But the missionaries would not have had a case to make without the actions of the slaves, whether the rebels were their parishioners or not. As far as Parliament was concerned, however, neither slaughtered slaves nor missionaries tarred and feathered were as effective as the general threat posed to the imperial economy — to the empire itself — by the virtual civil war between the slaves and their masters. The question for Parliament was essentially a political one; it was a matter of morality only in the sense that, in a liberal world, empire can only be maintained if its morality is justified. What Buxton was able to show in his great speech of 24 May, was that the actions of the slaves and the planters' counter attack showed up both slavery's immorality and its political impracticality. 'Was it certain', asked Buxton, 'that the colonies would remain to the country if we were resolved to retain slavery? ... How was the government prepared to act, in case of a general insurrection of the negroes? ... a war against people struggling for their rights would be the falsest position in which it was possible for England to be placed. And did the noble Lords think that the people *out of doors* would be content to see their resources exhausted for the purpose of resisting the inalienable rights of mankind?' In perhaps his most brilliant and telling passage, Buxton then quoted Thomas Jefferson, a statesman by then universally respected but one of the most tortured of slavery's defenders. 'A [slave] revolution is among possible events; the Almighty has no attributes which would side with us in [such a] struggle.'[43]

In sum, then, slave resistance and emancipationism were clearly intertwined in British slavery's final phase. News of slave resistance was disseminated more quickly, more widely and more thoroughly than ever before, while more and more slaves heard, if not always accurately, about Emancipationist activity in Britain. Moreover, slave resistance rose to a climax, in

Emancipation from below?

Jamaica, at the very point that the process was set in motion which led to the passing of the Emancipation Act on 31 July 1833. It remains to be decided, though, to what degree slave resistance and emancipationism, respectively, actually caused or speeded each other.

At the most obvious level, the Emancipation Act of 1833 was simply the political culmination of a widespread movement or campaign in the metropole. In conjunction with the general movement towards liberal reform, the small nucleus of convinced Emancipationists were able to carry the country towards a conviction that colonial slavery must be abolished. Through the interweaving of events — some of them, such as the victory of the Whigs and the passage of the Great Reform Bill, almost fortuitous — this popular conviction became translated into legislative fiat. This interpretation naturally plays down — if not actually denies — the effect of the actions of the slaves themselves in swaying first the British populace and then a sufficient majority in Parliament.

In an immediate sense, all the slave protests were certainly failures, and the slave rebellions of 1816 and 1823 actually set back the Emancipationist cause. Yet the slave resistance, not only rising to a crescendo but increasingly well publicised, gradually drove home the realisation both of the falsity of the assertion that the slaves were contented and of the plantocracy's claim to enjoy effective control. More than this, the increasingly paranoid behaviour of the colonial Whites both outraged and dismayed all levels of metropolitan opinion.

Servile rebellion was never to be condoned — least of all by Emancipationists and missionaries. For Wilberforce, for example, there was too close a congruence between the anti-Corn Law mob which threatened his house (and, he thought, his life) in 1815, and black slave rebels threatening planters' property (and perhaps their lives) in the sugar colonies. Slave rebellion was to be avoided at whatever cost; yet contradictory differences arose over the means required to prevent or control it. The response of British liberals was to ameliorate the slaves' condition and to guide them towards the Christian mode of 'civilisation', perhaps thereby fitting them to become effective wage labourers rather than slaves. The colonial regimes, on the other hand, fearing the ultimate outcome, fought a rearguard action against amelioration and resisted the spread of Evangelical Christianity as best they could. Their response to slave unrest remained traditional: savage repression of a kind no longer acceptable to metropolitan sensibilities, especially when it was accompanied by the persecution of Christian missionaries and the most nearly 'civilised' of slaves.

At least some of the slave leaders — including the authors of the subversive slave ditty of 1816 with which we began — saw the political problem in its full dimensions. To achieve the aim of freedom, they realised, the slaves needed not only solidarity among themselves, but the strengthening of links with metropolitan allies against their immediate oppressors. Christianity was, at the least, a universalising medium, with the white missionaries as messengers and mediators; mediators not so much with God, or even that other Big Massa, the English king, but with the larger congregation of fellow Christians among the British populace. And, in the event, what was most impressive of all to this larger constituency (though the pro-slavery forces did their utmost to mask it) was that the rebel slaves, though resolute in their aims, were initially more pacific in their means than the plantocratic regimes which they confronted, only resorting to force (as the 1816 ditty had it) when met by actual force.

Thus, the resistance of the slaves unequivocally contributed — if not only in direct and obvious ways — to the fact that the slave system was increasingly seen in Britain to be not only morally wrong and economically inefficient, but also politically unwise. So, in assessing the contribution of the slaves themselves to the achievement of emancipation in 1833, one can conclude that while Richard Hart's 1980 claim that British West Indian blacks were 'slaves who abolished slavery' is rather overstated, the earlier contention of Eric Williams that 'the alternatives were clear: emancipation from above or emancipation from below' is much more than simply plausible.

But wait; that peroration cannot be my final conclusion. Permit me, if you will, a John Fowles-like alternative ending, or epilogue, to my argument. So far, our analysis has concentrated on what the slaves contributed to the passing of the Emancipation Act of 1833. This line of argument is predicated on the

Emancipation from below? 127

assumptions that what was achieved in 1833−4 was both true freedom and what the slaves were striving for. Both assumptions are, to say the least, debatable.

Throughout this paper I have stressed that above all what the slaves demanded was what they termed 'freedom'. How was this freedom visualised by them? Elsewhere I have argued that this was freedom to make a life of their own; freedom to develop, under their own terms, elements of a lifestyle already achieved in prototypical form in the creolisation of the slavery system. I believe that the essential aim of the creolised slaves was to become peasant farmers. In Marxian terms, they wanted to relate to the larger market as small commodity producers. In their special context, they did not aim to destroy the plantations; they were even prepared to work for them, as long as they themselves could determine when, for how long and for what returns in the way of wages.[44]

To the degree that these aims were achieved, the ex-slaves were, by and large, contented; and thus, to the degree that they had brought about emancipation, they were the authors of their own contentment. But, as we all know, the aims were not achieved everywhere, or anywhere for long; and, especially after the worldwide slump in commodity prices in 1845, sporadic and then endemic unrest recurred.

The granting of emancipation on 1 August 1834, and of 'full freedom' four years later, were, in other words, great moments for British Emancipationists, but much less so for the newly freed slaves. The changes brought about were far from a defeat for British capital, which, under the illusory banners of free trade and *laissez-faire*, was now quite capable of exploiting peoples and territories without having slaves, plantations, or even formal colonies of its own. Despite its claims about beggary and maltreatment, the West Indian plantocracy, too, showed powers of adaptation, gaining from whatever concessions the imperial government continued to make, and reasserting its mastery over the mass of former slaves even in those Crown colonies ostensibly ruled directly by the Colonial Office through appointed governors and their nominated councils. Both at the imperial and local levels, then, the years after 1834 provide a classic illustration of Antonio Gramsci's principle of hegemony; that socio-economically dominant forces are prepared to shift their ground quite radically if doing so is the best, or only, means of retaining real power. For emancipated slaves everywhere, the struggle continued.

In all colonies, the newly freed were continually harassed by the extension of British police, vagrancy and masters and servants laws, applied by JPs who were usually planters, or by stipendiary magistrates strongly under plantocratic influence. The freedmen's ambitions to be peasant smallholders were hampered by relatively high prices for land, taxes that grossly favoured the large landowners and the enforcement of laws against squatting. Political expression was stifled, and where there were elections the franchise was denied to the black masses by loaded property qualifications. Though they could not control the larger economy, the colonial Whites also made sure that they remained a local oligarchy, controlling all wholesale and most retail trade, and obtaining legislation against the former slaves' informal marketing networks.

In the colonies with little spare land, the freedmen had no option but to labour on their former owners' terms, but in less crowded territories, particularly Jamaica and the Crown colonies of Trinidad and British Guiana, many did establish peasant smallholdings and independent villages in the first few years after emancipation. After 1845, though, the price of peasant commodities tumbled along with those of plantation staples in a worldwide slump, speeded by the adoption of completely free trade by the British imperial government. In marginal colonies, plantations failed, so that the opportunities for labour were non-existent even at wages below subsistence level. Elsewhere, would-be peasants were compelled to accept any wages offered to eke out the pitiful return from peasant farming. Formal slavery, in other words, had become a modified – and peculiarly West Indian – form of wage slavery.

Thus we would maintain that, from the larger perspective, the formal emancipation enacted on 31 July 1833 was part of a colossal hegemonic trick. If so, the first phase was the process of debate that between May 1832 and July 1833 hammered out the details of the Emancipation Act, in particular, the clauses which determined that the ex-slaves would continue to work for their former masters as so-called 'apprentices', and those which compensated the owners for their lost property in their slaves, to the unprecedented tune of £20,000,000.[45]

Emancipation from below?

If we accept this alternative, hegemonic, interpretation, surely it sheds fresh light on William Wilberforce's famous dying words on 26 July 1833: 'Thank God that I have lived to witness a day in which England is willing to give twenty millions sterling for the Abolition of Slavery.'[46] Does it not make Wilberforce seem to have been, at the least, an extremely equivocal Emancipationist – pessimistic about the chances of an idealistic emancipation, and taking it for granted that slaveholders should be generously compensated for their property? For more dedicated sceptics, or for devoted followers of Antonio Gramsci, William Wilberforce's dying words simply underline the conclusion that twenty millions sterling was the price that, in the event, the ruling class was prepared to pay to preserve its hegemony – or at least to delay the inevitable revolution.

NOTES

1. M. G. Lewis, *Journal of a Residence Among the Negroes in the West Indies*, London, Murray, 1845 edn, pp. 114–16.
2. Lewis's posthumous journal is said to have been printed from the ms. he had with him when he died at sea on his journey home in 1818. The original ms. has not survived. Despite its very imperfect dialect form, the ditty was said to be from a copy found upon the person of the Eboe King. The credibility of the plot itself, with its thousand alleged adherents, is eroded by the fact that, according to Lewis, only one ringleader – presumably the Eboe King – was condemned to death. *Ibid.*, pp. 114–15.
3. For the development of this concept, see Michael Craton, *Testing the Chains: Resistance to Slavery in the British West Indies*, Ithaca, Cornell University Press, 1982, particularly pp. 11–17.
4. Eric Williams, *Capitalism and Slavery*, London, André Deutsch, 1964 edn, p. 208; Richard Hart, *Blacks Who Abolished Slavery*, Kingston, ISER, 1980.
5. Sir Robert Schomburgk, *The History of Barbados*, London, 1847, p. 395. For the 1816 Barbados revolt in general see also Craton, *Testing the Chains*, pp. 254–66; Karl Watson, *The Civilised Island: Barbados, A Social History*, Barbados, 1979, pp. 125–35.
6. Codd to Leith, 25 April 1816, in Leith to Bathurst, 30 April 1816, C.O. 28/85; Craton, *Testing the Chains*, p. 264.
7. *Ibid.* and pp. 372–3, n. 37.
8. Codd to Leith, 25 April 1816, quoted in Michael Craton, 'Proto-Peasant Revolts? The Late Slave Rebellions in the British West Indies, 1816–1832', *Past & Present*, 85, Nov. 1979, p. 104.
9. *The Report from a Select Committee of the House of Assembly Appointed to Inquire into the Origins, Causes and Progress of the Late Insurrection*, Barbados, 1818, pp. 29–31; Craton, *Testing the Chains*, pp. 260–1.
10. Codd to Leith, 25 April 1816, *ibid.*, p. 258.

11. 'The Examination of Colonel Eversley', in *Report from a Select Committee*, pp. 28–9, *ibid*., p. 262.
12. The Registry Bill had got as far as a first reading in 1815, but was withdrawn for that session; Robert I. Wilberforce and Samuel Wilberforce, *The Life of William Wilberforce*, five vols, London, Murray, 1838, IV, pp. 282–6.
13. *Ibid.*, pp. 286–95. James Stephen had already resigned his seat in Parliament in 1815 in disgust with the government for not pressing the Registry Bill; Sir George Stephen, *Anti-Slavery Recollections, in a Series of Letters Addressed to Mrs. Beecher Stowe* ..., London, 1854, p. 26. The phrase about resting on their oars was used by Wilberforce in a letter to Zachary Macaulay on 27 Jan. 1817; *Life*, IV, p. 307.
14. *Ibid.*, p. 292. The possibility occurs that it was Wilberforce himself who advised Lewis not to publish his journal, though it seems more likely that Lewis did intend publication after his return to England in 1818 – an intention frustrated by his death on the voyage. On his previous return, Lewis arrived at Gravesend on 5 June 1816; *Journal of a Residence*, p. 135.
15. Robin Furneaux, *William Wilberforce*, London, Hamish Hamilton, 1974, pp. 358–83.
16. Sir Reginald Coupland, *Wilberforce: A Narrative*, Oxford, Clarendon Press, 1923, pp. 470–91; William Law Mathieson, *British Slavery and its Abolition, 1823–1838*, London, Longman, 1926, pp. 115–27; Peter Dixon, *Canning: Politician and Statesman*, London, Weidenfeld and Nicolson, 1976, pp. 255–58. For the most up-to-date discussion of the Demerara revolt, see Craton, *Testing the Chains*, pp. 267–90; 'Proto-Peasant Revolts?' pp. 105–9.
17. Entry for 16 October 1822; Rev. John Smith, 'Copy of a Journal', C.O. 111/46; Craton, *Testing the Chains*, p. 269.
18. *Ibid.*, pp. 277–88. For Jack Gladstone's testimony at Smith's trial, see *British Sessional Papers, Commons, Accounts and Papers, 1824, XXIII (333)*, pp. 530–32.
19. Murray to Bathurst, 24 August 1823, C.O. 111/39; Joshua Bryant, *Account of an Insurrection of the Negro Slaves in the Colony of Demerara*, Georgetown, 1824, p. 6; Craton, *Testing the Chains*, p. 283.
20. Bryant, *Account*, pp. 9–10; Craton, *Testing the Chains*, pp. 284–5.
21. *Ibid.*, pp. 285–8.
22. *Ibid.* See also, Rev. Edwin Angel Wallbridge, *The Demerara Martyr: Memoirs of the Rev. John Smith, Missionary of Demerara*, London, 1846; Cecil Northcott, *Slavery's Martyr: John Smith of Demerara and the Emancipation Movement*, London, Epworth Press, 1976.
23. Macaulay to Wilberforce, 11 Nov. 1823 in *Life*, V, p. 202. Macaulay was countering the reported remark of Chinnery, private secretary to Canning, that the Demerara revolt was instigated by 'Wilberforce, Buxton and Co'.
24. Diary entry of 16 February 1824, Charles Buxton (ed.), *Memoirs of Thomas Fowell Buxton, Bart*, London, Murray, 1849, p. 73.
25. *Ibid.*, p. 78. 'The Case of the Rev. John Smith', in Henry, Lord Brougham, *Speeches on Social and Political Subjects*, two vols, London, 1857, II, pp. 113–90.
26. *Ibid.*, p. 160.
27. Wilberforce and Wilberforce, *Life*, V, p. 223.
28. Mathieson, *British Slavery and its Abolition*, pp. 130–50; Michael Craton, *Sinews of Empire: A Short History of British Slavery*, New York, Doubleday and London, Temple Smith, 1974, pp. 271–7.
29. Michael Craton, 'We Shall Not Be Moved: Pompey's Slave Revolt in Exuma Island, Bahamas, 1830', *Nieuwe West-Indisches Gids*.

Emancipation from below? 131

30. For the most recent discussions of the Jamaican rebellion of 1831–2, see Craton, *Testing the Chains*, pp. 291–321; Mary Turner, 'The Jamaican Slave Rebellion of 1831', *Past & Present*, 40, July 1968; *Slaves and Missionaries: The Disintegration of Jamaican Slave Society, 1787–1834*, Urbana, University of Illinois, 1982.
31. Craton, *Testing the Chains*, p. 250; Norman Cohn, *The Pursuit of the Millenium: Revolutionary Millenarianism and Mystical Anarchists in the Middle Ages*, 2nd ed., London, Secker & Warburg, 1961, pp. 13–16.
32. Rev. Henry Bleby, *The Death Struggles of Slavery*, London, 1853, pp. 128–9; Craton, *Testing the Chains*, p. 300.
33. Trial of Samuel Sharpe, 19 April 1832, C.O. 137/185, 304–313; Craton, *Testing the Chains*, p. 300.
34. *Ibid.*, pp. 313–16.
35. Bleby, *Death Struggles of Slavery*, p. 116; Craton, *Testing the Chains*, p. 321.
36. Graham Wallas, *The Life of Francis Place, 1771–1854*, London, Allen & Unwin, 1928, pp. 295–313. For the latest work on the socio-political forces at work in the general movement for reform, see Christine Bolt and Seymour Drescher (eds), *Anti-Slavery, Religion and Reform*, Folkestone and Hamden, 1980; David Eltis and James Walvin (eds), *The Abolition of the Atlantic Slave Trade*, Madison, University of Wisconsin Press, 1981; James Walvin (ed.), *Slavery and British Society, 1776–1846*, London, Macmillan, 1982. The best work on the direct relationship between the Jamaican revolt and the political process in the metropolis is now Mary Turner, 'The Baptist War and Abolition', *Jamaica Historical Review*, XIII, 1982, pp. 31–41.
37. David J. Murray, *The West Indies and the Development of Colonial Government, 1801–1834*, Oxford, Clarendon Press, 1965, p. 191; Buxton, *Memoirs*, p. 238.
38. *Parliamentary Debates, 3rd series, X*, 10 March 1832.
39. *Ibid.*, XI, 23 March 1832.
40. Mathieson, *British Slavery and its Abolition*, pp. 223–4; George Spater, *William Cobbett: The Poor Man's Friend*, two vols, Cambridge, CUP, 1982, II, pp. 496–99.
41. *Parliamentary Debates, 3rd series, XIII*, 24 May 1832; Buxton, *Memoirs*, pp. 245–6; Craton, *Testing the Chains*, p. 323.
42. Philip Wright, *Knibb, 'The Notorious': Slaves' Missionary, 1803–1845*, London, Sidgwick & Jackson, 1973, p. 112. For the Graham Committee report and the concurrent campaign, see *British Sessional Papers, Commons, Reports, 1831–2, XX*; Buxton, *Memoirs*, pp. 242–50; Murray, *Colonial Government*, p. 94; Wright, *Knibb*, pp. 56–133; John Howard Hinton, *Memoir of William Knibb, Missionary in Jamaica*, London, 1849.
43. *Parliamentary Debates, 3rd series, XIII*, 24 May 1832; Buxton, *Memoirs*, pp. 245–6; Turner, 'Baptist War and Abolition', pp. 40–41.
44. This, and what follows, is essentially the argument of *Testing the Chains*, as first proposed in 'Proto-Peasant Revolts?' and more fully developed in 'Continuity Not Change: The Incidence of Unrest among Ex-Slaves in the British West Indies, 1838–1876', forthcoming.
45. For detailed descriptions of the final emancipation debates, see Lowell J. Ragatz, *The Fall of the Planter Class in the British Caribbean, 1763–1833*, New York, AHA, 1928, pp. 149–152; W. L. Burn, *Emancipation and Apprenticeship in the British West Indies*, London, Cape, 1937, pp. 102–20; Murray, *Colonial Government*, pp. 193–202; Craton, *Sinews of Empire*, pp. 277–80; William A. Green, *British Slave Emancipation: The Sugar Colonies and the Great Experiment, 1830–1865*, Oxford, OUP, 1976, pp. 112–25.
46. Wilberforce and Wilberforce, *Life*, V, p. 307.

8

West Indian Society 150 Years after Abolition: a Re-examination of Some Classic Theories*

LLOYD BEST

A MISPLACED REGION

The Caribbean is a misplaced region. That is its first distinguishing feature. Latin America, in contrast, is hopelessly misnamed, as is the Far East. Mr Nehru was once asked what he thought would happen there. 'Far from where?' he replied. Latin America is another of these Eurocentric conceptions but it is less a Latin than an American civilisation whether in Bolivia, Paraguay, Peru, Guatemala or even Mexico. It is an American civilisation with a Spanish garland.

The Caribbean entered world society as a result of a search for the Pacific by way of the Atlantic, an attempt to find the sunrise in the sunset, if you like. Long distance trade in the Mediterranean was trying to go around the Saladin's roadblock as Celso Furtado has reminded us. Going West, Columbus took island for mainland and even thought he had found the Khans. But in spite of the hopes and the dreams of the Admiral of the Fleet, the Caribbean has remained resolutely island. The islands are therefore not North America; they are not South America; and not Central America either. Trinidad's northern Archipelago

---

*This is a drastically revised and shortened version of the public lecture originally delivered at the University of Hull.

West Indian Society 150 Years after Abolition

is no more than ten kilometres from Venezuela and I doubt that we even know it exists, conflicts over marine oil and fishing rights notwithstanding.

The Caribbean is clearly a case apart. When I went to Allende's Chile in their fall of 1972, it was only shortly after Fidel Castro had been there. 'What did you think of our modern Enriquillo?' I kept on asking.

'*Bueno*, Fidel is a good boy; *pero un poco más tropical para nosotros.*' A little too tropical for them, indeed. It was sheer illusion on the part of the Ché Guevara and Fidel Castro to think that they could export a Caribbean revolution to American America. It was almost as arrogant as those Europeans who believe that in 500 short years they have Latinised and civilised the Aztecs and the Incas. Fidel's most fertile ground is not there but right here in the Indies.

American America is an entirely different world from the Latin Mediterranean. It is different even from European America in Argentina, Southern Brazil and North America. And the Caribbean is something else again. The islands are marked by an imported Afro-Asian population in America operating European institutions. This absence of roots and ruins does have its limitations. But it also provides us with corresponding opportunities. There exists a definite psychology of rootlessness but it would be a mistake to take that for any simple floating condition. The whole culture is anchored in institutional arrangements requiring us, therefore, to scrutinise the other characteristics.

PLANTATION ECONOMY

The second distinguishing feature of the region is the all-pervasiveness of what the historians first described as 'plantation economy'. The expositors have made a great deal of this concept in the contemporary literature. Here we need to dwell on just a few characteristics germane to the current discussion.

We know that the plantation economy has its moorings in external dependence. It relies on the outside world for its enterprise, for its management, for its organisation. Necessarily, the surplus generated by production accrues to venturers outside the region. Even in modern times, there has been a vast gap between the domestic product and what is retained at home as national income. This we all know and it is extremely important. What, however, is crucial at this moment is that this type of dependence limits the options for adjustment when there is crisis. Partly because the entrepreneurs and the risk takers live outside, and partly because the social and political structures are rigid, the adjustment to crisis is not through intrinsic development such as technological or organisational change. Rather it is expansionist, evasive, escapist even. You do not attempt to burst the bonds of your integument, if we may borrow a phrase from Marx; you do not innovate and reorganise your ways of doing and thinking; you go around instead by moving the same old operation to somewhere else. Or you carry the same old attitudes into other lines of production where natural conditions offer you easy options.

It was the whole matrix into which the society and its politics were cast which dictated this pattern of adjustment to economic crisis in terms of falling productivity, rising costs and declining markets. I am, of course, ruthlessly simplifying the story. But the theory of business management which underlies our work on plantation economy is meant deliberately to focus this mode of adjustment. Rather than introduce new techniques on given land, planters under the extreme conditions of slavery would instead engross the plantation by acquiring more land or new land.

The sugar industry expands by the identical type of adjustment. It shifts terrain. The industry moves from North East Brazil to Barbados, Antigua, St Kitts, Martinique and the Virgin Islands. As soil exhaustion and declining profitability set in, it moves to Jamaica and then to Saint Domingue, right up to Trinidad and Cuba in the nineteenth century. When the West Indians become high cost producers, technological developments do not bring long-run costs down; the industry expands to embrace East India. What makes this possible is not just that the market is outside; that is the least of the apostles. What makes that adjustment almost mandatory is that the enterprise is uncommitted to the environment. Moreover, the surplus necessary to facilitate new commitments elsewhere by the entrepreneurship conveniently accrues outside. It accrues in the hands of the metropolitan merchant venturers.

So the adjustment is by a widening rather than a deepening.

West Indian Society 150 Years after Abolition

The corollary of this is that the economic system employs more labour per unit of output as well as per unit of land. You do not train or equip existing labour to raise its skills or its productivity. Instead, you bring more bodies in at existing levels of skill and productivity. Thus engrossment, shifting of terrain and induction of additional labour are all of a piece in the theory of plantation economy. In terms of the business management involved, account needs also to be taken of overwork and underfeeding as means of adjustment, meant to increase the milkable surplus in times of crisis. But the full theory of plantation management, rich as it is, is not the issue here on this occasion.

Important here is not the economics but the sociology. New populations are being repeatedly introduced through this pattern of expansionist adjustment. This describes a highly turbulent demographic situation. The facts about the economics are intriguing, concerned with the international divison of labour and the international distribution of income. There is a full theory of growth and development. But it is the demography which must now detain us, since that is what complicates the crucial question as to what social cleavages and what political conflicts came to be characteristic of the West Indian environment since the abolition of slavery.

We need not begin with any simple, one-dimensional model of cowboys and indians. In the Caribbean we have both social stratification and social fragmentation, at one and the same time and of equal importance. The nineteenth-century Western European mind simply refuses to entertain it. But there is no law which requires us to choose between class and race and colour and religion as causes of cleavage. We can and do have all of them at once. In any given situation, we do have to rank them and to determine, in Mao Tse Tung's terminology, which is primary and which secondary contradiction. But the answer is not pre-ordained by nineteenth-century Marxist political sociology or indeed by any other given 'bible'.

FRAGMENTED SOCIETY

The economics suggests to me that there may be three types of cleavage and contradiction which we need to acknowledge in the West Indies and the Caribbean. I suspect that the primary cleavage opposes the residentiary groups, on the one hand, to plantation groups on the other. By the residentiary groups, I mean those involved in the kind of activity which predated the hegemony of the large sugar plantation. Before 1640 these were small peasant settler-farmers; later they were on the whole Maroons until the slave system broke up in the middle of the nineteenth century. Of course, these settlers produced mainly for export. The colonies needed foreign exchange in order to pay for their food and material imports and to defray the capital costs of establishment. They were not, however, export-specialised in the sense that exporting and earning foreign exchange were their very reason for existence.

In the nature of the case, this contradiction was for a long time disguised by that other contradiction between plantation *staff* on the one hand — the management elites — and the plantation *inmates* on the other — the multitude of the subjugated slave population. Neither staff members nor inmates were substantially settlers in any important sense. The one had no interest in settlement; the other had no means to achieve it. Psychologically and culturally, the whole of the order was absentee. At the same time, the long-run options open to the slave population tilted the latter's commitment towards a settler interest even if the short-run possibilities generated enormous ambiguity.

The third contradiction in the traditional social system of the Caribbean emerges from the two wings of plantation existence. Amongst the staff, four categories of members are to be distinguished. First of all, there are the lords proprietors who enjoy the proprietary patents and draw their share of the surplus in rent. Secondly, there are the merchant venturers who are the entrepreneurs of the economic system and are well placed to extract their share of the surplus in the form of venture profit. The theory of income distribution of plantation economy shows that the location which the merchants enjoy at the source of imported supplies and at the destination of exports is crucial. Absenteeism confers on them two advantages. Firstly, they can increase their share of the product by taking part of it as head office charges on imports and exports. Secondly, they can switch their investible funds to new terrain whenever profit opportunities dictate that option.

West Indian Society 150 Years after Abolition   137

The merchants and the lords proprietors are, therefore, manifestly in a somewhat different position from the planters, and, indeed, from the attorneys involved in the day-to-day management. There rages a running battle between them over the distribution and sharing of surplus. Eric Williams and Douglas Hall have both noted that there was little love lost between them until deteriorating business conditions drove them together very late in the eighteenth century. But even under conditions of collaboration – jointly to urge the case for imperial preference – the attorneys and the planters have markedly different options from those of the lords proprietors and the merchants. In spite of themselves, the former are saddled with some sort of implicit settler interest. In times of crisis, idle capacity takes the form of unemployed labour. They are, therefore, obliged to realise their surplus not in terms of foreign exchange earned in the metropolitan market but in terms of an output of domestic services and even goods available and consumable only within the colonial economy. Here, therefore, is a potent source of conflict amongst the management interests of the plantation economy.

Amongst the inmates equally, there exists a developing cleavage. Edward Kamau Brathwaite has singled out 'domestic slaves, female slaves with white lovers, slaves in contact with missionaries, traders or sailors, skilled slaves anxious to deploy their skills, and above all, urban slaves in contact with the "wider" life'. Doubtless there are powerful forces driving the inmates together; but we cannot always assume that they constitute a single united interest. Depending on issue and situation, the differences in their ambiguities are exceedingly potent. To explain their political behaviour we have no choice but to trace their careers. What we cannot do is to deduce it *a priori* from any given theoretical dissertation. We certainly cannot conclude that there emerges a conflict between the bourgeoisie and the proletariat.

There has never existed any bourgeoisie in the Caribbean. For one thing, there have been no *bourgs* in the region. The *bourgs* and the *faubourgs* which grew up outside the medieval manor and produced St Michel and St Germain, involved a specific cultural and social response to the revival of long-distance trade between the Mediterranean and the maritime countries of Western Europe. Pirenne has carefully established the particular context. The mere ownership of property outside of these cultural conditions does not automatically reproduce a bourgeois conspiracy or a capitalist ethic. Capitalism has arisen from a set of property relations cast in the mould of a given society and culture, blessed or cursed by its own psychology, its own history, its own sense of past and present and future. It, therefore, does not make much sense to me to assume that the mere transposition of European enterprise and European capital into India or Bolivia or the West Indies under widely different cultural, social and psychological conditions, can have produced the capitalist world system that is so highly touted in the literature today.

There does, of course, exist a set of common denominators. But, equally, there exists a set of differentiating factors. It stands to reason that the capitalist world system is a congeries of different hybrid cultures, each resulting differently from penetration by Atlantic enterprise, capital and management into very varied initial conditions. It is sheer arrogance to assume that all of these differing initial conditions have been summarily remade in one individual image. It is sheer ignorance to sweep so many explosive differences under the convenient carpet terminology of 'underdeveloped, Third-World systems'. The so-called problems of underdevelopment in the Caribbean and elsewhere are not problems of underdevelopment at all. They are the consequences of structures and cultures forged by the particular relationships of history but systematically misunderstood in the context of the one-dimensional, nineteenth-century Atlantic analytic paradigm.

The other way of understanding and unravelling the problem of viable development is simply to trace the actual career of these social and cultural systems. From this point of vantage, we are faced in the Caribbean, as we have seen, with first, a historically misplaced region; secondly, a plantation economy; thirdly, a social system both stratified and fragmented and marked by several levels of conflict, cleavage and contradiction.

PLURAL CULTURE

There is a fourth feature of Caribbean society which needs to be adduced in a factually-based assessment of the region's viability. The factor in question is plural culture which, however, is distinct from M.G. Smith's 'Plural Society'.[1] Here we perceive in culture a dimension separate from that of social order. Cleavages attributable to social differences such as race, colour, religion, economic class, occupation and income level are enhanced by an additional factor. That factor is national, or more properly, ethnic tradition. In other words, what is being evoked is the ancestral aspect of social identity. It is the unconscious element in the consciousness of self and of group. It is more a Freudian than a Marxian dimension, though Marx was clearly groping for it in his attempt to establish ideology as a property inherent in mere being. This ancestral element in the make-up of identity is to be distinguished from what we may call the existential element in the consciousness of self. The latter describes a much more current and, therefore, much more concrete aspect of existence.

It follows that plural culture describes not a given state but a dynamic process of the social system. In the Caribbean this has been true in two separate ways. First of all, the demographic turbulence which is inherent in the patterns of business management and economic adjustment has entailed a repeated inmigration or import of new ethnic formations. In time, it comes to entail a steady outmigration and export of populations with ethnic biases that in important ways govern feedback, but to explore this point here would be too much of a complication.

The pluralisation of culture resulting from demographic instability has been most pronounced in such territories as Trinidad, Guyana, Suriname and Cuba where the plantation emerged as a late developer. The abolition or the diminution of the slave trade, followed by the emancipation of the slaves, had led to a widening of the catchment for plantation labour. The heterogeneity of the population, therefore, took on a higher visibility. But the ethnic diversity had, of course, always been present in the transfer to America of huge multitudes of African servants drawn from different culture areas and put to serve an elite of European managers that was in itself surprisingly heterogeneous. What has happened is that the fact of wide diversity has been masked by historical interpretations which emphasise race and class as against ethnic identification, in response to the dominant paradigm of the North Atlantic.

This first dynamic element in the plural culture of the Caribbean derives, then, from the movement of people. As the sugar economy expands or adjusts, we might say that there is a corresponding movement on the external margin of the population. This is a widening or expansionist tendency, at least in the conditions of the Golden Age. (When gall and wormwood come, the same tendency shows up of course from the negative aspect, i.e. by way of contradiction.) The second dynamic element involves a deepening or an intrinsic tendency. You might say it represents a movement on the internal frontier of population. It is on this second aspect that most of West Indian social theory has focused.

Theorists such as Lloyd Braithwaite and Raymond Smith have tended to perceive interaction of the initially separate ethnic strands as ultimately yielding ground to an overriding pattern of social stratification. In other words, they have emphasised the existential element in social identity under conditions where the lines of interest dividing the managerial elites from the labouring inmates sometimes achieved a caste-like separation. By contrast, other theorists such as M. G. Smith, Leo Despres and Harry Hoetink have tended to stress the ancestral element of group identity thereby projecting an enduring political dissensus.[2]

The view taken here is that both these tendencies represent valid options on first approximation. The historical outcome of the cultural interaction is in no way determinate. As in every concrete situation, it depends on the particular interventions achieved by policy and, therefore, to some extent on the clarity, realism and the relevance attained by theoretical and historical interpretation. From that point of view, stratification theory may or may not have been more helpful than pluralist theory but not because it has been more optimistic or less pessimistic about social dissensus and political violence in Caribbean society. If it has been more powerful, it has been because it has captured more of the ambiguities and the contradictions in the interactions which have been playing themselves out on the internal margin of the Caribbean populations.

From this point of view, the work which perhaps comes closest to capturing and distilling the process of adaptation between initially competing ethnicities in the Caribbean is a work of profound contemplation put out by Edward Kamau Brathwaite under the title *Contradictory Omens*. The focus lies on the many-sidedness of the adjustment pattern by processes formal and informal, conscious and unconscious, involving capitulation as much as confrontation. *Contradictory Omens* improves on the vital distinction offered by Sylvia Wynter between creolisation and indigenisation but it effects this improvement by the device of regarding the two as one single process enjoying, however, a dual aspect.

Here Kamau Brathwaite postulates a colonial arrangement. The society is multi-racial but organised for the benefit of a minority of European origin.

'Creole society' is the result therefore of a complex situation where a colonial polity reacts, as a whole, to external metropolitan pressures and at the same time to internal adjustments made necessary by the juxtaposition of a master and labour, white and non-white, Europe and colony, European and African (mulatto creole), European and Amerindian (mestizo creole), in a culturally heterogeneous relationship.[3]

In this process of adaptation, one face presents 'the process of absorption of one culture by another'. This is acculturation. In Sylvia Wynter's meaning, it is simply 'creolisation'. Wynter's other concept, that of 'indigenisation' is equated with 'inter-culturation'. This is the second face to the process of adaptation. It presents 'a more reciprocal activity, a process of intermixture and enrichment, each to each'.[4]

The view of this lecture is that this interpretation could profitably be extended to uncover yet a third face to the process of Caribbean adaptation. It is a face which was somewhat subsumed in Wynter's extremely suggestive if not wholly completed notion of indigenisation. If we allowed it, this third face would acknowledge a deliberate and necessary involvement in insurgency against the process of acculturation. It would recognise a necessary affirmation of selfhood and, therefore, an unyielding if not unflinching resolve to pursue the paths of the subordinated culture by creating sundry repositories of the ancestral or ethnic tradition. This third face might appropriately be termed 'anti-culturation'. In the nature of the case, the activity is insurgent and subversive; it is necessarily illegitimate and, therefore, underground, devious and correspondingly eclectic. The balance of institutional power in both the slave society and the colonial condition — particularly in business and the economy as in government and administration — dictates both an attitude of negation and a concentration in those cultural areas where formal institutions cannot easily penetrate: in the arts, in sport, family life and in folk religion.

It is precisely the placing of this absolute necessity to indulge a cultural insurgency against the background of an institutional powerlessness which made West Indian society the tinderbox it has been throughout its post-Columbus history, as the Moyne Commission noted when reporting the disturbances in the English-speaking islands during the turbulent 1930s. What is more, the combination also explains the tremendous ambivalence in the chosen techniques and methods of subversion, to such a degree that limitation and self-censorship were transformed into some of the most potent forms of cultural insurgency. The plain fact is that, in the particular context, adaption through acculturation, certainly the strategem of calculated acculturation was often the most effective and, therefore, the most menacing form of anti-culturation if only because its end result was to establish the fitness for freedom, in the coloniser's terms, of the subjugated ethnic groups, what Norman Manley used repeatedly to term 'our fitness to rule'.

A methodological problem, therefore, exists here, as much for historians and social scientists as for men of affairs and action. It arises from the fact that the dynamics of plural culture within the specific framework of Caribbean colonial institutions, as distinct from the dynamics of plural culture within, say, North American post-1776 or even pre-1776 colonial institutions, is a process with many nuances. It is a process which cannot be easily fitted into the single-plane, one-dimensional paradigm of social movement which has come to capture the Western (though not so much the non-Western) mind ever since the nineteenth century triumph of materialist political philosophy both in the west of the West and the east of the West.

In the Caribbean, as in so many parts of the 'capitalist world system', there has been no simple historic confrontation of classes. The field has not been so ruthlessly ordered as in eighteenth-century England. The Industrial Revolution precipitated the whole of English society over a veritable cliff of history and took the whole of the Atlantic civilisation along, in the process harnessing huge multitudes of proletarianised labour to the treadmill of urban life, from morning until night, for twelve or fifteen hours a day, six days a week, for a lifetime, from childhood to early and final retirement. The factory environs were so encompassing of proletarian personality that there could be no contradiction between the Freudian and the Marxian dimensions of political psychology. The only surviving contradiction was that which threatened a final and definitive resolution of conflict between capitalist and worker. It was, at least, a plausible hypothesis even if one ultimately devastated by ethnic ambiguity and new national tradition. The workers of the world still believed in 'proud' England and in France and in Bingen-on-the-Rhine. Up to this day they can be persuaded to fight for commissar and king. And yet, capital and labour can be said to have a deep-seated sense of being pitted one against the other in mortal combat.

In the Caribbean, class ambivalence has been for much longer the dominant theme of the system. What has engaged the popular imagination as carrying the seeds of a fight to the finish has always been the jarring clash of ethnic tradition, particularly the clash of Africa and Europe in America. In the nature of the case, the surrounding conditions of economy and society in the region have never permitted a fight to the finish to be anything but an idle daydream. In Saint Domingue and again in Cuba, attempts have been made – from opposite sides – at genocide and at definitive extermination. In the end, the people of the Caribbean came to realise that they had nothing in the world to save but their chains.

The process of creolisation has been marked by upward and downward cycles, both around a trend of inescapable interculturation and around a changing pattern of anti-culturation. As Kamau Brathwaite points out, there has been a necessary acculturation of all ethnic groups from Africa, Asia or Europe to their new Caribbean environment. But there has also been an acculturation of black norms to white norms as well as interculturation between white norms and black norms. With virtually all the islands save Jamaica and Barbados perpetually in what Williams has called 'a state of betweenity', certain necessary overlapping contexts developed, to use Wilson Harris's felicitous phrase. Overlaps developed as much in relation to what have been regarded as the British, French, Dutch or Hispanic versions of white or European norms as on the relation established between these elite norms and the different African and later Asian ethnic traditions.

The process of creolisation, therefore, has been marked by changes of pace, changes in acceleration, changes in specific ethnic content and changes in specific ethnic proportions. And nowhere, not even in Haiti, has the framework of intercourse been so irretrievably fixed as to anchor the process in viable civic order. There have, therefore, been, in an important sense, as we shall see later on, important changes of social direction, changes brought about by revolutionary or at least fundamental developments, instanced as much from above as below. The Haitian revolution, following on the American and the French revolutions, was one such instance. Emancipation, following on abolition of the slave trade, was another. The post-war accession of Cuba (1959), Santo Domingo (1961) and many of the islands (post-1962) to a new kind of political independence, following on the post-war break up of the Atlantic empire, marks another such watershed in the political record of the island region.

AFRO-SAXON PERSONALITY

It has been a most bewildering movement of modern history. Fortunately, the record of events is so compressed in both historical time and geographical space that it, nevertheless, yields a wide range of extremely graphic concepts which capture its essence. From that point of view, the notion of the Afro-Saxon personality is nothing short of transcendental. In the limiting case of its arithmetic, it describes a mimic-man, an African slave in a bowler hat, manifestly fit to rule on account of his Oxbridge training and Oxford accent. The Afro-Saxon personality, therefore, captures all the absurdity of the Caribbean condition. But as Raymond Smith has remarked, its potency lies precisely in its irony. For when 'Afro-Saxon' translates itself into algebra and becomes a model which embraces the mulatto, the dougla and, indeed, every caricature of the Caribbean hybrid, it suddenly ceases to be absurd and becomes instead that paradigm which discovers the enormous power of generality and simplification and, by cutting through the dense foliage of cultural adjustments, exposes the core of our dilemma with a brutal directness.

This concept of Afro-Saxon personality is not at all loaded. It points clinically to the two basic cultural traditions which have created a mid-Atlantic civilisation, responding out of America to both Africa and Europe, hopelessly torn between two lovers. In the West Indies the European component is Saxon only because England in that case was the source of the European tradition. But the algebra holds good for the whole of the region. And yet, clinical as it is, or perhaps because it is clinical, the concept provokes a vast resentment at different levels.

The Afro-Creole resents it because there is an implicit ranking of the two traditions. Kamau Brathwaite's two mothers — Africa and Europe — are not on par in the initial founding conditions. There exists a hierarchy in which acculturation takes precedence over cultural insurgency. What is more, the great number of ethnic formations involved in the process of creolisation means that there are several different streams of insurgents, all of which are also subject to ranking. As the ethnic catchment widens over time, the later insurgents are forced to adapt not only to the dominant or great 'Saxon' tradition; they are also obliged to adapt to earlier versions of the little 'Afro' tradition.

It is in this sense that there is no such thing as an Indo-Saxon or a Sino-Saxon. The Indians and the Chinese resent having had to adapt to the metropolitan culture which dominated formal existence in the Caribbean; but they resent that less than having had to adapt to the creolised versions of that culture with which they had been endowed by the prior interaction between the African and the European mother traditions. What we have, therefore, is Afro-Saxon but Indo and Sino-Creole. And precisely because acculturation enjoys a higher status than anti-culturation, the Afro-Saxon enjoys a higher ranking than any breed or variant of Creole.

Here again there seem to be some interesting oddities of historical interpretation. It is in precisely those parts of the West Indies where the ambiguities of the creolisation process have been easiest to discern that the apparently simpler models of social stratification have tended to emerge. Lloyd Braithwaite and Raymond Smith have dealt in evidence from the new lands, which after abolition imported comparatively larger amounts of plantation labour, thereby widening their catchment of ethnic traditions. We refer here particularly to Trinidad and Guyana. On the other hand, M. G. Smith made his field observations in Jamaica and Grenada (Carriacou). The latter are the older, more settled and more mature of the colonies, not so marked by demographic turbulence (other than outmigration). They have experienced a much longer process of acculturation, which has come to mask the myriad cross-currents. Yet, it is within the latter context that the plural hypothesis has been most cogently advanced, which is certainly a paradox worth unravelling. To do so, we have only to agree that the obsession with insurgent activity in the form of independent affirmation of ancestral tradition by multiple cultural fragments is itself the evidence for the all-pervasiveness of the tradition according to which the Euro is ranked higher and the Afro (and therefore the Creole) lower in the scale of values.

The theorists of stratification have simply followed through the logic of the creolisation process. They acknowledge that what divides Creole society is a cleavage between those who had been more enmeshed in the process of acculturation from those who had been less enmeshed. In practical terms, the line of cleavage is no more indistinct than that which has forced Marxian and Marxist theory to invent the notion of 'the bourgeoisification of the proletariat'. It is no point denying that although there undoubtedly were uncompromising Maroons at both ends of the spectrum, virtually the whole of the population, in different degrees at different times, has been ambiguously and ambivalently caught up in acculturation as well as insurgency though, inevitably, with different results, depending, as it were, on group and individual life chances.

Where these theorists may have engendered misunderstanding if not confusion was in omitting to concede to the pluralists that Caribbean stratification did not (so much) rank capitalists and workers or the middle and the lower classes. The very notion of middle class in the Caribbean is absurd, since the Ricardian economic model on which class theory is based simply does not apply, there being no history of landlords, capitalists and workers. Even if, therefore, we were to approach the problem by this route, we would have to settle for two classes: upper and lower. But in any event, stratification would rank them only incidentally. What it does rank centrally are ancestral traditions, thereby uncovering specifically Caribbean cleavages and, therefore, providing clues to political parties which may appear to be 'race' parties or 'class' parties but which are really ethnic parties which resolutely exclude race and class kin parading different ethnicity or culture. In other words, in the Caribbean, ethnicity is the vital basis of class, if, for a moment, we were to accept that conventional way of conceptualising the problem. (And it is sometimes useful to be deliberately acculturated to that metropolitan tradition for the simple reason that the act of doing so is an act of identification with the 'little' as against the 'great' metropolitan tradition, thereby constituting an act of insurgency.)

Ethnicity is certainly the most fissionable issue in the region – even in so-called communist Cuba, where Fidel Castro's Africa policy cries out for a domestic explanation as distinct from the facile Atlantic perception of a 'Soviet surrogate pressed into action'. There exists no issue so bearing on the primordial as does ethnicity, none so likely to torpedo civil order and trigger violence. Raymond Smith had a penetrating insight into the matter. In his book, *British Guiana*, he seemed to be hinting that the ultimate source of the violent confrontation then developing in that country might not at all be Dr Jagan's advocacy of 'alien ideology'.[5]

Dr Smith seemed to be saying that the problem lay instead in the accession to political office, under the terms of adult suffrage then current, of a majority group which, against the background of Creole cultural expectation, was infinitely less fit to rule than Mr Burnham's Demerara minority. Here, indeed, was a brilliant insight. The evidence suggests that even Dr Jagan regarded and regards, in a curious kind of way, Mr Burnham as the man most fit to rule Guyana, in terms of the cultural skills the latter undoubtedly commands in the world of the North Atlantic. Perhaps Dr Jagan's communism, which is extremely otherworldly, and enjoys little or no vital life in the practical world of his political constituency, is largely another act of identification with the 'little tradition' of the North Atlantic and therefore a symbolic act of anti-culturation.

It is, therefore, unfortunate that Dr Smith's insight was not systematically pursued to its logical conclusion. It could provide clues to the working of the political system further afield in the Caribbean than British Guiana. The processes of land acquisition, escape to the city, churching and schooling, as well as the whole thrust towards 'fitness to rule' evident in later days of slave society and which have been described by Elsa Goveia, and which increasingly featured in post-emancipation society as described by a growing number of historians including Sewell, Hall, Wood, Eisner, Brereton and Marshall, have undoubtedly provided a basis for political division of Caribbean society even while developing a central Creole civilisation and Afro-Saxon culture.[6] It should not have to be repeated that here alone in this social history, before and after abolition, can we find the clues to our present day political prospects.

DOCTOR POLITICS

We must now turn to the political underpinnings of Caribbean society. The fifth and final feature of Caribbean society is the prevalence of what I have described in the Trinidad and Tobago context as 'doctor politics'.[7] In terms of the political algebra of the region, we are focusing here on the all-pervasive caudillo figures, the 'maximum leaders', who are called upon to play a transcendental role. To my mind, the continuing domination of the Caribbean political system by these single individuals is a much more important phenomenon than the emergence, in recent years, of so-called ideological diversity.

Left or Right, communist or capitalist, these strong figures arise to cross the frontiers of ideology and language and constitutional arrangement. In spite of the rich variety of window dressing, there may well be a cord which binds Gomez, Machado, Jiminez, Batista, Trujillo, Duvalier, Munoz Marin, Bustamante, Manley Senior, Bradshaw, Williams, Burnham, Jagan, Bird, *et al.*, into a single political tradition. If there is any merit in this hypothesis, we cannot simply be satisfied with the view that there is something askew with Caribbean man or with Caribbean political leaders. We cannot accept the facile political assertion that in Georgetown and Kingston, Havana, Santo Domingo and Port au Prince, there has been an over-endowment of king-sized political ambition. Rather, we must pose the question whether there might not be certain common underlying conditions which explain the recurrence of doctor politics almost everywhere in the region, even if we are forced to distinguish, as this observer has done elsewhere, between public school, grammar school, Sunday school and army school doctors.

No, the evidence suggests that you have large political ambitions in every part of the world. What we also have in the Caribbean is a new and unsettled social order and a plural culture. The perpetual movement of labour from diverse ethnic catchments has inevitably left behind community structures that are palpably weak. In this context, the political system is desperately short of the means of organisation. It is hard put to distil intelligence and to canvass opinion. It encounters extreme difficulty in elaborating community plans and in establishing machinery for collective action. The result is that crisis mobilisation tends to become a necessary substitute for long-term organisation. Leadership, therefore, emerges less as instrument and more as symbol. In the context, the theatre of political authority assumes more than usual meaning and the most enduringly charismatic candidates are necessarily those who add instrumental capacity to theatrical command.

This highly personalised and, therefore, centralised mode of political leadership is dictated equally by the corollary of weak community structures; which is to say, by external dependence or, in the extreme case, external domination. The Caribbean has been one of the most complete illustrations of the pure case of what Singham has described as a 'subordinate political system', not merely dependent on or dominated by the external world but actually deriving its legitimacy from an imperial centre.[8] Whether government was the military government established at acquisition through cession or conquest, or the planter governments which emerged in the eighteenth century to speak for the interest of the management elites, or indeed, the Crown colony governments deliberately instituted in the West Indies during the nineteenth century to govern from outside and above, political authority in the Caribbean has traditionally been devoid of any base in valid community support. In that context, even where such community support does appear, the choice of leadership tends to be disciplined by the demands of external negotiation. This is perhaps another way of saying that, quite apart from its subordinacy to metropolitan government under conditions of actual colonialism or informal supervision, the primacy of external transactions in the plantation economy, reinforced by the exceeding external exposure of small island states, exercises a definite impact on leadership patterns. Even in comparatively self-sufficient states, policy has shown a tendency to become bi-partisan and authority to become 'imperial', the better to admit expeditious and consistent central decision. This tendency is redoubled in the Caribbean. Doctor politics, whatever else it may mirror, must also be clinically regarded as one practical response to peculiar conditions.

There is another sense in which the personalisation of power is best taken as a response to the demands of external negotiation. In this case, what is at issue is not policy foreign to country but policy foreign to party. Cleavages, we have urged, are mainly ethnic and ancestral rather than existential. Parties, therefore, like leaders, are more symbolic in their substance than they are instrumental. They exist more for what they are and what they stand for than for what they do or are able to achieve. Their importance to the difficult task of mobilisation in a fragmented political community is much greater than it is in that of managing the affairs of the state. They are typically more adept at electioneering and campaigning than they are at government and administration. This also is a self-perpetuating condition. The lack of experience of responsibility provides a context congenial to the breeding of irresponsibility and, therefore, a continuing predominance of symbol over instrument. So, the whole of the polity poses a greater challenge by far to political management than could ever be posed by the sum of its parts.

Some of the corollaries here should be made explicit. We have implied that the political managers who tend to be selected are only incidentally those whose skills are addressed to the requirements of government. This is what sets up pressures, by what seems to be an invisible hand, to create informal structures parallel to and, therefore, subversive of the formal agencies of state and society. It helps to explain cases where appointed houses and nominated members are called upon to play a disproportionate part in relation to elected houses and elected members; where handpicked task forces replace bona fide functionaries of the Civil Service and where the processes of informing and instructing the executive by validly elected parliamentary representatives are replaced by *ad hoc* and semi-formal consultations and similar assemblies, all invariably distinguished for being instruments of controlled participation by the chief executive.

Such an authority and a responsibility then devolves on the maximum leader that even if he were genuinely polyvalent he would still not be able to cope with the impossible burden. The only choice left is now to invent a superhuman leader, larger than life. This explains in part the developing delusions of caudillo or charismatic politics, *The Autumn of the Patriarch*, to borrow the title of Gabriel Garcia Marquez' magnificent novel about Caribbean dictatorship.

The syndrome is once more self-perpetuating. In the context, all informal alignment and formal voting, whether legislative, municipal, cantonal or other, necessarily becomes uncompromisingly presidential. The electors cannot but opt for the man or against the man. There is no other issue of policy, programme or plan; nothing else matters but the maximum leader. It follows that the supporting cast become less and less likely to be the standardbearers of expertise. Institutional incapacity then becomes institutionalised for good, and all processes need to become progressively more informal if any tasks at all are to be accomplished. The ultimate absurdity is achieved when the process is pushed so far that the political system becomes locked into a world of total delusion, with a universally lionised leader who not only does not but need not deliver anything save chaos but whose survival in the transcendental role must be made to persist even after his death. The cost of returning to reality is even more prohibitive than that of continuing to inhabit the world of sustained and deliberate delusion.

The contemporary Caribbean is not without examples of this situation, a factor which will need to be carefully weighed in assessing its viability. It is worth repeating that this factor is likely to be much more potent than the development of so-called ideological diversity. But it also enjoys relevance to a field much wider than the Caribbean. The thesis here is that this mode of politics does not arise by accident but arises from a disjunction of structure in society and culture. It is, therefore, to be wondered how much real difference exists between the so-called underdeveloped countries marked by the ascendancy of personal power and the so-called developed ones featured more and more by a brand of politics centred on charismatic iron leaders. What is there to be discerned about the underlying structures in these metropolitan societies? Might it not be that the politics as well as the economics of underdevelopment can be achieved at any level of machine technology and income? If so, we are obliged to pose the question as to whether those Atlantic countries whose structures have been highly specialised in the domination of empire can be much better placed than those which have been specialised at the other end of the tandem − in subordination to empire − but which have been summarily cut loose in the few heady years since India broke away in 1947.

VIABILITY?

Misplaced region, plantation economy, fragmented society, plural culture and doctor politics, all revolving around the Afro-Saxon personality: these are some of the elements of a theory of Caribbean society. They set out some of the main ingredients with which to embark on a more valid historical interpretation of the region's viability. They offer a background against which to evaluate what might be the critical events and what the crucial moments. In this latter regard, the accession to new forms of freedom which, as we have noted, began with the Cuban revolution, was advanced by the fall of Trujillo and was then pursued through the independence of Jamaica as the first of a series of similar developments in the Dutch and British territories, marks a manifest watershed in the evolution of the record.

What it marks is the culmination of a process the start of which might be dated, in the case of the West Indies, from about the middle 1880s when the walls of Crown colony government were breached in Jamaica with the turn to representative government and with that, the opening of the gate to more responsible forms of government. On the way to adult suffrage and full self-government, in Kingston in 1944 and then in Port of Spain in 1946 and in most other capitals thereafter, the first ever general elections in 1925 to the Legislative Council in Trinidad (not Tobago), the model Crown colony, represents another important date following on the Wood Commission. By acknowledging that government needed to be anchored in the home community, the elections, limited as was the franchise, constituted a definite attack on the subordinate political system, unleashing repercussions that we may still be experiencing.

In other terms, the Caribbean did not begin in the year 1982 with the grandiose announcement of the Caribbean Basin Initiative. Nor did it begin in 1917, which opened the possibility of the current 'ideological diversification'. It did not even begin with emancipation in the middle nineteenth century, which in importance stands on a par with independence in the middle twentieth century. If the latter put an end to colonialism, the former put an end to slavery. Both events vastly changed the options. Indeed they both altered the ranking of priorities in the creolisation process, in the terms which we have already discussed. Emancipation, paradoxically, increased the premium on strategic acculturation. It definitely enhanced the prospect of successfully beating the system by capitulating to it. Independence, however, made that strategy completely obsolete. In contrast, it emphasised the value of cultural insurgence. No longer was it necessary to establish a fitness to rule, in the terms of the coloniser. The problem of the succession, therefore, expressed itself not in the affirmation of the Creole condition but in asserting a certain distance and a careful difference from it. While emancipation strengthened centripetal forces, independence released centrifugal ones. The pluralists were right but it was not simply that metropolitan might and power withdrew and left a vacuum in plural society, but that the contradictions of the plural culture were an autonomous source of confusion.

It ought not at all to be surprising that independence legitimated 'black power' all over the West Indies. In a society bred to dependence on metropolitan fashion, the legitimation first required the long hot summers of civil rights agitation in the United States of America, with all of its international news coverage and its television images. And yet, as Gordon Rohlehr has insisted, the assertion of an insurgent position fed not on imported but on internal sources of anxiety. This lecturer suspects that we have not yet been privileged to live to the very end of the story. Certainly, the escalation of an otherwise puzzling violence in Jamaica during the second half of the 1970s is very much a sequel.

The orthodox interpretation of the last days of Michael Manley's People's National Party administration adduces an ideological confrontation between conservative, North American backed, liberal democracy, espousing Caribbean basin capitalism, on the one hand, and on the other, a radicalising, communist and Castro-supported social democracy, on the way to socialism. This, however, is little more than mindless Mickey Mouse rhetoric, with little grounding in the world of empirical facts. Neither capitalism nor socialism has enjoyed any footing in Jamaica. All the evidence suggests that Norman Manley introduced merely the symbolism of socialism as part of the entirely valid strategy of capitulation when the PNP was formed under the distinguished patronage of Sir Stafford Cripps. The moment socialism arose as a policy option, it was summarily abandoned and the three celebrated Hs (Hill, Hart, Henry) were expelled from the ranks of the party. They were sidelined for the very good reason that the modalities of socialist reconstruction, with its emphasis on nationalisation and co-operatives and procedures that emerged from the Western European experience, do not respond to the perceptions which Jamaicans and West Indians have of necessary collective action. Norman Manley was wise enough to appreciate that it would be sheer folly to turn the sugar industry over to co-operatives owned and run by the workers. He probably sensed that what was needed was a form of 'morning sport', that is to say, an ancestral reference in collaborative endeavour, known and understood by the population and, therefore, capable of inciting them to work together for the general good in the existential situation of the contemporary Indies. In the context, he had no such practical proposals on offer. The intellectuals in his milieu had failed to distil and to deliver any kind of praxis relevant to the region. The whole basis of their legitimacy lay in their ability to master bookish concepts in the coloniser's idiom. The founder of the PNP died still a sane and serious man, capable of more than token sacrifices. He died in search of another vision, one based on a different moral insight into his own and Jamaica's particular condition.

Such a vision would offer an alternative to the orthodox interpretation of the sequel to Norman Manley, which played itself out in terms of the hopes and the disappointments of the critical 1970s. It would notice that the two traditions formed by the creolisation process had been pushed by events into a certain polarisation. The alignments had been there all along, separating those who had been more fully caught up in the idiom of the coloniser from those less fully or only minimally so involved. On the whole, Mr Bustamante and the Jamaica Labour Party represented the latter. The constituency included both white and black, both the very rich and the very poor, mainly people beyond the portals of schooling and feeling less pressure or less need to acculturate to the dominant tradition. Norman Manley and the PNP represented the other constituency, drawn mainly from the middle or intermediate ranks of society, intermediate by colour, occupation and income but above all, most torn by the ambiguities of option. It is precisely the ambivalence of this group which prevented any inflexible polarisation and rendered possible several times over the alternation in office of the two political parties. What may have triggered the polarisation and the hardening of position was the change in the ranking of the two traditions brought on by the advent of independence.

The PNP had come to office in 1972 not merely on the normal swing of the pendulum. More significantly, its leadership had also understood how — in the new dispensation — black power had become not only fashionable but potent, even explosive. The language, the style, the conceptualisation and the historic intentions of the Maroon had suddenly come of age, particularly in its Rastafarian version which had somehow discovered, in its reggae and ganja culture, the software of an international significance. All the campaign resources of the PNP were assiduously addressed to the capture of this constituency which, by 1976, delivered a colossal landslide victory in the general elections.

The contradiction lay in the fact that the PNP at its core was, in conventional terms, the party most fit to rule while its leader, more perhaps than any figure in the entire West Indies, was regionally regarded as having the most complete command of the relevant idiom. Michael Manley had 'emerged from the appropriate stable; he was a thoroughbred of West Indian culture; he looked right, spoke right and was right'. That is how one distinguished commentator from the University of the West

Indies once put it in a private interview with this lecturer. The view was universally shared in the Caribbean.

It seems to follow that the origins of the subsequent crisis must have been in the fact that the black power revival was led by a group the premises of which had always been more or less the negation of cultural insurgency. The conflict moreover was more than symbolic. In instrumental terms, it expressed itself in a total incapacity of the PNP government to devise practical policies responding to the perceptions and the capacities of the people it was leading. The relevance of the whole pattern of leadership formation in Jamaica (and the West Indies) was subjected to the test of practicality by a hugely legitimated administration, vastly supported and enjoying every opportunity to transform the society. The resulting programme of action can only be described as tragically amateur.

When the cadres of the party needed to address the complex realities of the Jamaican economy, they could nowhere find the rigour and the resolve to abandon symbolic rhetoric. Destabilisation was ritually adduced as a major factor, coupled with the constraints of the old international economic order and capitalist wickedness. Little or no attempt was made to locate the crisis in the currents of the domestic cultural tradition and to situate the exceptional violence of the response in autonomous frustrations having little to do with Cold War politics. To the end, the PNP intellectuals continued to respect the dominance of the great tradition. By far the smaller part of the story is that many of them physically retreated to other countries and situations. The larger part lies in an all-pervasive psychological retreat from reality into a world of endless declamation, particularly by those who remained at the centre. There was not even a serious fight over the leadership of the movement, even though doctor politics was delivering encompassing chaos.

This failure to adduce an algebra capable of making sense of contemporary developments has not affected Jamaica alone or even Jamaica principally. The other explosive illustration of the bankruptcy of the conventional paradigm comes from the record of events in Trinidad and Tobago. In that country, one party will have remained in office for thirty unbroken years, if it arrives safely at 1986. The orthodox explanation adduces the magical properties of the founder of the ruling party, the incompetence of the opposition, the backwardness of the population, the flood of petro-dollars, the failure to found a socialist party and every manner of escapist analysis except one that locates the functioning of the system in the context of the inherited ethnic structures. The consequence here too has been the survival of doctor politics in its most absurd incarnation. The country had become so locked into worship of the virtue of the maximum leader that on his disappearance the only possible candidate for the succession was the minimum leader.

I am happy to be able to say here and now that, fully two clear years before the succession, we were able to provide an exact account of the subsequent scenario. Needless to say, we are not by this revelation aiming to ascribe or attribute the gift of prophecy. What we are pointing to is an aid to judgment, which in the case of Trinidad and Tobago is to be found by acknowledging that there is a framework of some nine ethnicities which explain much of the apparently absurd life of the political system and its constituent parties. We have elsewhere attempted to elaborate the features of this framework. What we insist on here, by way of closure, is that there can be no substitute for independent thinking. More than fifteen years ago, this lecturer made the case for independent thought as the major ingredient in Caribbean freedom. He offers no apology for today's restatement of the case in a different version.

NOTES

1. M. G. Smith, *The Plural Society in the British West Indies*, Berkeley, University of California Press, 1965.
2. See, for example, Lloyd Braithwaite, 'Race Relations and the Industrialization in the Caribbean', in G. Hunter (ed.), *Industrialization and Race Relations*, London, Oxford University Press, 1965; Raymond Smith, 'Social Stratification, Cultural Pluralism and Integration in West Indian Societies', in S. Lewis and T. G. Mathews (eds), *Caribbean Integration*, Rio Piedras, 1967; M. G. Smith, *op. cit.*; Leo Depres, *Cultural Pluralism and Nationalist Politics in British Guyana*, Chicago, Rand McNally, 1967; Hermannus Hoetink, *The Two Variants in Caribbean Race Relations*, London, Oxford University Press, 1967.
3. E. K. Brathwaite, *Contradictory Omens*, Mona, Jamaica, Savacou Publications, 1974, pp. 10–11.
4. Sylvia Wynter, 'Jonkonnu in Jamaica. Towards the Interpretation of Folk Dance as a Cultural Process', *Jamaica Journal*, June 1970, pp. 34–48. On 'inter-culturation', see Brathwaite, *loc. cit.*, pp. 52–5.

5. Raymond Smith, *British Guiana*, London, Oxford University Press, 1962.
6. Elsa Goveia, *Slave Society in the British Leeward Islands at the End of the Eighteenth Century*, New Haven, Yale University Press, 1965; Donald Wood, *Trinidad in Transition: The Years After Slavery*, London, Oxford University Press, 1968; Gisela Eisner, *Jamaica 1830–1930: A Study in Economic Growth*, Manchester, Manchester University Press, 1961; Douglas G. Hall, *Free Jamaica, 1838–1865: An Economic History*, New Haven, Yale University Press, 1959; William Grant Sewell, *The Ordeal of Free Labour in the West Indies*, New York, 1861; Bridget Brereton, *Race Relations in Colonial Trinidad, 1870–1900*, Cambridge, Cambridge University Press, 1979; Woodville K. Marshall, 'Notes on Peasant Development in the West Indies since 1838', *Social and Economic Studies*, vol. 17, 1968, pp. 252–63. Also by Woodville Marshall 'Aspects of the Development of the Peasants', *Caribbean Quarterly*, vol. 1 and no. 1, 1972; 'A Review of Historical Writing on the Commonwealth Caribbean since 1940', *Social and Economic Studies*, vol. 2 and no. 3, 1975.
7. On 'doctor politics', see *Trinidad Express*, 31 May 1969 and early issues of *Tapia*.
8. A. W. Singham, *The Hero and the Crowd in a Colonial Polity*, New Haven, Yale University Press, 1968.

9

'Some in Light and some in Darkness': the Long Shadow of Slavery

SHRIDATH S. RAMPHAL

THE CRITICAL CONJUNCTURES

This series of lectures commemorates two events which an irony of fate conjoined in 1833: the abolition of slavery within British dominions overseas and the death of William Wilberforce who, perhaps more than any single mortal, is associated in men's minds with the mighty struggle which led to that landmark in history. Hull gave Wilberforce to the world in 1759, and sent him to the nation's Parliament twenty-one years later in 1780, little knowing that it was initiating service to a wider world that would be universal in its beneficence and immemorial in its inspiration. Indeed, in relation to Wilberforce's service to humanity, what we might be marking in Hull is not 150 years of his passing but a little over 200 years of that first decision by the electors of Hull to send him to Westminster, where he was to begin a career destined to bring great and lasting distinction to this ancient city. The first tribute I wish to pay is to Hull itself.

A while after Wilberforce's death, Thomas Hill, in a little poem which he called 'The Grave of Wilberforce', composed at Chesterfield Vicarage, wrote these words:

> *Conspicuous on his native coast,*
> *The storied obelisk shall boast*
> *The first-fruits of his fame.*[1]

That was, of course, a reference to the resolve of the people of Hull to erect such an obelisk in commemoration of the public and private virtues of their townsman. The obelisk was duly erected at St John's Street and is now a Wilberforce shrine in its new location at the Queen's Gardens. But what attracts me so much to these lines of Thomas Hill is the perception that abolition of the slave trade and emancipation itself were but 'the first-fruits' of the struggle against human bondage. It is about that perception that I wish to speak – the perception that Wilberforce's contribution did not end with the enactment of the Abolition of Slavery Act 150 years ago, but continues to inspire man's efforts to seek release from other servitudes and inequalities.

In the early 1830s, the Agency Committee in its formidable address for the 'Universal Abolition of Negro Slavery and the Slave Trade throughout the World' used words of import far beyond even their own perspectives when they wrote:

Slavery, wherever it exists, is the same moral deformity, – the same crime before God, and ought to be viewed with detestation, and reprobated with boldness, by every man who professes to act on Christian principles.[2]

They were concerned that the slave trade, though abolished under British law, continued to be 'sustained by British capital and screened by British ingenuity';[3] that slavery itself, though abolished by Act of the Westminster Parliament, continued in foreign lands with, for example, 'the mines of Chili and Peru ... peopled with miserable, though guiltless, victims whose blood is drained by a system of unparalleled horror, to fill the pockets of English shareholders'.[4] They were protesting that human bondage, though formally banished by legislative enactment from the British colonies, was still yielding inhuman gains.

Bondage still takes many forms; some directly as pernicious as slavery itself, others less direct; still screened by ingenuity; all a continuing testament of man's inhumanity to man. They constitute an unbroken line of human servitude stretching from slavery and summoning us, a century and a half after Wilberforce's life of service ended, to continue the work that he began and to match the zeal and resolution that he brought to it in his time.

Slavery did not begin with the British Empire and did not end with emancipation in 1834. It is as old as man, casting its long shadow across centuries of human conflict between justice

'Some in Light and Some in Darkness' 161

and degradation, need and aggrandisement, freedom and oppression. That is why the memorial in Hull marks but the first-fruits of Wilberforce's fame. It is a permanent reminder that such human conflicts will continue until man himself outgrows his baser instincts of greed and bigotry and lust for power. But remembrance of the life and work of Wilberforce is also a great renewal of faith in the capacity of each generation to record its own victories against servitude. Our generation needs that faith as much as any other; we need, also, to record our own successes.

In our endeavours, how encouraging it is to recall that the campaign Wilberforce successfully led from his representation of this city and region had a human impact that was virtually worldwide. As far east as Mauritius, as far west as Jamaica, and, of course, throughout the vast continent of Africa, the impact of abolition was direct. But it would gradually, all too slowly, but inexorably, spread to the slave trade of other European powers, especially Portugal. Between 1810 and 1846 no less than 120,000 slaves were liberated from foreign slave ships;[5] and, although slavery was also officially abolished in the United States in 1807 the thriving illicit trade with the Southern States was eventually ended only by the Civil War. Cuba, as late as 1859, received 30,000 African slaves;[6] but there, too, the trade ended with victory for Lincoln on mainland America.[7] Both the trade in slaves and the institution of slavery were tenacious in their resistance. But yield they had to. And when eventually they did, it was capitulation to the forces that Wilberforce and the Anti-Slavery movement had begun to muster so very many years earlier. The ripples of freedom that went out from Hull touched many shores.

That human impact of Wilberforce's life and work thus confirms as well what we too often forget; namely, the power of the committed, dispassionate, resolute individual, righteous in humanity's cause, to change the world. It is both sobering and an encouragement that so many of the great individuals who now stand out as the true heroes of their generation were men who, like Wilberforce, took their stand on the side of a universal morality and in this very area of human bondage. Gandhi and Martin Luther King are of our own time but already of all time.

But let me not imply that abolition of the slave trade and

emancipation from slavery were the triumph of one man. They were the incremental results of a gruelling effort lasting more than half a century, conducted not only in Parliament but on the hustings and in churches and assembly halls throughout the nation. It was, moreover, a campaign, a crusade, against which apathy, no less than open hostility, was always a countervailing force.[8] It is worth remembering that abolition might have come in 1796, not 1807, had not the parliamentary motion for it been lost (by seventy-four votes to seventy) when the floating voters on whom Wilberforce counted were tempted away to the performance of a new Italian opera, *I dui Gobi* or 'The Two Hunchbacks'.[9] An irony, at the very least a subliminal abstention, it is tempting to say, when we recall how substantially the ivory for Europe's piano keys was carried with the slave caravans from Africa's hinterland to the coast.[10] That the anti-slavery campaign recovered from that setback of 1796 and, having achieved abolition of the slave trade in 1807, pressed on with renewed energy in the 1820s for full emancipation, is one of the great success stories of popular movements driving governments to noble endeavours beyond their own ambition.

Wilberforce personified the cause in Parliament and remained an inspiration even when he had handed on the leadership to Thomas Buxton. But we cannot fail to remember also those who resembled Wilberforce in the strength of their humanitarian commitment based on religious principles and who motivated the whole campaign: the Quakers who founded the Abolition Committee, the Evangelical 'Saints' of the Clapham sect; John Wesley, with his great cry: 'Whether you are a Christian or no, show yourself a man'; Granville Sharp, who pioneered the drive towards legal recognition of the slave's human rights, and who was also instrumental in founding Sierra Leone in 1787 as a colony for freed slaves.[11]

Wilberforce was buried with much ceremony in Westminster Abbey. In 1834, a small book was published called *The Bow in the Cloud or the Negro's Memorial*, intended to illustrate the evils of slavery and commemorate its abolition. In it is a funeral oration by John Ely 'supposed to be delivered at the grave of Wilberforce'.[12] It is a moving oration with a passage which represents to me a true synthesis of Wilberforce's life and work:

'Some in Light and Some in Darkness'

If on the tombs of victors are inscribed the dates of their victories, a simple date shall constitute the most splendid epitaph of Wilberforce's sepulchre, — that of the day when he achieved his great triumph: write upon his memorial stone that one simple date,

THE 25TH OF MARCH, 1807

and all shall comprehend its import and admire it as expressive and sublime. Yet may other victories be inscribed beneath that first and signal one, — victories achieved partly by his aid, and partly consequent upon that grand preliminary triumph. When merchandise in the persons of men was denounced as a crime, the purchaser and the holder of slaves were denounced as criminal; and the advocates of the slave trade argued justly, that its abolition would lead to the emancipation of the slave. It was reserved for the author of the former, to witness the consummation of the latter: his last public act was the vindication of that martyred missionary's character, who had devoted his life to the instruction of the African in West Indian bondage; the last tidings that fell on his dying ear announced the final triumph of the cause, achieved cheaply, yet nobly, at the cost of twenty million sterling. Inscribe then the tomb of Wilberforce with this three-fold achievement:

THE SLAVE-TRADE ABOLISHED —
THE MISSIONARY OF DEMERARA VINDICATED —
SLAVERY EXTINGUISHED.[13]

How can we hope to improve on that summation? But historians have raised issues which impugn so large a claim, which question, in particular, whether abolition was not influenced more by economic than humanitarian concerns. Some of these questionings have come from my part of the world, as in Eric Williams's *Capitalism and Slavery*.[14] As Wilberforce's most recent biographer, Robin Furneaux, has himself acknowledged,[15] some questionings were long overdue if only to provide a rounded account of the forces contributing to abolition.

It is clear enough that by the early nineteenth century the slave trade, in the West Indian context in particular, was beginning to yield diminishing returns to the country. The sugar monopoly could not be squared with the regime of free trade which Britain's new industrial capitalism required. But it is equally clear that there were powerful forces within Britain itself, indeed within Parliament, and dominant forces in the colonies, and in many foreign lands, that sought to preserve the slave trade and slavery itself.[16]

Were it not for the Anti-Slavery movement, with Wilberforce

at its helm and with men like Thomas Clarkson, James Stephen, Zachary Macaulay, Thomas Buxton and the many others in whose name Wilberforce spoke in Parliament; were it not for the public outcry against slavery that their collective work generated; were it not for what virtually became a people's movement for abolition, these intransigent enclaves of economic and political power might well have held at bay over a much longer period the new but wider economic interests. It was the conjuncture of public indignation with the longer term economic argument for abolition that induced Britain to abolish first the trade and then slavery itself.

Such a conjuncture is often essential to radical change. Where morality and material interest, where principle and prudence, thus combine to dictate reform the change itself is not less worthy because morality alone has not wrought it. Where self-interest is served in doing what is right, that does not make the doing of it any less wholesome. When all elements have been assayed in the crucible of history, I have no doubt that the contributions of Wilberforce and his colleagues, and through them the contributions of hundreds and thousands of ordinary people for whom slavery sustained under their laws was no longer an acceptable face of civilisation, will be seen to have been profound in their impact upon events.

It is also important to recognise that the essential success of the Anti-Slavery movement was in its effect on public opinion. Joseph Sturge described his fellow Abolitionists in his memoirs as 'the excellent men who laboured so long and so successfully to put the traffic in men under the ban of law and opinion'.[17] That juxtaposition of 'law' with 'opinion' is significant; and opinion was far from being the lesser of the two. Sturge spoke also of the need 'to engage the sympathy of the people', and 'to awaken the slumbering conscience of the nation', not forgetting 'the official class'.[18] From the 1780s onwards, the fires of the Abolitionist cause were fanned by religious revivalism in the industrialising cities of Britain, whose own toiling masses, assured of a soul and a future salvation, could not see them denied to the slaves across the seas. Anti-slavery was to become a truly popular movement. Its parallel in our day can only be the worldwide peace movement, which has yet to run its course, and could have equally far reaching results.

I dwell on this matter awhile because I believe that it is to such conjunctures that we must look again as we face the continuing legacy of servitude: never abandoning morality, but never ignoring either the degree to which material interest might converge with it. If we really want progress, these are the conjunctures devoutly to be wished and assiduously to be pursued; never ceasing to exhort governments, but never forgetting that people move governments; that, indeed, sometimes, only people can.

This commemoration has been a comprehensive act of remembrance. Wilberforce and the Anti-Slavery movement would have been proud of your treatment of their memory. And they would have been pleased that it has been in so many ways a West Indian occasion: with honorary degrees to C. L. R. James, Clive Lloyd, Aston Preston, David Pitt and myself; a lecture series featuring Lloyd Best and Orlando Patterson also, and a conference on Wilberforce and slavery that will include many scholars from and of the Caribbean. In a real sense we are all here because the anti-slavery cause survived and eventually overcame a myopic readiness to sacrifice principle at the altar of what its opponents conceived of as 'practicality'. And how supremely fitting and resonant of hope for our collective future that all this should have been done by a University of Hull whose Chancellor is another Wilberforce (Lord Wilberforce of Kingston-upon-Hull, formerly a Lord of Appeal in Ordinary) – a kinsman of that great son of Hull, and one who by the quality of his own work in the law has added lustre to even so shining a name as Wilberforce. And how doubly fitting that at the academic helm of the university should be Roy Marshall – a scholar of distinction risen out of the West Indian nation, a nation that ambition may yet mould from the archipelago that was once the 'sugar colonies'.

Let us in return acknowledge that a rather special obligation devolves upon us as children of slavery, of indenture, of colonialism. It is an obligation to ensure that no trace of servitude lingers or re-emerges in our societies under whatever guise. The legacy of servitude is a continuing one; one which only a vigilant humanity can eradicate. Wherever racism, oppression, intolerance, authoritarianism, dominion of whatever kind, encroaches on human freedom it stalks in the shadow of slavery. We must never allow ourselves the complacency of believing that that long shadow has been lifted for all time from our region. The one hundred and fiftieth anniversary of emancipation is a good time for the West Indies to reaffirm — West Indian people and their leaders alike — that the freedom won in 1833 shall never perish or again be sequestered. The inhuman gulf that once yawned between master and slave must never have a modern day equivalent in the West Indies of today or tomorrow.

THE GUYANA CONNECTION

A vignette of Wilberforce's service to the anti-slavery cause which has escaped the studied attention of his biographers but has a rather special interest for me, illustrates well both the steadfastness with which the Abolitionists laboured and the strength of the forces they were eventually to overcome.

Berbice is today a county of Guyana — the county of my birth. Initially a separate colony of the Dutch, it fell finally to Britain in 1803. Sugar estates in Berbice which were the property of the Dutch government became the property of the British Crown — along with the slaves attached to them. Managed at first by the new colonial administration,[19] the estates and the condition of the slaves appear to have 'sustained a progressive deterioration in all respects'.[20] A proposal to lease the estates to a private individual fell through when he refused to accept conditions affecting the welfare of the slaves attached to the lease by the Abolitionist, James Stephen, acting on behalf of the Crown.

Convinced of 'the impossibility of disposing of the Estates in any way so as to prevent the destruction of the Slaves, without retaining them in the possession of The Crown',[22] the Chancellor of the Exchequer concurred in a plan for ensuring in relation to the estates 'such improvements as the Government itself ... had recommended to the colonial assemblies to adopt and enforce upon private masters';[23] arrangements which 'could not, it was thought, be safely left to the colonial Government, or to individual agents on the spot, without the intimate superintendence and control of some authority in England'.[24]

It should occasion no surprise that that 'authority in England' turned out to be Wilberforce and five others (including James

'Some in Light and Some in Darkness' 167

Stephen) duly appointed as commissioners for the management of the Crown's estates in Berbice, 'and for the preservation, protection and improvement of the negro and other slaves belonging thereto'.[25]

Wilberforce must have seen the 'Berbice Commission' as a heaven sent opportunity to demonstrate the practicality of the humanitarian approach – to refute the constant argument that the ideas of the Abolitionists spelt ruin for the estates, their owners and the trade in their produce. Certainly he welcomed the commission and, with kindred spirits as fellow commissioners, was well set to carry the campaign to the plantations, and to some of the worst plantations anywhere – as that pioneer of modern West Indian writing, Edgar Mittelholzer, a fellow Berbician, so well dramatised in his Kaywana Trilogy.[26]

Wilberforce's zeal was in sharp contrast to the disfavour with which the intervention of the commissioners was viewed in the colony. Even after the commission had been appointed, the governor was urging the Crown to lease or sell the estates 'on almost any terms';[27] 'I see not the least prospect', he wrote (on 3 May 1811) 'of benefit to The Crown by holding these properties.'[28]

The attitude of the planters was open hostility. Wilberforce and his friends, after all, had carried the Slave Trade Abolition Bill through the British Parliament only a few years earlier over the fierce objections of the West India lobby and the sugar planters in the West Indies in particular. What is more, the approaches to that Abolition Act of 1807 had been skilfully prepared by Wilberforce and his friends through the 'Guiana Order' of 1805 abolishing the slave trade to the captured Dutch colonies in Guiana by an executive order (authorised as a war measure) and then building on it the Foreign Slave Trade Act of 1806, confirming the Guiana Order, and deftly attaching to it all the prohibitions of previous and defeated Foreign Slave Bills.[29] The Guiana planters nurtured a special hatred for Wilberforce.

But abolition of the trade did not render slavery itself illegal. Despite the nuisance of exhortations from Whitehall, life could go on much as usual – for master and for slave. In Berbice, most of the planters were still Dutch, among the most brutal and tyrannical anywhere, and the prospect of Wilberforce and

168   *Out of Slavery*

his band of 'Saints' running the Crown's plantations in Berbice excited predictable consternation.

The confrontation was given a sharper edge by the circumstance that among the estates was Dageraad — a name that has passed into the history of Guyana and of slavery generally as a symbol of the bestiality of slavery and the courage of its victims in resisting it. Dageraad was part of the scene of one of the earliest slave uprisings, a rebellion starting at Magdalenenberg in Berbice in 1763, that came close to succeeding. Today, Cuffy, the rebellion's leader, is commemorated as Guyana's first national hero. But the rebellion failed; it was eventually put down at Dageraad with terrible vengeance.[30]

The first act of the commissioners was to draw up regulations for the management of the estates and slaves. They ran to seven closely printed pages[31] and covered such matters as providing 'a copious and permanent supply of native provisions for the slaves'; guaranteeing 'their rest on the Sunday'; supplying them with 'abundant and comfortable clothing'; keeping their 'houses in proper repair'; making 'the preservation of their health, and their due medical treatment in sickness, the object of special care and attention'; never employing slave labour 'where cattle or machinery could be substituted'; accepting 'as a fundamental maxim' that making the estates more productive 'was not to be pursued by a culture more extensive or laborious than might be consistent with the most scrupulous regard to the health and comfort of the slaves'; directing 'that the cart-whip in the hands of the driver, as an instrument of compelling labour, should be laid aside'.[32]

These instructions must have seemed to the planters of Berbice a model of subversion not to be endured or by example enlarged. Both the planters and the colonial government struck out against them and not only against the commissioners but the slaves themselves. On 17 October 1815 the agent in Berbice wrote to the authorities in London:

> You are aware ... of the general prejudice which exists here against the wise and benevolent system of the Commissioners; and you also know that notwithstanding the seeming support of the Colonial Government, and all our own exertions, several instances have occurred in which individuals have not only attempted, but have actually succeeded in wreaking their vengeance upon the poor people, who have experienced the blessings of that system.[33]

'Some in Light and Some in Darkness'

The agitation for the withdrawal of Wilberforce's hand was vigorously conducted and at levels of high influence. To withdraw the Berbice Commission would have been unthinkable at so high a point in the campaign of the Anti-Slavery movement. Instead, what was sought by the planters was accomplished with all the semblance of propriety. By the convention between Great Britain and the Netherlands relative to the colonies of Demerara, Essequibo and Berbice in 1815, the British government agreed that the estates in Berbice would revert to their former owners — now identified not as the Dutch government but as the 'Berbice Association'.[34] Wilberforce was aghast, and he and his fellow commissioners pleaded against this retrogression. They quoted the poignant report of the Rev. John Wray, their ardent representative in Berbice, who had written on 11 January 1816:

> The Dutch here are very much prejudiced against every thing the Commissioners have done or are doing; and I believe it is the general opinion of well-disposed people that the poor Negroes will suffer very much out of spite. Several of the Negroes came crying last Saturday evening, to know if it was true. They are well aware what must be their fate, if the Dutch become their masters.[35]

Their principal agent had written earlier in outraged distress: 'Methinks I hear the whip sounding again without mercy.'[36] But the pleas were to no avail. The convention with Holland was concluded and the plantocracy returned to the estates in the guise of the Berbice Association. Reform by example was not to be. The planters and the Colonial government could not be fought in the lands where slavery flourished. Only emancipation would suffice; and that was a goal for which the Anti-Slavery movement had to struggle in London.

Berbice, Guiana, would not be fully rid of the blight of slavery for another twenty years, if we take account of the post-emancipation transition to true freedom. In those years the mantle of the Anti-Slavery movement would pass to sturdier shoulders than those of the aging and ailing Wilberforce but his connection with slavery and Guiana's connection with both would not end. The neanderthal myopia of the planter class was eventually to contribute directly and significantly through its own excesses to the ultimate victory which the Anti-Slavery movement sought. In the end, Wilberforce's defeat at the hands of the Berbice planters was the signal that his final victory was at hand.

While the planters kept up their implacable opposition to emancipation and the British government temporised in the face of the growing militancy of the new Abolitionists, the slaves themselves moved; and nowhere more effectively than in Demerara. On 18 August 1823, a revolt broke out on two plantations with the demand for immediate emancipation — which they genuinely believed the Crown had approved but was being denied them locally. They were in essence not so very far from the truth. Let Furneaux's account tell the story. Having attempted to negotiate,

> The Governor returned to Georgetown with some loss of dignity and that night 13,000 slaves from 37 plantations joined the rebels. They were badly armed and easily subdued, but while they were in control of their plantations, their restraint was unusual. This clemency was not returned. Nearly 50 slaves were hanged and three were given the dreadful sentence of 1,000 lashes and condemned to be worked in chains, two for the remainder of their lives.[37]

Wilberforce's pamphlets calling for emancipation had been circulating on the estates. The local 'Gazette' did not conceal the planters' wrath: 'Perhaps the intriguing saints at home had a hand in it — if so, they will hear with disappointment and pain that a Superintending and just Providence has frustrated their diabolical intentions.'[38]

But the very brutality of the planters in response to the revolt hastened emancipation; most pointedly in the death of the Rev. John Smith, a nonconformist minister on one of the estates where the revolt started. Smith was a consumptive and two months after the revolt, as he was about to return to England for health reasons, he was arrested and charged with complicity. He was vilified by the planters, tried by courtmartial, convicted and sentenced to death, though with a recommendation for mercy. The governor referred the case to England but before a reply could be received Smith died in prison.[39] The revolt gave the Abolitionists what they needed most — a dramatic event with which they could stir instincts of abhorrence, revulsion and shame against the system of slavery; and the Demerara planters had provided a martyr.

On 11 June 1824 the debate on Smith took place in the House of Commons. A feeble Wilberforce testified against the 'scandalous injustice' meted out to Smith; but there were many other

'Some in Light and Some in Darkness' 171

champions: Brougham was formidable and Smith's trial was condemned by all save the West India lobby as a tragic parody of justice.[40] But more than the missionary's fate was being debated; in the result, the Demerara revolt and the 'martyrdom' of John Smith dealt slavery a blow from which it never recovered. Hence John Ely's inclusion of the vindication of the 'missionary of Demerara' among Wilberforce's triadic achievements.

But, most decisive of all, the slaves themselves were no longer prepared to wait. The tension was mounting and spreading. A slave revolt had taken place in Barbados in 1816. The year after the Demerara revolt in 1824 came the turn of Jamaica. In 1831 an insurrectionary movement developed in Antigua. But the climax came with the revolt in Jamaica during Christmas of that year.[41] Eric Williams sums up well the situation that had been reached on the eve of emancipation:

> In 1833, therefore, the alternatives were clear: emancipation from above, or emancipation from below. But EMANCIPATION. Economic change, the decline of the monopolists, the development of capitalism, the humanitarian agitation in British churches, contending perorations in the halls of Parliament, had now reached their completion in the determination of the slaves themselves to be free. The Negroes had been stimulated to freedom by the development of the very wealth which their labor had created.[42]

On 29 August 1833, as Wilberforce (and Zachary Macaulay) lay dying, the Abolition of Slavery Bill passed its second reading in the House of Commons. The 'first-fruits' of their labour were at hand.

INDENTURE: ANOTHER SLAVERY

But I have run ahead of myself in speaking as I did a while ago of Berbice as the county of my birth; for it could not be until emancipation had released the slaves from forced labour on the plantations. Only then would my forebears be brought to take their places on those same sugar estates under another kind of slavery. Through a strange twist of fate I speak to you tonight in Hull 150 years after slavery's abolition as a descendant of those who endured this other kind of slavery that emancipation spawned. There is a sense in which my identity as a West Indian might be thought to begin with the abolition of slavery. In truth, it arises from a continuum with slavery itself. Indeed, the links with Guiana were to have an uncanny persistence.

Within three years of emancipation, indeed, before the brutal apprenticeship system which followed had itself been aborted, planters of Demerara had started the search for alternative labour. One of the plantations on which the Demerara revolt had started (indeed, the plantation on which the Rev. John Smith had his chapel), was owned by Sir John Gladstone, the father of Britain's future Liberal Prime Minister. In fact, as Eric Williams relates, the future Prime Minister was to make his maiden speech as MP for Newark in May 1833, speaking in defence of slavery on the family estates in Demerara; testimony, let it be allowed, more to filial feelings than Liberal principles.[43]

By January 1836, John Gladstone was writing to an English firm in Calcutta asking them to provide 100 coolies for five to seven years. A new traffic was beginning. It had, in fact, been foreshadowed some years earlier with the transport of Indian labourers to the Indian Ocean territories of Réunion and Mauritius. The reply, written in what their ablest chronicler, Hugh Tinker, describes as a 'curiously proto-Darwinian tone', reveals well that though much had changed with abolition, very much remained the same.

> We are not aware that any greater difficulty would present itself in sending men to the West Indies (than to Mauritius), the natives being perfectly ignorant of the place they go to or the length of voyage they are undertaking ... The Dhangurs are always spoken of as more akin to the monkey than the man. They have no religion, no education, and in their present state no want beyond eating, drinking and sleeping: and to procure which they are willing to labour.[44]

Satisfied, John Gladstone arranged for the transportation of his coolies, who were duly allocated to two of his other estates. The continuum could hardly be more pointed. But in truth, it was too pointed for comfort. While the planters were keen for a general scheme of immigration the government of India was uneasy and the newly formed British and Foreign Anti-Slavery Society began to be vigilant. In 1839 the government of India prohibited 'overseas emigration for manual labour'[45] and the following year, despite pressure from the planters, Lord John Russell informed Parliament that he was not prepared to relax the prohibition on 'coolie emigration' to the West Indies.

'I should be unwilling', he said, 'to adopt any measure to favour the transfer of labourers from British India to Guiana ... I am not prepared to encounter the responsibility of a measure which may lead to a dreadful loss of life on the one hand, or, on the other, to a new system of slavery.'[46]

But Russell's was not to be the last word. The measure, *indenture*, was to come, and with it both the dreadful loss of life and the new system of slavery from which he had recoiled.

It came about because, wherever possible, the freed slaves fled from the land, or if not from the land, the master. The planters, therefore, needed labour, and from this need grew the successor form of slavery. In 1842, a House of Commons committee blamed declining production in the West Indies on lack of labour, and declared 'that one obvious and most desirable mode of endeavouring to compensate for this diminished supply of labour, is to promote the immigration of a fresh labouring population, to such an extent as to create competition for employment'.[47] This blatant proposal to force the freed slaves back on to the land and bring down wages signposted the way to the massive use of Indian immigrant indentured labour on colonial plantations.

In 1844, only four years after Russell's rejection of it, the decision was taken to support and theoretically to control Indian emigration to the West Indies, condoning what was indeed to endure as 'a new system of slavery' for hundreds of thousands of Indians right up to the First World War.

Between 1830 and 1870, possibly as many as two million Indians were transported overseas under the indenture system to labour on tropical plantations; of these, some half million went to the French and British sugar colonies[48] — among them my widowed great-grandmother and her young son. The bulk of the earliest immigrants was provided by the hill tribesmen, the Dhangurs, described in the reply to John Gladstone which I quoted in the cynical, dehumanised language of slavery. Later the main recruiting was in the heavily populated regions of Benares and North Bihar, and later still among the landless Tamil labourers of South India, many of them Untouchables already crushed into semi-slavery by high caste landlords. Many Indians exchanged a familiar servitude at the base of the Indian caste system for an even more alienated inequality as indentured plantation labourers.[49]

But first they had to endure their own passage across the Kala Pani — 'the Black Waters'[50] — their own diaspora, not so unlike that earlier pernicious traffic in human cargo. A Guyanese poet, Arthur Seymour, has described the Middle Passage in these terms:

> *A ferry of infamy from the heart of Africa*
> *Roots torn and bleeding from their native soil*
> *A stain of race spreading across the ocean.*[51]

And so indeed it was. It remains an apt description of the ferry that was to succeed it, crossing from the heart of India, spreading another stain of race across the ocean.

For three-quarters of a century, in what amounted for the great majority to an 'exile into bondage',[52] the plantations imposed their servitude on the Indian labourers, who were but mute pieces on the chequerboard of worldwide colonialism. Although nominally free, they were little more than slaves. Often their emigration was as a result of fraud and outright force. They endured cruel and degrading conditions of work, frequently under the former slave masters or their descendants. Perhaps the truest symbol of the unbroken chain between slavery and indenture was the tenement range or logie of the inherited 'nigger yard' — the squalid, foul, degenerate, huddled pens that passed for housing for slave and indentured labourer alike. Nigger yard, coolie yard, bound yard, were all one; only the labels changed to match the changing style of servitude. Like the slaves, the Indian migrants were subject to the coercion of the whip, and to the new coercion of the criminal law applied for labour offences such as absenteeism and lack of identity documents which were not crimes under the general law.[53] The minimal wages, which were the inducement for the whole vast dislocation, were subject to arbitrary stoppages. Pay was sometimes withheld for years. The 'double cut' was often applied — two days' pay docked for one day's absence; and throughout the eighty years of indentured labour another type of 'double cut' remained the rule: one day's pay fined for every day absent, but with an extra day added to the period of indenture.[54]

A Royal Commission in 1870 described the indentured Indian as trapped by the law, 'in the hands of a system which elaborately twists and turns him about, but always leaves him face to face with an impossibility'.⁵⁵ In his foreword to Walter Rodney's brilliant work, *A History of the Guyanese Working People, 1881–1905*, the celebrated West Indian author, George Lamming, sums up the cruel realities of indenture thus:

> Indentured labour was bound labour. It was deprived of all mobility and was therefore condemned to provide that reliability of service a crop like sugar demanded. The planter class, with the full permission of the metropolitan power, had given itself the legal right to deploy this labour as it pleased. As Rodney emphasizes here, with great relevance to many a contemporary situation, what the ruling class could not acquire by the normal play of the market forces had now been appropriated through legal sanctions. Indentured Indian labour was enslaved by the tyranny of the law that decided their relations to the land where they walked, and worked and slept.⁵⁶

Rodney himself emphasised the link between indenture and slavery with characteristic penetration:

> ... indentured labour has as its ultimate function the guaranteeing of planter control over the entire labour process, ... this alone justified the continuation of indentureship, irrespective of the cost to the individual proprietor and to the general taxpayer ... More than anything else, it was the regimented social and industrial control which caused indenture to approximate so closely to slavery.⁵⁷

It is ironic that the death knell of the virtually worldwide indenture system was sounded in South Africa, where labour conditions today are among the closest to organised slavery. In 1895 the young Gandhi began his lifelong struggle for freedom and decolonisation by opposing the conditions of Indian indenture.⁵⁸ As the cause gathered public support in India, viceroys such as Curzon and Hardinge added their considerable weight in favour of just treatment of Indians overseas. Gandhi's protest was part of the turning of the tide. Indentured emigration to Mauritius was stopped in 1910 and to Natal in 1911; in 1909 free emigration to Malaya now replaced indenture, which was ended in Assam in 1913.⁵⁹ By 1915, when Gandhi returned to India, indenture had become the central issue.⁶⁰

The last bastions were in the West Indies and Fiji. The revelations of Gandhi's friend, the Rev. C. F. Andrews and others about the conditions of Indians in Fiji, and particularly the moral degradation of Indian women, aroused Indian public opinion to such an extent that in 1917 the whole tottering system of indenture was declared at an end.⁶¹ For the generations that came after, similarly to the Africans after emancipation, there would be a struggle of a different kind; but the process of recovery could begin. The Rev. C. F. Andrews, I am told, held me as a tearful infant in his arms when he visited Guyana in 1929. Later, in the 1930s, at the end of a sentimental visit to Fiji, he placed his faith in the powers of recovery of the indentured Indians⁶² — a quality which the children of indenture shared with those of African descent who are the children of slavery in its cruellest form. Both can say, in the words of Guyana's contemporary poet, Martin Carter, and say with truth and with hope:

> From the nigger yard of yesterday I come with
> My burden.
> To the world of tomorrow I turn with
> My strength.⁶³

The poverty-belts of India were not, of course, the only sources of unequal labour for the nineteenth-century plantations. The chronically poor anywhere were easily persuaded and exploited. Poor Europeans and especially Portuguese from Madeira had been employed earlier, but they were not enough and, unlike the Indians, could not be induced to re-indenture. China was a potential source, but of the first shipload of Chinese to British Guiana in 1852 no less than forty-eight per cent were dead on arrival, many of them from the fumes of poisoned rice. Moreover, Chinese women could not be recruited at all except, as the emigration agent in Hong Kong pointed out, by outright purchase; this direct form of slavery did not appeal to the Colonial Office.⁶⁴ However, it was possible to obtain some Chinese labourers from the barracoons of Portuguese Macao, Amoy and Canton, by purchase of prisoners or large-scale kidnapping. Over 125,000 were imported into Cuba between 1852 and 1874 in what was eventually condemned as a cruel return to slavery. From the 1860s some Chinese families emigrated from Southern China to British Guiana and to Trinidad.⁶⁵ Chinese labourers from the Straits Settlements also indentured for Mauritius. Later, the idea of cheap Chinese labour occurred to South Africans and 47,000 Chinese were admitted in 1905. The trade stopped after Chinese labour on the Rand was roundly condemned as slavery by British public opinion, including labour leaders, the following year.⁶⁶

It seemed that wherever sugar flourished, so grew the bitterness of servitude. Even in the sugar plantations of Queensland, in tropical Australia, there was an attempt to solve labour problems by the practice of 'blackbirding' — the kidnapping from the New Hebrides (now Vanuatu), the Solomon and the Gilbert Islands (now Kiribati) of labourers who were supposed to sign contracts they could not read. This traffic was paralleled by a similar French trade in African 'engagés' to the French Indian Ocean islands, which was eventually replaced by indentured Indian labour.[67] The 'ferry of infamy' continued to ply; and across many oceans.

APARTHEID: SLAVERY'S MODERN FACE

Slavery is more than a system; indeed, for slavery to be formalised by law and institutionalised into a system, a measure of bigotry is essential — often gross, sometimes subtle. In this sense, slavery begins in the human mind, in the distorted manner in which one man looks upon another and makes a perverted judgement enabling him to deny that those enslaved are equal members of one human race. Slavery rests on an assumption of superiority by the enslaver. And it is always 'the other', consciously perceived as different, who is enslaved. In this difference lies the beginning of the denial of common humanity.

The basis of 'otherness' may be religion: European Christians and Circassians were for centuries enslaved as 'infidels' by the Islamic Turks and Moors. The difference may be one of class: the West Indian and American plantations were worked in their earliest decades by indentured poor whites or by white criminals. The ruling groups within some African tribes sold their own serf class into the plantation slave trade. The simple distinction between one nation and another, or between one tribe and another, has often been the basis for slavery; which explains why warfare has historically been the most frequent source of slaves.

Race has been a primal reason for 'otherness', with the white race mainly as slave owners and the black race mainly as slaves. But, as we have seen, slavers are nothing if not eclectic; after emancipation brown men and yellow, Indians and Chinese, made acceptable substitutes. Academics dispute whether the motivation behind the beginnings of plantation slavery in the New World was purely economic, or whether it was from the start racial, as it certainly became. What is clear is that perceived differences of race and colour allowed awareness of otherness to be placed readily at the service of the economic system of slavery. It was dangerously easy, if appallingly unjust, to proceed from the observed reality that most slaves were black men and women to the irrational belief that black men and women were, and should be, slaves.

The history of our own time affords the most complete example of otherness as a reason for enslavement. Nazi Germany used pseudo-scientific theories based on perverted Darwinism to justify the persecution and enslavement of the Jews; for what were the concentration camps but the ghettos of the vast slave labour force? Even the motto on the entrance gates of one camp, Sachsenhausen, cynically underlined the point: 'Arbeit Macht Frei' – 'Work Makes Free'.[68] But the camps were not reserved only for the Jews, their most numerous victims; within them were to be found any who had opposed themselves by their otherness to the Nazis: political dissenters, members of religious minorities, gypsies, homosexuals, Slavs, prisoners of war, even (another irony in that supremely sick system) the mentally ill. Indeed, the category of the other was on the verge of encompassing anyone who was not an Aryan German Nazi, and in the end the psychosis was becoming self-destructive, with the masters forced to look among themselves for their slaves.

That brings us dangerously close to the present; close enough to put us on notice for our own times. Frantz Fanon recognised the totalitarian impulse as springing from the assumption of superiority when he wrote: 'It is the racist who creates his inferior', and asked the question: 'Superiority? Inferiority? Why not the quite simple attempt to touch the other, to feel the other, to explain the other to myself?'[69] No question is more pertinent amid the anomy and anonymity of our multi-racial modern cities where it is all too easy to become alienated from one's fellows, to perceive them as strangers, transforming them into the others from whom we can justify withholding what Wilberforce so well described as 'that equitable consideration and that fellow-feeling which are due from man to man'.[70] But who better to explore

'Some in Light and Some in Darkness'

these contemporary challenges within this series than Lord Scarman who will be speaking on them later.

The Martinique poet, Aimé Césaire, correctly perceived that Nazism was the importation into Europe of a system with which black people were all too familiar, the seeds of which had already been sown by the Europeans themselves. 'Before they became its victims', he wrote, 'they were its accomplices; that Nazism they tolerated before they succumbed to it, they exonerated it, they closed their eyes to it, they legitimated it because until then it had been employed only against non-European peoples.'[71]

It is one of the least pardonable crimes against contemporary humanity that under the label of 'apartheid' false doctrines of racial superiority continue to be employed against the non-European peoples of South Africa, and most viciously against its black people. And apartheid is not without its accomplices beyond South Africa; those who, failing to identify with its victims as fellow humans, would tolerate, exonerate, close their eyes to, and legitimate it. Yet, apartheid is the most cruel legacy of slavery — carrying the stain of race into the end years of the twentieth century.

One hundred and fifty years after Wilberforce, consider the reality of South Africa: eighty-seven per cent of the land reserved for four and a half million whites; twenty to twenty-two million blacks, seventy per cent of the population, relegated to the remaining thirteen per cent of scrub land — denied even the right to belong; legislated out of their own country; deemed to be migrant workers from fantasy 'black homelands'. In the same way as the slavery of the plantation colonies, the laws of apartheid discriminate overtly between one class and another; in South Africa, between the whites and all others, with the totally disenfranchised black Africans the most oppressed of all. As with slavery, apartheid is rooted in otherness, the otherness of 'separate development'. As with slavery, it is the otherness of race that sustains apartheid's evil creed.

Apartheid resembles slavery also in its economic rationale. Its basic motive is to provide a permanent subject labour force kept rigidly separate from the ruling class. The Bantustans to which every black South African must by law belong, and the townships where the great majority actually live, are nothing other than segregated pools of cheap labour. The mines and farms of South Africa could not function without that labour. And the means of ensuring control and domination of the labour supply is the rigidly enforced 'pass laws', regulating movement, entrenching insecurity, denying civil liberties, even dividing husbands from wives and children. Pass laws, let us remember, were a feature also of the system of plantation slavery. It was wide protest against apartheid's pass laws which led to the Sharpeville massacre in 1960: shades of the West Indian slave rebellions of the 1820s and the last-ditch intransigence of the West Indian planters.

Apartheid is another slavery; yet, it is possible to descend through the apartheid system, as through the circles of Dante's hell, to a condition of ultimate repression indistinguishable from slavery at its worst. South Africa rejects every exposé as propaganda — as do its apologists. So let us look to the British press. On 30 March 1983 the *Guardian* reported on the protests of black leaders in Namibia at the token six-year prison sentence passed on a white farmer found guilty of battering to death a twenty year old black parole prisoner sent to work on his farm.[72] A photograph produced at the trial showed the farmer holding a chain securing his badly beaten victim. Even the shackles of slavery have been bequeathed to apartheid. The manacles in the Wilberforce Museum are not mere relics to remind us of past evils; they are grim testimony of apartheid's present inhumanities. What we are dealing with here is an imprisoned labour force being worked and beaten to death with impunity.

In 1980 the number of black prisoners working for white farmers was at least 90,000, about one-eighth of the total agricultural work force.[73] After arrest for minor pass laws infringements, many of these forced labourers are directed straight to the farms without trial, under the 'parole' scheme. Others who cannot find employment accept placement on farms by the 'aid centres' as an alternative to deportation to the Bantustans. Another mechanism to achieve the same effect is the 'youth service camp'. The aid centres are administered by the euphemistically named Department of Cooperation and Development — a new name for the Department of Native Affairs. Even private enterprise mental hospitals have provided contract labour under conditions of brutal compulsion for major national and international companies and for the gold mines, with the patients often paid only in sweets or cigarettes; 11,000 are believed to have been thus abused in 1975; since then an Act of Parliament has prevented the publication of further information.

The true depth of the system is reached in the farm prisons. These are built at farmers' cost and long-term prisoners allocated to each farmer in proportion to his investment; thereafter the prisoners effectively become the farmers' property. A 1971 advertisement for the sale of a grain, wine and sheep farm mentioned 'winery shed and ten convicts' as among the assets. Here, still, is the dehumanisation, the reification, of true slavery. It is a monstrous system, with atrocities (such as the recent example from Namibia), floggings, torture and extremes of sadism a frequent occurrence. Court sentences on anyone charged are often minimal or not even implemented, and the police sometimes aid farmers in their brutality.

[Since this lecture was delivered, *The Times* of 6 June 1984 carried a report from its own correspondent in Johannesburg on the 'white man who celebrated his nineteenth birthday by going out and beating a black man to death with karate sticks'.[74] He was found guilty of culpable homicide by the Pretoria Regional Court and sentenced to 'serve only 2000 hours "periodic imprisonment" at the weekends, of which 800 hours have been suspended conditionally for five years ... He will be free to continue his job on the railways during the week'.]

History will record as a twentieth-century aberration our failure to show resolution in the completion of this unfinished business of slavery's abolition. How can the future judge the power-brokers of our age save in terms of hypocrisy and double standards when they justify their acquiescence in apartheid in terms of solicitude for 'allies' in the contest between East and West, or simply in terms of national interest in relation to 'trade and investment'? The former is wholly misguided and contradictory and antithetical to the true interests of any who seek the goodwill of Africa. The latter is the modern day equivalent of what a nineteenth-century parliamentary critic of those who wished to ban slave-grown goods while not attacking the system at source called 'lucrative humanity'.[75] A moral choice is incumbent on all who would trade with apartheid, and there can be only one decision: morality and expediency, humanitarianism and 'policy' demand that South Africa be made to dismantle apartheid.

But I go further. I invite each and every one of you, citizens of Hull and other friends, to question whether any can take pride in the work and achievements of Wilberforce and the Anti-Slavery movement if, as individuals, as a nation, as a world community, we fail to take a righteous and uncompromising stand against apartheid. By what quirk of logic, what twist of values can we celebrate emancipation and tolerate apartheid? We tarnish and depreciate the memory of Wilberforce so long as slavery South Africa style flaunts its evil and defies our will to curb it, sensing our resolve to be a fragile thing.

Yet, South Africa defies that will as demonstrated by acts of aggression against Mozambique, compounding illegality with untruth. Let us be clear of one thing. Those who struggle against apartheid, who are driven to take up arms against it, are not the ones we ought to condemn as 'terrorists'. They are the counterparts, 150 years later, of the slaves who in rebellion and uprising throughout the West Indian plantations threw off their chains and made a stand for freedom. Oppression is no less terrorism because it wears an official uniform. Those who fight for freedom do not become terrorists merely because they cannot form themselves into conventional armies. The real terrorists in Southern Africa are not those who help the oppressed, but the oppressors themselves who command the heights of economic, social, political and military power in South Africa to sustain an evil system of racism that is itself the alpha and omega of terrorism against the human personality, a system that ineluctably will breed its own responses of violent retribution.

Can any act of commemoration of the historic achievement of 1833 be anything but a charade unless it rouses in us something of the passion of Wilberforce and the Saints in renouncing for our world and our time the legacy of slavery that is apartheid? Two hundred years ago the citizens of Hull sent Wilberforce to Westminster. Is there any truer way of commemorating his life of service to mankind than to send out from Hull this year the message that his memory demands? — that apartheid is the same 'moral deformity', the same 'crime before God', as slavery is; that it must be viewed with the same detestation, and

'Some in Light and Some in Darkness' 183

reprobated with the same boldness as was slavery 150 years ago; that Britain that led the way then must lead the way now; this time reinforced by a Commonwealth which itself became possible because of that first step in acknowledgement of the universality of the dignity of man which Wilberforce and Hull helped Britain to take.

And what a moral compulsion devolves upon West Indians to yield to none in abhorrence of apartheid and in resolve to stand against it. The spirit of every slave worked and beaten and degraded on West Indian sugar plantations, of every rebel against slavery hanged in the cause of freedom from Guiana to Jamaica, rises up to demand of us that abhorrence and resolve. They suffered in vain if the societies their suffering moulded can be ambivalent, or unequivocal and passionate only in words, towards another slavery against other Africans 150 years after their own freedom was won. We have no trade or investments to forgo; but our sportsmen can help the world to make a stand against apartheid; and we can, we must, help our sportsmen to do so. It will not be hard to be resolute if we remember what our forebears endured 150 years ago, and how much they needed the support of others in both moral and political terms to win their own freedom from enslavement.

A FEUDAL WORLD

Yet one further word remains to be spoken in reminder of the struggle against those inequalities that are at least in part the legacy of slavery. When 150 years ago the British Parliament took the final step in the abolition of slavery in lands under British jurisdiction, it was to be the beginning of a wider process of the abolition of slavery worldwide. It was, alas, the beginning also of the colonisation of Africa.[76] Great humanitarian instincts had played a powerful role, even if not an exclusive one, in putting an end to the systematic enslavement of man by man. But neither those instincts nor the religious mandates to which they were a response were a match for the economic forces which underpinned Europe's unseemly 'scramble for Africa' and the legacy of racism which slavery bequeathed to imperialism.

That legacy made the decolonisation process immeasurably harder and longer and in places more embittered than it should have been. But, by and large, the process itself has been accomplished. The Commonwealth was made possible because of it and because of the manner of its accomplishment. Yet, in one sense, decolonisation was a notional equalisation; the deeper economic disparities remained — inequalities embedded in the structures of a world economic system that had not yet recognised the convergence of principle and policy, the conjuncture of human solidarity and global interdependence. The moral imperatives for change, the hard-headed compulsions of mutual need which demand it, are unavoidable. As Barbara Ward once memorably declared: 'We dare not forget the really poor, who are the great majority, because prosperity, like peace, is indivisible'.[77]

Yet, the reality of life within the poverty belts of Africa and Asia and within the many enclaves of absolute poverty beyond them, is that about one billion of the world's 'huddled masses' are caught in the trap of poverty and are still yearning to be free. Theirs, to use former World Bank President Robert McNamara's stark description, 'is a condition of life so limited by illiteracy, malnutrition, disease, high infant mortality and low life-expectancy as to deny its victims the very potential of genes with which they are born'.[78] How far are they from the margins of slavery? Are they not bound hopelessly in servitude to economic forces they cannot even comprehend, much less resist? In his book, *India — A Wounded Civilization*, V. S. Naipaul described the reality of grinding poverty as he found it in a village in Bihar:

> In the village I went to, only one family out of four had land; only one child out of four went to school; only one man out of four had work. For a wage calculated to keep him only in food for the day he worked, the employed man, hardly exercising a skill, using the simplest tools and sometimes no tools at all, did the simplest agricultural labour. Child's work; and children, being cheaper than men, were preferred; so that, suicidally, in the midst of an over-population which no one recognised ... children were a source of wealth, available for hire after their eighth year for, if times were good, fifteen rupees, a dollar fifty a month. Generation followed generation quickly here, men as easily replaceable as their huts of grass and mud and matting ... Cruelty no longer had a meaning; it was life itself.[79]

What Naipaul saw in India was but a sample of the hellholes of absolute poverty that exist in all the continents of the South.

Even in those countries that we categorise euphemistically as 'low income' and 'least developed', a year's earnings amount to just about two weeks' social security benefit for an unemployed worker in Europe. In the report of the Brandt Commission which we called 'North–South: A Programme for Survival', we said this:

> The crisis through which international relations and the world economy are now passing presents great dangers, and they appear to be growing more serious. We believe that the gap which separates rich and poor countries — a gap so wide that at the extremes people seem to live in different worlds — has not been sufficiently recognised as a major factor in this crisis. It is a great contradiction of our age that these disparities exist — and are in some respects widening — just when human society is beginning to have a clearer perception of how it is interrelated and of how North and South depend on each other in a single world economy.[80]
>
> The extent to which the international system will be made more equitable is essentially a matter for political decision. We are looking for a world based less on power and status, more on justice and contract; less discretionary, more governed by fair and open rules.[81]

Power and status again, the old enemies of freedom; justice and contract, the goals towards which Wilberforce reached. But between the idea and the reality still falls the long shadow of slavery. How much has changed, how much remains the same! Servitude within the feudal societies of Europe preceded slavery in the dominions abroad, just as domestic reform preceded abolition; both were essentially inhumanities within national societies. We must now widen our horizons, looking to our global society and the unequal relations of states and people within it. It is a fearful prospect; one that should fill us with resolve to ensure that the malignancy of otherness deepened by the stain of race does not perpetuate such rank divisions in the state of man. In one sense, the difference between the eighteenth and nineteenth centuries, on the one hand, and the twentieth, on the other, is that we are now confronted not with so many separate feudal societies but with a human society that bears all the attributes of a feudal state: not with one state and two peoples but with one earth and two worlds. The latter cannot endure any more than could the former. Challenge is now unavoidable, not least because interdependence of the human condition has acquired a sharper focus in so many areas — in international security, in the preservation of the environment, in conservation of the resources of a small planet that an expanding human race must share, but, most pointedly of all, in the world economy.

For even the strongest economies, policies, it is clear, now have to be informed by the fact that the 'global economy' is a reality; that the self-interest of any nation can only be pursued effectively through taking account of the mutual needs and interests of all nations. In the area of international co-operation for development, therefore, not only is it right to do good, it has become necessary as well. It was not lightly that the Brandt Commission urged that if the world fails 'to become stronger by becoming a just and humane society' it will move towards its destruction.[82] We have lost the option of ignoring our interdependent state — of ignoring the reality that we have become one world. And since we can no longer ignore it, we must respond to it.

Indeed it is remarkable how true today rings the argument of mutual interest that Wilberforce used in the 1820s in a narrower context. As he girded himself in 1823 for the foundation of the Anti-Slavery Society and the long push towards emancipation, he was not afraid to bolster the claims of humanity and justice by the argument of self-interest. In his 'Appeal to the Religion, Justice and Humanity of the Inhabitants of the British Empire on behalf of the Negro Slaves in the West Indies' he asserted that: 'While we are loudly called on by justice and humanity to take measures without delay for improving the condition of our West Indian slaves, self-interest also inculcates the same duty, and with full as clear a voice.'[83] The appeal to self-interest was not the core of a case coated with humanitarian concern; that concern itself was central; the call to self-interest was designed to bring along those whom the moral imperative was not strong enough to move.

The free trade doctrines of Adam Smith had by then taken deep root; they provided the conjuncture which Wilberforce needed. It was an age, he declared, in language that is as apposite to our age as well:

in which it has been incontrovertibly established by the soundest of our political economists, — that the base and selfish, though plausible, views, which formerly prevailed so widely among statesmen, and taught them to believe that the prosperity and elevation of their country would be best promoted by the impoverishment and depression of its neighbours, were quite fallacious; and when we have now learned the opposite and beneficent lesson — that every nation is, in fact, benefitted by the growing affluence of others and that all are thus interested in the well-being and improvement of all.[84]

Accordingly, as was so regarding slavery 150 years ago, the demands of compassion, of morality, of humanitarianism, even of human solidarity, do not today stand alone; they need not contend in vain against the claims of national interest. They are, in fact, being constantly reinforced by the compulsions of mutual interest. We have reached in our global society that conjuncture of principle and prudence, of morality and 'sound policy', that made the abolition of slavery possible 150 years ago and makes inevitable now the eradication of its continuing legacy of servitude and inequality.

There is no higher need than that we should understand this convergence well, should acknowledge that we have to find in our minds the way to do what we know in our hearts to be right; should recognise that poverty is not only a stain spread across our civilisation, but also an economic blight that will ultimately destroy the first fruits of that civilisation and the prosperity of those who would reap them. Humanity must respect worldwide the precept that Wilberforce laboured for all his life in the context of slavery and knew at the end had prevailed; namely, that justice and survival are conjoined; that the task is to bring man's mutual interests and his moral impulse together; that Auden's words do remain true: 'We must love one another or die'.[85]

Wilberforce was driven forward by a profound conviction that slavery transgressed the limits of immorality within community. We must look now to a wider community and to a new morality, but the limits are the same. Why do we not answer the call of their transgression? Is it because we have lived for so long in a world of separate worlds that we find it hard to recognise the one world we have become? Or are we reluctant to give up our comforting illusions of otherness, to acknowledge our inseparable humanity, fearful lest morality prove too fragile a support for oneness, or our self-interest be left unprotected and unserved?

Our political and economic systems must now provide conceptual space for the reality of an interdependent world economy. We talk, all of us, about that 'world economy' and we accept its interdependent character even as we acknowledge its existence. Yet, we continue to act as if the world economy is merely the sum total of national economies, a statistic extrapolated from national economic reality.

At a time which has seen interest rates reach unprecedented levels, which has produced greater unemployment in the industrialised world than at any time in the living memory of anyone under fifty, which has produced a debt problem of such staggering proportions that it threatens countries whose creditworthiness has previously been beyond question; which has seen commodity prices fall in real terms to their lowest levels since the 1930s; which has produced foreign exchange deficits for the vast majority of developing countries so severe that they are depriving many an economy of even the capacity for survival: in a time such as this, can we any longer pretend that the answers are in the keeping of individual states; that the solutions can be produced through domestic policies alone?

Yet, while the world has accepted at one level of perception the reality of a world economy, while governments themselves speak of commitments to world economic recovery, most continue to act as though that world economy does not itself need attention and management. Governments, international institutions, the banking community, transnational corporations, all know that it does; yet the skills of management so exalted at home remain withheld at the global level. The collective search for world economic recovery is deferred and we rush like lemmings – separately but together – towards the abyss of economic disaster, continuing the pretence that our fate is ours alone, that humanity is separable.

Two hundred years after Wilberforce went from Hull to Westminster, are we willing to accept for our human society the kind of world satirically endorsed in Brecht's *Threepenny Opera?*

> *Some in light and some in darkness*
> *That's the kind of world we mean.*
> *Those you see are in the light part.*
> *Those in darkness don't get seen.*[86]

'Some in Light and Some in Darkness'

Do we really believe that such a feudal world could now subsist? If we do, we will have learnt nothing from the history of the Anti-Slavery movement. We will be as purblind and myopic as the old plantocracies, unable to recognise that they could not hold back the dawn and that if instead they welcomed it they too would share in the light and warmth it shed.

'One day', said Martin Luther King, speaking of his dream — not just a dream for America but for all the world: 'One day the sons of former slaves and sons of former slave-owners will be able to sit down together at the table of brotherhood.'[87] We are all bidden to that feast, but until we bridge the differences that still divide mankind, barriers of race and poverty, of ideology and of religion, above all, the barriers in our minds that preserve the prejudice of otherness, we cannot hope to reach that table. We must begin to make our way towards it; how better to do so than by following the signposts established by Wilberforce over 150 years ago in his exhortation against slavery:

Let us act with an energy suited to the importance of the interests for which we contend. Justice, humanity and sound policy prescribe our course, and will culminate our efforts.[88]

NOTES

1. M. A. Rawson (ed.), *The Bow in the Cloud, or The Negro's Memorial. A Collection of Original Contributions, in Prose and Verse, Illustrative of the Evils of Slavery, and Commemorative of its Abolition in the British Colonies*, London, Jackson and Walford, 1834, p. 301.
2. *Ibid.*, preface p. vii.
3. *Ibid.*
4. *Ibid.*, preface p. viii.
5. Christopher Lloyd, *The Navy and the Slave Trade. The Suppression of the African Slave Trade in the Nineteenth Century*, London, Cass, 1968, p. 117.
6. *Ibid.*, p. 167.
7. *Ibid.*, pp. 181–2.
8. R. Coupland, *Wilberforce. A Narrative*, Oxford, Clarendon Press, 1923, *passim*; R. I. Wilberforce and S. Wilberforce, *The Life of William Wilberforce*, five vols, London, John Murray, 1838, *passim*; M. Craton, J. Walvin and D. Wright, *Slavery: Abolition and Emancipation. Black Slaves and the British Empire. A Thematic Documentary*, London, Longman, 1976, pp. 231–5 ff, 279–82 ff; E. Williams, *Capitalism and Slavery*, London, Deutsch, 1981, pp. 179–83.

9. Roger T. Anstey, 'Capitalism and Slavery: A Critique' in *The Economic History Review 2nd Series*, vol. XXI, no. 2, Welwyn Garden City, Broadwater Press for the Economic History Society, Aug. 1968, pp. 315–6; Coupland *op. cit.*, pp. 224–50.
10. Walter Rodney, *How Europe Underdeveloped Africa*, London, Bogle-L'Ouverture Publications, 1972, pp. 94–5.
11. Craton, Walvin and Wright, *op. cit.*, p. 217, pp. 195–275 *passim*.
12. Rawson, *op. cit.*, pp. 282–99.
13. *Ibid.*, pp. 289–90.
14. Williams, *op. cit.*
15. Robin Furneaux, *William Wilberforce*, London, Hamish Hamilton, 1974, p. 257.
16. Christine Bolt and Seymour Drescher (eds), *Anti-Slavery, Religion and Reform: Essays in Memory of Roger Anstey*, Folkestone, Dawson, 1980, pp. 22, 29–30, 339–40, 355–6.
17. *Memoirs of Joseph Sturge*, London, 1864. Quoted in Craton, Walvin and Wright, *op. cit.*, p. 288.
18. *Ibid.*, p. 290.
19. A. R. F. Webber, *Centenary History and Handbook of British Guiana*, British Guiana, The Argosy Company Ltd, 1931, pp. 127, 141; James Rodway, *History of British Guiana*, three vols, Georgetown, Thomson, 1891–4, *Vol. II 1782–1833*, pp. 267–8, 274–5.
20. *Report of the Commissioners appointed for the management of The Crown Estates in the Colony of Berbice*, London, 20 May 1816, p. 1.
21. *Ibid.*, p. 2.
22. *Ibid.*, p. 3.
23. *Ibid.*
24. *Ibid.*
25. *Commission appointing William Wilberforce Esquire, et al. to be Commissioners for the Management of The Crown's Estates in Berbice and on the Continent of South America*, London, 23 April 1811, p. 1.
26. Edgar Mittelholzer, *Children of Kaywana*, London, Peter Nevill, 1952; *Kaywana Blood*, London, Secker and Warburg, 1958; *Kaywana Stock*, London, Foursquare, 1962.
27. *Report of the Commissioners appointed for the management of The Crown Estates in the Colony of Berbice*, p. 6.
28. *Ibid.*
29. John Pollock, *Wilberforce*, London, Constable, 1977, pp. 189, 201–14; Bolt and Drescher, *op. cit.*, p. 13, citing Roger Anstey, *The Atlantic Slave Trade and British Abolition 1760–1810*, London, Macmillan, 1975.
30. Rodway, *op. cit.*, *Vol. I 1668–1781*, pp. 171–214; Webber, *op. cit.*, pp. 58–62.
31. *Report of the Commissioners appointed for the management of The Crown Estates in the Colony of Berbice*, pp. 25–31.
32. *Ibid.*, p. 10.
33. *Ibid.*, p. 20.
34. *Convention Between Great Britain and The Netherlands, relative to the Colonies of Demerara, Essequibo, and Berbice. London, 12 August 1815, British State Papers, Vol. 3 1815*, London, Ridgway, 1838, pp. 394–5.
35. *Report of the Commissioners appointed for the management of The Crown Estates in the Colony of Berbice*, p. 22.
36. *Ibid.*, p. 21.
37. Furneaux, *op. cit.*, p. 416.
38. Rodway, *op. cit. Vol. II*, p. 240.

39. Furneaux, *op. cit.*, p. 417.
40. *Ibid.*, pp. 418–9.
41. Williams, *op. cit.*, pp. 205–6.
42. *Ibid.*, p. 208.
43. *Ibid.*, p. 93.
44. Hugh Tinker, *A New System of Slavery. The Export of Indian Labour Overseas 1830–1920*, London, Oxford University Press for the Institute of Race Relations, 1974, p. 63.
45. *Ibid.*, p. 69.
46. *Ibid.*, pp. v, 71.
47. Craton, Walvin and Wright, *op. cit.*, p. 344.
48. Tinker, *op. cit.*, pp. 113–4.
49. *Ibid.*, pp. 52–60.
50. *Ibid.*, pp. 46, 97.
51. Arthur Seymour, 'First of August' in *Selected Poems of A. J. Seymour*, Georgetown, 1983, p. 12.
52. Tinker, *op. cit.*, p. 60.
53. *Ibid.*, p. 105.
54. *Ibid.*, pp. 186, 188–9.
55. *Ibid.*, p. 244.
56. G. Lamming in Walter Rodney, *A History of the Guyanese Working People, 1881–1905*, London, Heinemann Educational Books, 1982, p. xxii.
57. *Ibid.*, p. 39.
58. Tinker, *op. cit.*, p. 283 *et seq.*
59. *Ibid.*, pp. 314–8.
60. *Ibid.*, pp. 335 *et seq.*
61. *Ibid.*, pp. 346–57.
62. *Ibid.*, p. 381.
63. Martin Carter, 'I come from the nigger yard' in *Poems of Resistance from Guyana*, Georgetown, Guyana Printers, 1979; first published London, Lawrence and Wishart, 1954, p. 38.
64. Tinker, *op. cit.*, pp. 94–5.
65. F. R. Augier, S. C. Gordon, D. G. Hall and M. Reckord, *The Making of the West Indies*, London, Longman, 1960, p. 202.
66. Tinker, *op. cit.*, pp. 299–300.
67. Lloyd, *op. cit.* Appendix G, 'Blackbirding in the Pacific', pp. 291–2.
68. F. V. Grunfeld, *The Hitler File*, London, Weidenfeld and Nicolson, 1974, p. 318.
69. Frantz Fanon, *Black Skin White Masks*, London, Granada/Paladin, 1972, pp. 65, 165.
70. William Wilberforce, *An Appeal to the Religion, Justice and Humanity of the Inhabitants of the British Empire in behalf of the Negro Slaves in the West Indies*, London, Hatchards, 1823, p. 43.
71. Aimé Césaire, *Discours sur le Colonialisme*, Paris, Présence Africaine, 1956, pp. 14–15, quoted in Fanon, *op. cit.*, p. 64.
72. *The Guardian*, 30 March 1983.
73. Allen Cook, *Akin to Slavery: Prison Labour in South Africa*, London, International Defence and Aid Fund, 1983, passim for this and subsequent paragraph.
74. *The Times*, 6 June 1983.
75. Williams, *op. cit.*, p. 170.
76. Bolt and Drescher, *op. cit.*, pp. 363 *et seq*; Lloyd, *op. cit.*, pp. 156–62.
77. Barbara Ward, cited by Brian Johnson, *The Environmentalist, Vol. I*, Lausanne, Elsevier Sequoia SA, 1981, p. 96.

78. Robert McNamara, cited by S. S. Ramphal, *One World to Share. Selected speeches of the Commonwealth Secretary-General, 1975–9*, London, Hutchinson Benham, 1979, p. 78.
79. V. S. Naipaul, *India: A Wounded Civilization*, London, Deutsch, 1977, p. 28.
80. *North-South: A Programme for Survival. The Report of the Independent Commission on International Development Issues under the Chairmanship of Willy Brandt*, London, Pan Books, 1980, p. 30.
81. *Ibid.*, p. 65.
82. *Ibid.*, p. 33.
83. Wilberforce, *op. cit.*, p. 68.
84. *Ibid.*, pp. 69–70.
85. W. H. Auden, 'September 1, 1939' in *Selected Poems*, London, Faber, 1979, p. 88.
86. Bertolt Brecht, tr. R. Manheim and J. Willett (eds), *The Threepenny Opera*, London, Methuen, 1979, p. 84.
87. Martin Luther King, speech to Civil Rights March on Washington 28 August 1963, cited in D. L. Lewis, *Martin Luther King, A Critical Biography*, London, Allen Lane The Penguin Press, 1970, p. 228.
88. Wilberforce, *op. cit.*, p. 77.

10

The English Judge and the Ethnic Minorities*

LORD SCARMAN

In 1772 Lord Mansfield, giving judgment in Somersett's case, declared that slavery has no place in the common law of England. He was not creating law: he was asserting a basic principle already recognised, as he well knew, in our courts of common law.

Wilberforce grew to maturity against this background. His concern was how the vigorous and prosperous slave trade based largely on Liverpool but operating outside the United Kingdom could be reconciled with the principle of the law and the ethic of our people. In 1807 he secured the legislation to abolish it. But this was not enough. Slavery was still lawful in the overseas dominions and plantations. He secured eventually the abolition of slavery in all lands under the sovereignty of the British Crown: but he died before the Act of Parliament was passed.

It can fairly be said that Wilberforce's triumphant campaign against the existence of slavery under the British flag proceeded from strength: it was an application of common law rule to the commerce and empire of Britain. In 1983 the one hundred and fiftieth anniversary of his death, if he were alive, would he be content with the British scene? He would be confronted not with slavery in British dominions overseas but with the plight of ethnic minorities at home. Would he be content with what he saw?

---

* This is a shortened version of the lecture delivered

I doubt it. He would not, of course, find slavery. But he would find racial disadvantage. The problem is different: but in terms of human wretchedness it is, or can be, severe. Men and women in our country are secure in their civil rights. They have their liberty and their property protected by law: they are not their master's chattels. But the ethnic minorities are socially and economically insecure: and politically they have little hope of influencing executive decision or legislation. They suffer because of their race. Wilberforce, alive today, would surely campaign against racial disadvantage, seeing it as an insidious and dangerous disease in British society.

How can we who are lawyers help the campaign which, if he were now living, he would assuredly mount to right the injustice and oppression of racial disadvantage? This is the question to which I shall address myself. Can the law help? Have the judges a useful contribution to make?

In his Hamlyn lectures of this year, the Lord Chancellor, Lord Hailsham, concluded (p. 83) that the state of human rights in Britain is excellent – socially, politically and economically. This is the truth, but not the whole truth. For beneath the smooth and tranquil surface of our national life lie dangerous rocks which can shipwreck our society. In principle, the ethnic minority groups in our midst enjoy the equal protection of our laws. But do they get equality? Their answer is 'no'. They cite the immigration and citizenship laws. They contend that even our education law is loaded against them. They see the race relations legislation as ineffectual to redress the balance of their disadvantage, and they find no comfort in the common law's philosophy of freedom. Freedom to do as you please so long as it is not prohibited by law is, they believe, a fertile mother of disadvantage. It affords no protection to the weak against the strong, to the minorities against the majority.

When they turn to our institutions for help, they find Parliament unsure. They lack representation or influence in the political parties. The House of Commons has at present no member of the Asian or Caribbean ethnic groups and the House of Lords has only a very few. They do, however, see a gleam of hope in the judicial system.

It is the duty of the English judge to secure to all who come before him the equal protection of our laws. And he has a wide

The English Judge and the Ethnic Minorities

ranging power to develop the judge-made common law so as to ensure justice and equality. The development by the judges of the principle of judicial review of the administrative decisions of government has not escaped the notice of the ethnic minorities. They are mounting a strong challenge by invoking the principle and have enjoyed a considerable measure of success in the courts.

The protection the courts can offer is necessarily limited. Judicial decision is not comparable with legislation. It makes law slowly and unevenly, advancing on a case by case basis. In countries under a written constitution the higher courts are entrusted with the protection of the constitutional rights of the individual not only against infringement by the executive but against legislation passed in breach of the constitution. Our courts have no power to protect against legislation even if it amounts to the infringement of a human right: for Parliament's legislation is sovereign. The judges, though they interpret it, must obey and apply it. This limitation upon the range of the court's power to protect human rights is in stark contrast with the powers of the courts in those common law countries which have accepted written constitutions. In the USA, Canada, India, Jamaica, Trinidad and Tobago, and in many others, the courts stand guard over the constitutional rights of the people.

The question must be asked. Is it not time to embody our human rights and fundamental freedoms in a constitutional instrument which the courts can safeguard? British experience with the European Convention on Human Rights and Fundamental Freedoms suggests an affirmative answer. We have ratified the convention, and have also accepted the right of the citizen to petition the European Commission of Human Rights if aggrieved by an infringement of the obligation imposed by the convention on member states to ensure that its rights and freedoms are secured to all within their respective jurisdictions. But we have not made the convention part of our law. In consequence, there is a steady, dismal and embarrassing flow of cases from the United Kingdom to the European Court of Human Rights in which infringements of the convention by our government are alleged: and too many of these cases are found to be justified. Immigrants, prisoners, British Rail employees, and a Sunday newspaper are among those who have succeeded in establishing by recourse to Europe infringements within the United Kingdom of their human rights and freedoms. But the process is expensive, slow and beset with difficulty. Why not incorporate the convention into our law, allow our judges to rule on these fundamental questions, and begin the progress, already achieved in other common law countries, towards judicial protection within our own frontiers of the human rights of our people? No single reform, I believe, could do more for the ethnic minorities and other disadvantaged groups within our society.

Though our courts lack this constitutional power, they do exhibit great strengths in the protection of the individual against abuse of power. In 1977 a procedural change was introduced into the Rules of the Supreme Court (which govern the procedure of the High Court and the Court of Appeal). The new procedure was 'judicial review'. It has been described by a commentator as 'a most beneficent reform in the practice and procedure relating to administrative law'. (White Book, note on O. 53) It enables the citizen to challenge in our courts administrative acts or omissions of government (central and local) and provides a range of remedies, which include the quashing of an order, declaration of illegality and injunction. The courts can insist on discovery of documents and the production of evidence.

Two recent cases show the efficacy of the procedure. The first arose under the education legislation. (*Shah* v. *Barnet LBC* 1 All.E.R. 226) Five foreign-born students, who had resided for more than three years in the United Kingdom applied to their local education authority for a mandatory grant to enable them to go to a university or other institution of higher education. They were refused on the ground that, being here for education, they were not ordinarily resident. The House of Lords held that in refusing them their grants the local education authorities had misinterpreted the law and required the authorities to reconsider the applications.

The second case concerned liberty and the protection of 'habeas corpus'. (*Khawaja and Khera* v. *Secretary of State, Home Department* [1983] 1 All.E.R. 765) A young man had entered the UK with his parents and was given permission to settle here. He did not tell the immigration officer that he was married, but he was not asked. His failure to volunteer the

The English Judge and the Ethnic Minorities

information unasked was treated by the Home Office as a deception, and he was arrested as an illegal immigrant with a view to deportation. He challenged the Home Office's action in the courts. The House of Lords ruled in his favour and set him free. The House asserted that it was the duty of the court to satisfy itself that the conditions justifying his detention existed. Mere silence, when no questions had been asked, was not fraud or deception. The Home Office had failed to establish a case of deception. The House reaffirmed the ancient principle of the common law that no imprisonment or detention is lawful unless it can be shown to the satisfaction of a court to be justified.

If Wilberforce were alive, he would, I believe, approve of what the courts are doing, but would deplore the constitutional limitations which our history imposes upon them. Dare I suggest that he would think the time ripe for constitutional reform? A Bill of Rights entrusted by Parliament to the protection of the courts would put our law on course to help the weak and the disadvantaged in our society. Wilberforce's life of endeavour teaches us to look at the ills not of his time but of our generation, and to tackle them with energy and dedication. That is the lesson to be learnt on this, the one hundred and fiftieth anniversary of the completion of his labours.

INDEX

Anti-Slavery Society, 4, 36, 43, 115, 123, 172, 186
Apartheid, 177, 179–82
Augustine, Saint, 17, 23–6
Baptists, 37, 41–2, 119
Barbados, 111–16, 118, 120, 134, 143, 171
Berbice, 166–9, 171
Brathwaite, Edward Kamau, 137, 141, 143, 145
British Empire, 47, 90, 160, 186
British Guiana, 94, 97, 101, 115–18, 128, 147–8, 167, 169, 172, 176, 183
Buxton, Thomas Fowell, 52, 101, 115, 118, 122–4, 162, 164
Calvin, John, 26, 74
Christianity, 19–26, 37, 41–2, 49–50, 58, 60–1, 63, 65–6, 69–85, 116, 120, 125–6
Cicero, 19, 23
Clarkson, Thomas, 35, 51, 55–6, 164
Cuba, 33, 94, 99, 101, 134, 139, 143–4, 147, 161, 176
Davis, David Brion, 25, 27, 49, 56
Demerara, 111, 116, 118–20, 124, 163, 169–72
Evangelicals, 34, 48–50, 59, 66, 69–85, 111, 162
Fox, Charles James, 55, 92
Gladstone, William Ewart, 116, 172
Guyana, 139, 147, 166, 168, 176
Indenture, 172–7
Jamaica, 30, 97, 110–11, 113, 115, 118–25, 128, 134, 143, 146, 152, 154–6, 161, 171, 183, 195
James, C.L.R., 2–4, 165
Macaulay, Zachary, 118, 164, 171
Manley, Norman, 142, 148, 154
Methodism, Methodists, 37, 40–2, 60, 70, 119
Mill, John Stuart, 5, 14, 21
Parliament, 31–2, 34, 37–9, 43–4, 49, 53–5, 60–1, 70, 81–2, 90–5, 122–5, 159, 170–3, 181, 183, 193, 197
Paul, Saint, 17, 20–3, 26–7
Pitt, William, 52–3, 59, 69, 71, 75, 81
Plato, Platonism, 15–17, 23, 26
Santo Domingo, 92, 96, 98, 110, 113, 134, 143–4, 148
Slave trade, 30–8, 41, 43–4, 49–58, 60, 66, 70, 86–95, 102, 160–4, 167

Smith, Adam, 103–5, 186
Smith, John, 116–18, 170–2
Stephen, James, 56, 115, 123, 164, 166–7
Sugar, 96–7, 116, 133, 154, 163, 165–7
Trinidad, 94, 97, 101, 119, 128, 134, 139, 148, 152, 156–7, 176, 195
Wilberforce, William, 1–5, 30–2, 34–5, 37, 39–41, 43–5, 47–66, 69–85, 87, 91, 101, 105, 110–11, 115, 119, 129, 159–67, 169–71, 179–80, 182, 185–9, 193–4, 197
Williams, Eric, 32, 34, 48–9, 89, 111, 137, 143, 148, 163, 171–2